VOICES IN
BLACK & WHITE

VOICES IN BLACK & WHITE

Writings on Race in America from HARPER'S MAGAZINE

With an introduction by Henry Louis Gates, Jr.
Edited by Katharine Whittemore and Gerald Marzorati

FRANKLIN
SQUARE
P·R·E·S·S

NEW YORK

Copyright © 1993 Franklin Square Press
All rights reserved.

Published by Franklin Square Press, a division of Harper's Magazine, 666 Broadway, New York, N.Y. 10012

First Edition.

No part of this book may be reproduced in any form without written permission from the publisher.

Library of Congress Cataloging in Publication Data:
Voices in Black & White: writings on race in America from Harper's Magazine/edited by Katharine Whittemore and Gerald Marzorati/introduction by Henry Louis Gates, Jr.
p. cm. — (The American retrospective series, v. I)
Articles published 1922–1992.
ISBN: 1-879957-07-8 $21.95
ISBN: 1-879957-06-X $14.95 (pbk.)
1. United States—race relations. I. Whittemore, Katharine. II. Marzorati, Gerald. III. Harper's Magazine. IV. Voices in Black and White. V. Series.
E185.61.V74 1992
305.8' 00973—dc20
92-30718 CIP

Book design by Deborah Thomas.
Cover design by Louise Fili.

Manufactured in the United States of America.

This book has been produced on acid-free paper.

CONTENTS

Introduction

Henry Louis Gates, Jr.

THE PROBLEM OF the twentieth century, W.E.B. Du Bois avowed in his now famous prophecy, would be the problem of the color line. Like a geological fault, it is a line along which tensions build and find at times violent release. But it is also a place where the larger contradictions and conflicts of a society are played out. Indeed, so integral have the dynamics of race become to American society that Andrew Hacker could begin his best-selling study, *Two Nations,* in effect a contemporary sequel to Gunnar Myrdal's *An American Dilemma,* with the statement, "Every one of us could write a book about race. The text is already imprinted in our minds and evokes our moral character."

As the title of Hacker's book suggests, it has become a commonplace that the racial divide in this country amounts to a split between "two nations." The reference, of course, is Benjamin Disraeli's depiction of rich and poor in Victorian England as "two nations, between whom there is no intercourse and no sympathy; who are as ignorant of each other's habits, thought, and feelings as if they were dwellers in different zones, or inhabitants of different planets." Often enough, it does seem as if black and white America inhabit different spaces, different worlds, different nations. And yet the relation is also and at the same time intimate and indissoluble. This truly is the American paradox.

In a sense insistently explicated by writers such as Ralph Ellison and James Baldwin—but also William Faulkner and William Styron—black American and white have each created the other, each defined itself in relation to the other, and each could destroy the other. As Baldwin wrote, America's "interracial drama" has "not only created a new black man, it has created a new white man, too." To him, therefore, "the history of the American Negro problem is not merely shameful, it is also something of an achievement. For even when the worst has been said, it must also be added that the perpetual challenge posed by this problem was always, somehow, perpetually met." If the black presence in this country were magically to disappear—these writers recognized—a polity might persist, but it would not be American.

This view of the valence of race in American culture takes us far beyond the familiar "contributionist" approach, in which labels of attribution are pasted upon the elements of our culture like tags at a bake sale: the Indians gave us maize, the blacks gave us jazz, and Mrs. Ellsworth made the carrot cake. However fortifying such an exercise may be for the grade-school pupil, it won't carry us far in understanding the nature of our own modernity. For the truth of the matter, as the philosopher Kwame Anthony Appiah notes, is that there are no white people—only people passing for white. Just as there are no black people, only people passing for black. For even the seemingly most brute aspects of our social identities are culturally constructed; "race" is always refracted and inflected by a mutable fretwork of assumptions and beliefs local to our time and place.

Mutable, I say, and yet astonishingly persistent across the years. With amazing durability, race continues to serve as a stage upon which various fantasies of otherness, of intimacy and alienation, deprivation and desire are enacted. Which makes it, perhaps, inevitable that *Harper's Magazine,* distinguished by its historical longevity, should have registered the American obsession in all its contradictory aspects. This book assembles pieces about North and South, about color and sex and class and culture. They are contributions that address the great American obsession in ways that make it impossible to view it as a unitary subject, impossible to view it, as it were, in black and white.

A chronology of reflections on race in America must also be a record of a nation's shifting moral compass—all in the aftermath of an abrupt upheaval, wherein a system that struck many as "natural" and unexceptionable came to name an undisputed social evil. Thus Mark Twain, our greatest novelist, illuminates the psychology of the white Southerner's relation to slavery in the course of telling us about his mother. Slavery, he observed, "stupefied everybody's humanity, as regarded the slave, but stopped there." Thus his mother, kindhearted and compassionate, had not the slightest inkling that slavery might be wrong. After all, "as far as her experience went, the wise and the good and the holy were unanimous in the conviction that slavery was right, righteous, sacred, the peculiar pet of the Deity, and a condition which the slave himself ought to be daily and nightly thankful for."

And what gives especial moral gravity to much Southern literature that contends with race is precisely the consciousness of change: witness the moral estrangement William Styron relates as the writer's educated sensibilities alienate him from his family, his ethical patrimony, and the community of his birth. Styron thus describes the outlook into which he was reared as "the typically ambivalent one of most native Southerners, for whom the Negro is taken simultaneously for granted and as an object of unending concern." The Negro becomes a subject of "an incessant preoccupation, somewhat like a monstrous, recurring dream populated by identical faces wearing expressions of inquietude and vague reproach." And yet the dream has become part of who one is. "Only when one reflects upon their possible absence, some magical disappearance, does one realize how unimaginable this absence would be: it would be easier to visualize a South without trees, without *any* people, without life at all."

Of course, a dream of the autochthonous black community proves equally alluring for the Negro—and equally elusive. For one thing, mixing and hybridity has been at times a physical as well as a cultural fact of life, as we are reminded by the interview here with an Alabama domestic. "I don't know if it was rape or money or lust or affection or what that caused the mingling-up," she muses. But the guilt payments offered by her white father only fed her sense of abandonment and dispossession, only reinforced the stigma of her mixed parentage.

That the Southern experience is modulated by class as well as color is made clear by the distinguished black writer and anthologist Arna Bontemps. At the same time as it insulated him from the insult of material deprivation, his thoroughly middle-class background could become a burden to him in other ways. "Now don't go up there acting colored," his father cautions him before sending him off to a white boarding school. Only in time does Bontemps rebel against the pre-suppositions of his father's imperative: "How dare anyone, parent, schoolteacher, or merely literary critic, tell me not to act *colored?*" And he bears down on the "conflict in which every educated American Negro, and some who are not educated, must somehow take sides." On the one hand, rank assimilation, a clean break with the past, and the "shedding of his Negro-ness"; on the other, "embracing the rich-ness of the folk heritage." In the end, as Bontemps and so many other black intellectuals were to conclude in the wake of the Great Migration, the "Southern Negro's link with his past seems . . . worth preserving."

Certainly it is a sentiment that Ralph Ellison confirms in his elo-quent meditation on Harlem. In Harlem, he writes, the response to the greeting "How are you?" is often "Oh, man, I'm *nowhere.*" Ellison mordantly reflects on the cultural losses sustained in the great migra-tion of Southern rural blacks to Northern cities, wherein the Negro "surrenders and does not replace certain important supports to his personality." Lost is his sense of being "at home in the world," the result, Ellison writes, of "accepting (for day-to-day living, at least) the obscene absurdity of his predicament." While "his folk wisdom is dis-carded in the mistaken notion that it in no way applies to urban liv-ing," Ellison knows these supports of the Southern Negro to be "of inestimable psychological value."

By mid-century, the twin vectors of migration and integration gave rise to what was for many the specter of miscegenation. "My

Daughter Married a Negro"—the title aptly evoking one of those Samuel Z. Arkoff horror flicks—tells a survivor's story, which is also a story of a sort of coming-to-consciousness. A few acquaintances "continue to greet us as though we had a death in the family." But the father has come through the other side, striving conscientiously for the mid-century liberal ideal of color-blindness.

"He and his race, the best of them, are on the make," the anonymous father of the bride writes. He is gripped by a sense of black futurity and potential that similarly animates William Faulkner's own intense and intensely ambivalent feelings about both Negroes and a social order built upon their exclusion. If, as the postbellum cry insisted, the South would rise again, Faulkner knew it would be a very different South. He believed that the enslaved Negro had been rescued from a state of timeless barbarity in Africa, and therefore that the swiftness with which he had adapted to an age of technology signified enormous if unrealized potential. (Needless to say, perhaps, his convictions about Africa are based on the colonialist folklore of his day, and bear little resemblance to the actual continent.) But his central theme resonates with one that the scholar Orlando Patterson would later demonstrate at length; namely, the conceptual linkage between the concept of enslavement and that of liberty. Thus for Faulkner, at the end of the day, "We will have to choose between not color nor race nor religion nor between East and West either, but simply between being slaves and being free."

The perplexities that confronted Roger Wilkins's coming-of-age, resolutely personal though they are, at the same time bespeak the ambitions, anxieties, and uncertainties of an emergent class of African-Americans. The dualities negotiated by Arna Bontemps would not have been foreign to him. Set against those crucial years of the Sixties and Seventies, years of transformation and tumult, Wilkins's memoir, both urbane and impassioned, presents an intimate perspective on what it meant to grow up middle-class and black. The non-coincidence of color and culture—the divisions internal to black America—didn't come as a revelation to him, it was something he had taken for granted. He knew he didn't feel any great sense of identity with poor blacks. And yet a subtly differentiated sense of the black community does not prevent the supervening interests of solidarity and activism to become the central mission of his life, a life devoted to public and intellectual service.

It was a sense of purpose—a sense that the destiny of black America and one's own personal destiny ran parallel—that infused James Baldwin's own remarkable career. And his account of Martin Luther King, Jr., is fraught with a sense of the significance, both personal and political, of their encounter. If King himself does not quite fit within his viewfinder, many of the episode's ancillary characters are beautifully preserved in the amber of Baldwin's prose. There is, for example, the white Southern bus driver who refuses to answer Baldwin when the writer politely inquires what the fare is. The driver was convinced the question was "but another Negro trick, that I had something up my sleeve, and that to answer my question in any way would be to expose himself to disaster. He could not guess what I was thinking, and he was not going to risk further personal demoralization by trying to. And this was the spirit of the town." This is a perfectly Baldwinian moment, both for the unnerving sympathy he extends to the racist driver and for the way that this most incidental of events is made to yield up a complex psychology of defensiveness, pride, and fear. Baldwin thus displays his talent for understanding white America better than it understands itself.

Baldwin's observations are, as always, mediated through his finely tuned sensibility. In arranging what is in effect a roundtable on the South in the throes of desegregation, the child psychiatrist Robert Coles presents the voices of Southerners, black and white, in a relatively unmediated forum. They speak of mingled hopes and frustrations, a sense of the fragility of either side of the racial divide. In the course of many books, Robert Coles has, of course, been particularly attuned to the distinctive perceptions and concerns of childhood. Certainly, it represents a passage whose vulnerability and acuteness of perception is memorably captured by Maya Angelou. Eschewing didacticism, she hints at the cultural deformation behind her youthful conviction that "I was really white," and that "a cruel fairy stepmother, who was understandably jealous of my beauty, had turned me into a too-big Negro girl, with nappy black hair, broad feet, and a space between her teeth that would hold a number-two pencil." But she can also convey the sort of transfiguration her grandmother undergoes when, subjected to a fury of racist taunts, she maintains an eerie, songful stoicism.

The time of watching and waiting that childhood affords is, however, limited in duration, and the burdens of adulthood are not long postponed. With his privileged Caribbean background and a "blue chip" educational experience, Orde Coombs came to political consciousness at a time when racial solidarity across class divisions had gained an especial urgency. In the scathing tradition of the great sociologist E. Franklin Frazier, Coombs exposes the black bourgeoisie to a pitiless light, decrying its insularity, its cultural insecurity, its political obtuseness: all expressed in its chronic and self-limiting need to distinguish itself from those "other Negroes"—to certify its difference, in short, rather than challenging the color-coded social order to which it was still and would always be captive. At the same time, Coombs is scarcely anti-elitist; he retains Du Bois's sense of the role that the "risen"—what Du Bois called the talented tenth—could play in the elevation of the race.

Privilege has a different meaning for Mary Richie, whose powerful set of observations ground, in concrete detail, her relation to the blacks with whom she shares a city as a complex of fear and desire, benevolence, disapproval, and guilt. A young black asks her the time, although two large clocks are visible over her shoulders. "I thought, he is testing himself against whites, that's good. I forgot it was I he was challenging; that whatever I said I was giving him an excuse to scorn me." It is a moment that seems to recapitulate the plight of Baldwin's bus driver, who fears his questioner is making a fool of him in some way he cannot quite fathom. But while Mary Richie, too, distrusts the question, there is a difference. She answers it.

As Richie suggests, a consequence of the proverbial color line is to reduce human beings to their color-coded images, so that human interaction becomes a matter of shadow as well as act. The theater of race takes place in a ghostly ether where blacks and whites are reduced to the essence of their official identities, and our personalities are left behind in the dressing room. And as spectators, we fear that we will become what we behold. That may be one reason why the relation of black Americans to their representations in mass media has always been a peculiarly anxious one. And by the mid-Seventies—at least from my perspective as the twenty-five-year-old African-American I was then—it seemed that our official reactions to such images had become more reflexive than reflective, and all too inclined to police a simplistic ideology of "positive" and "negative" images.

Polarities like these are no more tenable in representation than in life, but they do have the advantage of conserving on thought. The sharp ideological oppositions through which we parse political discourse offer a similar convenience, and at a similar price. This is not to minimize the very real and consequential distance between the Reverend Jesse Jackson, who surely remains the most prominent spokesman of the political left in this country, and Charles Murray, one of the intellectual architects of Ronald Reagan's domestic policies. And yet many will be surprised to find Jackson, in 1986, raising the same issues of welfare reform that would be staples of the 1992 presidential campaign. Jackson's support for enterprise zones, his proposals for reducing the disincentive effects of welfare, and his basic conviction that "this welfare system hurts people fundamentally" converge with many neo-liberal and conservative approaches, even while his sympathies and sense of constituency link him with the tradition of progressive populism.

In Shelby Steele's vocabulary, Jackson is, in uneasy alternation, both "bargainer" and "challenger"—both someone who charges white America with its injustice and someone who offers white America a kind of amnesty in exchange for its racial goodwill. But for Steele, these two postures are, in fact, the primary avenues through which "blacks have handled white society's presumption of innocence." Exploring the subtle politics of racial *ressentiment*, Steele is, perhaps, more Ellisonian than Baldwinian. In his view, the power that black bargainers wield is the sacerdotal power of absolution. Steele's critics, of course, accuse him of granting precisely such absolution; but surely his diagnosis of white America's need to claim innocence cannot be part of this act. If Steele is a bargainer, he is a self-conscious one. And his distrust of a politics of blame is, in the end, shared by many of his critics on the left. Thus the black legal scholar and critic Patricia Williams argues that "it does no one much good . . . to make race issues contests for some Holy Grail of innocence." For her, as for many progressives, "generalized notions of innocence and guilt have little place in the struggles for transcendence; there is no blame among the living for the dimensions of this historic crime, this national tragedy."

This is not an insight that all have found readily digestible. For urban communities increasingly isolated from the larger economy and buffeted by disease and disorder, the culture of conspiracy has had a powerful allure. James Traub wryly takes up the ways in which a "counter-reality" takes root in Harlem. In a pattern that bespeaks a larger alienation, the mainstream media is viewed with suspicion, even while an alternative mythology is given the sort of credence that is immune to countervailing evidence. The evolution of such a "counter-reality" is not, of course, peculiar to a forum like *The Gary Byrd Show*. As we know, Ronald Reagan promulgated his own counter-reality, populated by welfare queens in chauffeured limousines and a host of similar phantasms. (Reporters who went out in search of the empirical origins of these anecdotes invariably returned empty-handed, but—as is the way with such counter-reality—they had long since taken on a life of their own.) Similarly, the genetic theories of Dr. Frances Cress Welsing—whose crude assumptions any tenth grader should be able to see through—are not nuttier than, say, Shirley MacLaine's conjectures. Because of the peculiar vulnerability of the black urban community, however, they are clearly more dangerous; and the culture of conspiracy is maladaptive for black America in a way it cannot be for white America.

The mythologies with which David Updike, as a white American marrying a black African, had to contend attest to the way that buried assumptions about racial identity can inform the responses of even those who think they have left them behind. It also suggests we have not yet come so far from the world evoked in the 1951 testament "My Daughter Married a Negro"—or, for that matter, the 1967 film *Guess Who's Coming to Dinner.* The insidious question persists: "But what about the children?" As if blackness were a heritable disease, like Tay-Sachs or sickle-cell. As if a steel barrier of race would forever seal one parent off from his offspring. But Updike's musings speak also to the way in which the American race issue is peculiarly and locally *American.* For instance, it is obvious to his Kenyan wife that the cultural distance would be as great or greater had she married a Yoruba from Nigeria or an Asante from Ghana; but these are precisely the sort of differences that our own politics of pigment tends to elide.

Surveying the multifarious contents of this reader—extracted from the pages of a single magazine—I am more persuaded than ever that Hacker is right: that every one of us could write a book about race. But I am also persuaded of something else: they would all be different books. Race, as we have come to see, is less an essence than it is a text, one that is written and rewritten, singly and collectively. And so it is for the acts of remembrance and commentary—and the individuals, black and white, behind them—that this volume gathers together in bruising intimacy. To paraphrase Ralph Ellison's Invisible Man, who knows but that, on the lower frequencies, they speak for us?

—*Henry Louis Gates, Jr.*

SLAVERY IN HANNIBAL

(FEBRUARY 1922)

Mark Twain

AS I HAVE said, we lived in a slave-holding community; indeed, when slavery perished my mother had been in daily touch with it for sixty years. Yet, kind-hearted and compassionate as she was, I think she was not conscious that slavery was a bald, grotesque, and unwarrantable usurpation. She had never heard it assailed in any pulpit, but had heard it defended and sanctified in a thousand; her ears were familiar with Bible texts that approved it, but if there were any that disapproved it they had not been quoted by her pastors; as far as her experience went, the wise and the good and the holy were unanimous in the conviction that slavery was right, righteous, sacred, the peculiar pet of the Deity, and a condition which the slave himself ought to be daily and nightly thankful for. Manifestly, training and association can accomplish strange miracles. As a rule our slaves were convinced and content.

There was nothing about the slavery of the Hannibal region to rouse one's dozing humane instincts to activity. It was the mild domestic slavery, not the brutal plantation article. Cruelties were very rare, and exceedingly and wholesomely unpopular. To separate and sell the members of a slave family to different masters was a thing not well liked by the people, and so it was not often done, except in the settling of estates. I have no recollection of ever seeing a slave auction in that town; but I am suspicious that that is because the thing was a common and commonplace spectacle, not an uncommon and impressive one. I vividly remember seeing a dozen black men and women chained to each other, once, and lying in a group on the pavement, awaiting shipment to the Southern slave market. Those were the saddest faces I ever saw. Chained slaves could not have been a common sight, or this picture would not have taken so strong and lasting a hold upon me.

The "nigger trader" was loathed by everybody. He was regarded as a sort of human devil who bought and conveyed poor helpless creatures to hell—for to our whites and blacks alike the Southern plantation was simply hell; no milder name could describe it. If the threat to sell an incorrigible slave "down the river" would not reform him, nothing would—his case was past cure.

It is commonly believed that an infallible effect of slavery was to make such as lived in its midst hard-hearted. I think it had no such effect—speaking in general terms. I think it stupefied everybody's humanity, as regarded the slave, but stopped there. There were no hard-hearted people in our town or I mean there were no more than would be found in any other town of the same size in any other country; and in my experience hard-hearted people are very rare everywhere.

THIS QUIET DUST

(APRIL 1965)

William Styron

> *You mought be rich as cream*
> *And drive you coach and four-horse team,*
> *But you can't keep de world from moverin' round*
> *Nor Nat Turner from gainin' ground.*
>
> *And your name it mought be Caesar sure*
> *And got you cannon can shoot a mile or more,*
> *But you can't keep de world from moverin' round*
> *Nor Nat Turner from gainin' ground.*
> —Old-time Negro Song

MY NATIVE STATE of Virginia is, of course, more than ordinarily conscious of its past, even for the South. When I was learning my lessons in the mid-1930s at a grammar school on the banks of the James River, one of the required texts was a history of Virginia—a book I can recall far more vividly than any history of the United States or of Europe I studied at a later time. It was in this work that I first

3

encountered the name Nat Turner. The reference to Nat was brief; as a matter of fact, I do not think it unlikely that it was the very brevity of the allusion—amounting almost to a quality of haste—which captured my attention and stung my curiosity. I can no longer quote the passage exactly, but I remember that it went something like this: "In 1831, a fanatical Negro slave named Nat Turner led a terrible insurrection in Southampton County, murdering many white people. The insurrection was immediately put down, and for their cruel deeds Nat Turner and most of the other Negroes involved in the rebellion were hanged." Give or take a few harsh adjectives, this was all the information on Nat Turner supplied by that forgotten historian, who hustled on to matters of greater consequence.

I must have first read this passage when I was ten or eleven years old. At that time my home was not far from Southampton County, where the rebellion took place, in a section of the Virginia Tidewater which is generally considered part of the Black Belt because of the predominance of Negroes in the population. (When I speak of the South and Southerners here, I speak of *this* South, where Deep South attitudes prevail; it would include parts of Maryland and East Texas.) My boyhood experience was the typically ambivalent one of most native Southerners, for whom the Negro is taken simultaneously for granted and as an object of unending concern. On the one hand, Negroes are simply a part of the landscape, an unexceptional feature of the local scenery, yet as central to its character as the pinewoods and sawmills and mule teams and sleepy river estuaries that give such color and tone to the Southern geography. Unnoticed by white people, the Negroes blend with the land and somehow melt and fade into it, so that only when one reflects upon their possible absence, some magical disappearance, does one realize how unimaginable this absence would be: it would be easier to visualize a South without trees, without *any* people, without life at all. Thus at the same time ignored by white people, Negroes impinge upon their collective subconscious to such a degree that it may be rightly said that they become the focus of an incessant preoccupation, somewhat like a monstrous, recurring dream populated by identical faces wearing expressions of inquietude and vague reproach. "Southern whites cannot walk, talk, sing, conceive of laws or justice, think of sex, love, the family, or freedom without responding to the presence of Negroes." The words are those of Ralph Ellison, and, of course, he is right.

Yet there are many Souths, and the experience of each Southerner is modified by the subtlest conditions of self and family and environment and God knows what else, and I have wondered if it has ever properly been taken into account how various this response to the presence of the Negroes can be. I cannot tell how typical my own awareness of Negroes was, for instance, as I grew up near my birthplace—a small seaside city about equally divided between black and white. My feelings seem to have been confused and blurred, tinged with sentimentality, colored by a great deal of folklore, and wobbling always between a patronizing affection, fostered by my elders, and downright hostility. Most importantly, my feelings were completely uninformed by that intimate knowledge of black people which Southerners claim as their special patent; indeed, they were based upon an almost total ignorance.

For one thing, from the standpoint of attitudes toward race, my upbringing was hardly unusual: it derived from the simple conviction that Negroes were in every respect inferior to white people and should be made to stay in their proper order in the scheme of things. At the same time, by certain Southern standards my family was enlightened: although my mother taught me firmly that the use of "lady" instead of "woman" in referring to a Negro female was quite improper, she writhed at the sight of the extremes of Negro poverty, and would certainly have thrashed me had she ever heard me use the word "nigger." Yet outside the confines of family, in the lower-middle-class school world I inhabited every day, this was a word I commonly used. School segregation, which was an ordinary fact of life for me, is devastatingly effective in accomplishing something that it was only peripherally designed to do: it prevents the awareness even of the existence of another race. Thus, whatever hostility I bore toward the Negroes was based almost entirely upon hearsay.

And so the word "nigger," which like all my schoolmates I uttered so freely and so often, had even then an idle and listless ring. How could that dull epithet carry meaning and conviction when it was applied to a people so diligently isolated from us that they barely existed except as shadows which came daily to labor in the kitchen, to haul away garbage, to rake up leaves? An unremarked paradox of Southern life is that its racial animosity is really grounded not upon friction and propinquity, but upon an almost complete lack of contact. Surrounded by a sea of Negroes, I cannot recall more than once—and then briefly, when I was five or six—ever having played with a Negro child, or ever having spoken to a Negro, except in trifling talk with the cook, or in some forlorn and crippled conversation with a dotty old grandfather angling for hardshell crabs on a lonesome Sunday afternoon many years ago. Nor was I by any means uniquely sheltered. Whatever knowledge I gained in my youth about Negroes, I gained from a distance, as if I had been watching actors in an all-black puppet show.

Such an experience has made me distrust any easy generalizations about the South, whether they are made by white sociologists or Negro playwrights, Southern politicians or Northern editors. I have come to understand at least as much about the Negro after having lived in the North. One of the most egregious of the Southern myths—one in this case propagated solely by Southerners—is that of the Southern white's boast that he "knows" the Negro. Certainly in many rural areas of the South the cultural climate has been such as to allow a mutual understanding, and even a kind of intimacy, to spring up between the races, at least in some individual instances. But my own boyhood surroundings, which were semi-urban (I suppose suburban is the best description, though the green little village on the city's outskirts where I grew up was a far cry from Levittown), and which have become the youthful environment for vast numbers of Southerners, tended almost totally to preclude any contact between black and white, especially when that contact was so sedulously proscribed by law.

Yet if white Southerners cannot "know" the Negro, it is for this very reason that the entire sexual myth needs to be reexamined. Surely a certain amount of sexual tension between the races does continue to exist, and the Southern white man's fear of sexual aggression on the part of the Negro male is still too evident to be ignored. But the nature of the growth of the urban, modern South has been such as to impose ever more effective walls between the races. While it cannot be denied that slavery times produced an enormous amount of inter-breeding (with all of its totalitarianism, this was a free-for-all atmo-sphere far less self-conscious about carnal mingling than the Jim Crow era which began in the 1890s) and while even now there must logical-ly take place occasional sexual contacts between the races—especially in rural areas where a degree of casual familiarity has always obtained—the monolithic nature of segregation has raised such an effective barrier between whites and Negroes that it is impossible not to believe that theories involving a perpetual sexual "tension" have been badly inflated. Nor is it possible to feel that a desire to taste for-bidden fruit has ever really caused this barrier to be breached. From the standpoint of the Negro, there is indifference or uncomplicated fear; from that of the white—segregation, the law, and, finally, indif-ference, too. When I was growing up, the older boys might crack wan jokes about visiting the Negro whorehouse street (patronized entirely, I later discovered, by Negroes plus a few Scandinavian sailors), but to my knowledge none of them ever really went there. Like Negroes in general, Negro girls were to white men phantoms, shadows. To assume that anything more than a rare and sporadic intimacy on any level has existed in the modern South between whites and Negroes is simply to deny, with a truly willful contempt for logic, the monstrous effectiveness of that apartheid which has been the Southern way of life for almost three-quarters of a century.

I have lingered on this matter only to try to underline a truth about Southern life which has been too often taken for granted, and which has therefore been overlooked or misinterpreted. Most Southern white people *cannot* know or touch black people and this is because of the deadly intimidation of a universal law. Certainly one feels the presence of this gulf even in the work of a writer as supremely knowledgeable about the South as William Faulkner, who confessed a hesitancy about attempting to "think Negro," and whose Negro characters, as marvelously portrayed as most of them are, seem nevertheless to be meticulously *observed* rather than *lived*. Thus in *The Sound and the Fury*, Faulkner's magnificent Dilsey comes richly alive, yet in retrospect one feels this is a result of countless mornings, hours, days Faulkner had spent watching and listening to old Negro servants, and not because Dilsey herself is a being created from a sense of withinness: at the last moment Faulkner draws back, and it is no mere happenstance that Dilsey, alone among the four central figures from whose points of view the story is told, is seen from the outside rather than from that intensely "inner" vantage point, the interior monologue.

Innumerable white Southerners have grown up as free of knowledge of the Negro character and soul as a person whose background is rural Wisconsin or Maine. Yet, of course, there is a difference, and it is a profound one, defining the white Southerner's attitudes and causing him to be, for better or for worse, whatever it is he is to be. For the Negro is *there*. And he is there in a way he never is in the North, no matter how great his numbers. In the South he is a perpetual and immutable part of history itself, a piece of the vast fabric so integral and necessary that without him the fabric dissolves; his voice, his black or brown face passing on a city street, the sound of his cry rising from a wagonload of flowers, his numberless procession down dusty country roads, the neat white church he has built in some pine grove with its air of grace and benison and tranquillity, his silhouette behind a mule team far off in some spring field, the wail of his blues blaring from some jukebox in a backwoods roadhouse, the sad wet faces of nursemaids and cooks waiting in the evening at city bus stops in pouring rain—the Negro is always *there*.

No wonder then, as Ellison says, the white Southerner can do virtually nothing without responding to the presence of Negroes. No wonder the white man so often grows cranky, fanciful, freakish, loony, violent: how else respond to a paradox which requires, with the full majesty of law behind it, that he deny the very reality of a people whose multitude approaches and often exceeds his own; that he disclaim the existence of those whose human presence has marked every acre of the land, every hamlet and crossroad and city and town, and whose humanity, however inflexibly denied, is daily evidenced to him like a heartbeat in loyalty and wickedness, madness and hilarity and mayhem and pride and love? The Negro may feel that it is too late to be known, and that the desire to know him reeks of outrageous condescension. But to break down the old law, to come to *know* the Negro, has become the moral imperative of every white Southerner.

I suspect that my search for Nat Turner, my own private attempt as a novelist to re-create and bring alive that dim and prodigious black man, has been at least a partial fulfillment of this mandate, although the problem has long since resolved itself into an artistic one—which is as it should be. In the late 1940s, having finished college in North Carolina and come to New York, I found myself haunted by that name I had first seen in the Virginia history textbook. I had learned something more of Southern history since then, and I had become fascinated by the subject of Negro slavery. One of the most striking aspects of the institution is the fact that in the 250 years of its existence in America, it was singularly free of organized uprisings, plots, and rebellions. (It is curious that as recently as the late 1940s, scholarly insights were lagging, and I could only have suspected then what has since been made convincing by such historians as Frank Tannenbaum and Stanley Elkins: that American Negro slavery, unique in its psychological oppressiveness—the worst the world has ever known—was simply so despotic and emasculating as to render organized revolt next to impossible.) There were three exceptions: a conspiracy by the slave Gabriel Prosser and his followers near Richmond in the year 1800, the plot betrayed, the conspirators hanged; a similar conspiracy in 1822, in Charleston, South Carolina, led by a free Negro named Denmark Vesey, who also was betrayed before he could carry out his plans, and who was executed along with other members of the plot.

The last exception, of course, was Nat Turner, and he alone in the entire annals of American slavery—alone among all those "many thousand gone"—achieved a kind of triumph.

Even today, many otherwise well-informed people have never heard the name Nat Turner, and there are several plausible reasons for such an ignorance. One of these, of course, is that the study of our history—and not alone in the South—has been tendentious in the extreme, and has often avoided even an allusion to a figure like Nat, who inconveniently disturbs our notion of a slave system which, though morally wrong, was conducted with such charity and restraint that any organized act of insurrectory and murderous violence would be unthinkable. But a general ignorance about Nat Turner is even more understandable in view of the fact that so little is left of the actual record. Southampton County, which even now is off the beaten track, was at that period the remotest backwater imaginable. The relativity of time allows us elastic definitions: 1831 was yesterday. Yet the year 1831, in the Presidency of Andrew Jackson, lay in the very dawn of our modern history, three years before a railroad ever touched the soil of Virginia, a full fifteen years before the use of the telegraph. The rebellion itself was of such a cataclysmic nature as practically to guarantee confusion of the news, distortion, wild rumors, lies, and, finally, great areas of darkness and suppression; all of these have contributed to Nat's obscurity.

As for the contemporary documents themselves, only one survives: the *Confessions of Nat Turner*, a brief pamphlet of some five thousand words, transcribed from Nat's lips as he awaited trial, by a somewhat enigmatic lawyer named Thomas Gray, who published the *Confessions* in Baltimore and then vanished from sight. There are several discrepancies in Gray's transcript but it was taken down in haste, and in all major respects it seems completely honest and reliable. Those few newspaper accounts of the time, from Richmond and Norfolk, are sketchy, remote, filled with conjecture, and are thus virtually worthless. The existing county court records of Southampton remain brief and unilluminating, dull lists, a dry catalogue of names in fading ink: the white people slain, the Negroes tried and transported south, or acquitted, or convicted and hanged.

Roughly seventy years after the rebellion (in 1900, which by coincidence was the year Virginia formally adopted its first Jim Crow laws), the single scholarly book ever to be written on the affair was published—*The Southampton Insurrection,* by a Johns Hopkins Ph.D. candidate named William S. Drewry, who was an unreconstructed Virginian of decidedly pro-slavery leanings and a man so quaintly committed to the *ancien régime* that, in the midst of a description of the ghastliest part of the uprising, he was able to reflect that "slavery in Virginia was not such to arouse rebellion, but was an institution which nourished the strongest affection and piety in slave and owner, as well as moral qualities worthy of any age of civilization." For Drewry, Nat Turner was some sort of inexplicable aberration, like a man from Mars. Drewry was close enough to the event in time, however, to be able to interview quite a few of the survivors, and since he also possessed a bloodthirsty relish for detail, it was possible for him to reconstruct the chronology of the insurrection with what appears to be considerable accuracy. Drewry's book (it is of course long out of print) and Nat's *Confessions* remain the only significant sources about the insurrection. Of Nat himself, his background and early years, very little can be known. This is not disadvantageous to a novelist, since it allows him to speculate—with a freedom not accorded the historian— upon all the intermingled miseries, ambitions, frustrations, hopes, rages, and desires which caused this extraordinary black man to rise up out of those early mists of our history and strike down his oppressors with a fury of retribution unequaled before or since.

He was born in 1800, which would have made him at the time of the insurrection thirty-one years old—exactly the age of so many great revolutionaries at the decisive moment of their insurgency: Martin Luther,* Robespierre, Danton, Fidel Castro. Thomas Gray, in a foot-

---

*See Erik Erikson's Young Man Luther *for a brilliant study of the development of the revolutionary impulse in a young man, and the relationship of this impulse to the father-figure. Although it is best to be wary of any heavy psychoanalytical emphasis, one cannot help believing that Nat Turner's relationship with his father, like Luther's, was tormented and complicated, especially since this person could not have been his real father, who ran away when Nat was an infant, but the white man who owned and raised him.*

note to the *Confessions,* describes him as having the "true Negro face" (an offhand way of forestalling an assumption that he might have possessed any white blood), and he adds that "for natural intelligence and quickness of apprehension he is surpassed by few men I have ever seen"—a lofty tribute indeed at that inflammatory instant, with antebellum racism at its most hysteric pitch. Although little is known for certain of Nat's childhood and youth, there can be no doubt that he was very precocious and that he learned not only to read and write with ease—an illustrious achievement in itself, when learning to read and write was forbidden to Negroes by law—but at an early age acquired a knowledge of astronomy, and later on experimented in making paper and gunpowder. (The resemblance here to the knowledge of the ancient Chinese is almost too odd to be true, but I can find no reason to doubt it.)

The early decades of the nineteenth century were years of declining prosperity for the Virginia Tidewater, largely because of the ruination of the land through greedy cultivation of tobacco—a crop which had gradually disappeared from the region, causing the breakup of many of the big old plantations and the development of subsistence farming on small holdings. It was in these surroundings—a flat pastoral land of modest farms and even more modest homesteads, where it was rare to find a white man prosperous enough to own more than half a dozen Negroes, and where two or three slaves to a family was the general rule—that Nat was born and brought up, and in these surroundings he prepared himself for the apocalyptic role he was to play in history. Because of the failing economic conditions, it was not remarkable that Nat was purchased and sold several times by various owners (in a sense, he was fortunate in not having been sold off to the deadly cotton and rice plantations of South Carolina and Georgia, which was the lot of many Virginia Negroes of the period); and although we do not know much about any of these masters, the evidence does not appear to be that Nat was ill-treated, and in fact one of these owners (Samuel Turner, brother of the man on whose property Nat was born) developed so strong a paternal feeling for the boy and such regard for Nat's abilities that he took the fateful step of encouraging him in the beginnings of an education.

The atmosphere of the time and place was fundamentalist and devout to a passionate degree, and at some time during his twenties Nat, who had always been a godly person—"never owing a dollar, never uttering an oath, never drinking intoxicating liquors, and never committing a theft"—became a Baptist preacher. Compared to the Deep South, Virginia slave life was not so rigorous; Nat must have been given considerable latitude, and found many opportunities to preach and exhort the Negroes. His gifts for preaching, for prophecy, and his own magnetism seem to have been so extraordinary that he grew into a rather celebrated figure among the Negroes of the county, his influence even extending to the whites, one of whom—a poor, half-cracked, but respectable overseer named Brantley—he converted to the faith and baptized in a mill pond in the sight of a multitude of the curious, both black and white. (After this no one would have anything to do with Brantley, and he left the county in disgrace.)

At about this time Nat began to withdraw into himself, fasting and praying, spending long hours in the woods or in the swamp, where he communed with the Spirit and where there came over him, urgently now, intimations that he was being prepared for some great purpose. His fanaticism grew in intensity, and during these lonely vigils in the forest he began to see apparitions:

> I saw white spirits and black spirits engaged in battle, and the sun was darkened; the thunder rolled in the heavens and blood flowed in streams . . . I wondered greatly at these miracles, and prayed to be informed of a certainty of the meaning thereof; and shortly afterwards, while laboring in the fields, I discovered drops of blood on the corn as though it were dew from heaven. For as the blood of Christ had been shed on this earth, and had ascended to heaven for the salvation of sinners, it was now returning to earth again in the form of dew . . . On the twelfth day of May, 1828, I heard a loud noise in the heavens, and the Spirit instantly appeared to me and said the Serpent was loosened, and Christ had laid down the yoke he had borne for the sins of men, and that I should take it on and fight against the Serpent, for the time was fast approaching when the first should be last and the last should be first . . .

Like all revolutions, that of Nat Turner underwent many worrisome hesitations, false starts, procrastinations, delays (with appropriate irony, Independence Day, 1830, had been one of the original dates selected, but Nat fell sick and the moment was put off again); finally, however, on the night of Sunday, August 21, 1831, Nat, together with five other Negroes in whom he had placed his confidence and trust, assembled in the woods near the home of his owner of the time, a carriage maker named Joseph Travis, and commenced to carry out a plan of total annihilation. The penultimate goal was the capture of the county seat, then called Jerusalem (a connotation certainly not lost on Nat, who, with the words of the prophets roaring in his ears, must have felt like Gideon himself before the extermination of the Midianites); there were guns and ammunition in Jerusalem, and with these captured it was then Nat's purpose to sweep thirty miles eastward, gathering black recruits on the way until the Great Dismal Swamp was reached—a snake-filled and gloomy fastness in which Nat believed, with probable justification, only Negroes could survive, and no white man's army could penetrate. The immediate objective, however, was the destruction of every white man, woman, and child on the ten-mile route to Jerusalem; no one was to be spared; tender infancy and feeble old age alike were to perish by the axe and the sword. The command, of course, was that of God Almighty, through the voice of his prophet Ezekiel: *"Son of Man, prophesy and say, Thus saith the Lord; Say, a sword, a sword is sharpened, and also furbished: it is sharpened to make a sore slaughter . . . Slay utterly old and young, both maids and little children, and women . . ."* It was a scheme so wild and daring that it could only have been the product of the most wretched desperation and frustrate misery of soul; and of course it was doomed to catastrophe not only for whites but for Negroes—and for black men in ways which from the vantage point of history now seem almost unthinkable.

They did their job rapidly and with merciless and methodical determination. Beginning at the home of Travis—where five people, including a six-month-old infant, were slain in their beds—they marched from house to house on an eastward route, pillaging, murdering, sparing no one. Lacking guns—at least to begin with—they employed axes, hatchets, and swords as their tools of destruction, and swift decapitation was their usual method of dispatch. (It is interesting that the Negroes did not resort to torture, nor were they ever accused of rape. Nat's attitude toward sex was Christian and high-minded, and he had said: "We will not do to their women what they have done to ours.")

On through the first day they marched, across the hot August fields, gaining guns and ammunition, horses, and a number of willing recruits. That the insurrection was not purely racial, but perhaps obscurely pre-Marxist, may be seen in the fact that a number of dwellings belonging to poor white people were pointedly passed by. At midday on Monday their force had more than tripled, to the amount of nineteen, and nearly thirty white people lay dead. By this time, the alarm had been sounded throughout the county, and while the momentum of the insurgent band was considerable, many of the whites had fled in panic to the woods, and some of the farmers had begun to resist, setting up barricades from which they could fire back at Nat's forces. Furthermore, quite a few of the rebels had broken into the brandy cellars of the houses they had attacked and had gotten roaring drunk—an eventuality Nat had feared and had warned against. Nevertheless, the Negroes—augmented now by forty more volunteers—pressed on toward Jerusalem, continuing the attack into the next night and all through the following day, when at last obstinate resistance by the aroused whites and the appearance of a mounted force of militia troops (also, it must be suspected, continued attrition by the apple brandy) caused the rebels to be dispersed, only a mile or so from Jerusalem.

Almost every one of the Negroes was rounded up and brought to trial—a legalistic nicety characteristic of a time in which it was necessary for one to determine whether *his* slave, property, after all, worth eight or nine hundred dollars, was really guilty and deserving of the gallows. Nat disappeared immediately after the insurrection, and hid in the woods for over two months, when near-starvation and the onset of autumnal cold drove him from his cave and forced him to surrender to a lone farmer with a shotgun. Then he too was brought to trial in Jerusalem—early in November 1831—for fomenting a rebellion in which sixty white people had perished.

The immediate consequences of the insurrection were exceedingly grim. The killing of so many white people was in itself an act of futility. It has never been determined with any accuracy how many black people, not connected with the rebellion, were slain at the hands of rampaging bands of white men who swarmed all over Southampton in the week following the uprising, seeking reprisal and vengeance. A contemporary estimate by a Richmond newspaper, which deplored this retaliation, put the number at close to two hundred Negroes, many of them free, and many of them tortured in ways unimaginably horrible. But even more important was the effect that Nat Turner's insurrection had upon the institution of slavery at large. News of the revolt spread among Southern whites with great speed: the impossible, the unspeakable had at last taken place after two hundred years of the ministrations of sweet old mammies and softly murmured Yassuhs and docile compliance—and a shock wave of anguish and terror ran through the entire South. If such a nightmarish calamity happened there, would it not happen *here?*—here in Tennessee, in Augusta, in Vicksburg, in these bayous of Louisiana? Had Nat lived to see the consequences of his rebellion, surely it would have been for him the cruelest irony that his bold and desperate bid for liberty had caused only the most tyrannical new controls to be imposed upon Negroes everywhere—the establishment of patrols, further restrictions upon movement, education, assembly, and the beginning of other severe and crippling restraints which persisted throughout the slaveholding states until the Civil War. Virginia had been edging close to emancipation, and it seems reasonable to believe that the example of Nat's rebellion, stampeding many moderates in the legislature into a conviction that the Negroes could not be safely freed, was a decisive factor in the ultimate victory of the proslavery forces. Had Virginia, with its enormous prestige among the states, emancipated its slaves, the effect upon our history would be awesome to contemplate.

Nat brought cold, paralyzing fear to the South, a fear that never departed. If white men had sown the wind with chattel slavery, in Nat Turner they had reaped the whirlwind for white and black alike.

Nat was executed, along with sixteen other Negroes who had figured large in the insurrection. Most of the others were transported south, to the steaming fields of rice and cotton. On November 11, 1831, Nat was hanged from a live oak tree in the town square of Jerusalem. He went to his death with great dignity and courage. "The bodies of those executed," wrote Drewry, "with one exception, were buried in a decent and becoming manner. That of Nat Turner was delivered to the doctors, who skinned it and made grease of the flesh."

Not long ago, in the spring of the year, when I was visiting my family in Virginia, I decided to go down for the day to Southampton County, which is a drive of an hour and a half by car from the town where I was born and raised. Nat Turner was of course the reason for this trip, although I had nothing particular or urgent in mind. What research it was possible to do on the event I had long since done. The Southampton court records, I had already been reliably informed, would prove unrewarding. It was not a question, then, of digging out more facts, but simply a matter of wanting to savor the mood and atmosphere of a landscape I had not seen for quite a few years, since the times when as a boy I used to pass through Southampton on the way to my father's family home in North Carolina. I thought also that there might be a chance of visiting some of the historic sites connected with the insurrection, and perhaps even of retracing part of the route of the uprising through the help of one of those handsomely produced guidebooks for which the Historical Commission of Virginia is famous—guides indispensable for a trip to such Old Dominion shrines as Jamestown and Appomattox and Monticello. I became even more eager to go when one of my in-laws put me in touch by telephone with a cousin of his. This man, whom I shall call Dan Seward, lived near Franklin, the main town of Southampton, and he assured me in those broad cheery Southern tones which are like a warm embrace—and which, after long years in the chill North, are to me always so familiar, reminiscent, and therefore so unsettling, sweet, and curiously painful—that he would like nothing better than to aid me in my exploration in whatever way he could.

Dan Seward is a farmer, a prosperous grower of peanuts in a prosperous agricultural region where the peanut is the unquestioned monarch. A combination of sandy loam soil and a long growing season has made Southampton ideal for the cultivation of peanuts; over 30,000 acres are planted annually, and the crop is processed and marketed in Franklin—a thriving little town of 7,000 people—or in Suffolk and Portsmouth, where it is rendered into Planters cooking oil and stock feed and Skippy peanut butter. There are other money-making crops—corn and soybeans and cotton. The county is at the northernmost edge of the cotton belt, and thirty years ago cotton was a major source of income. Cotton has declined in importance but the average yield per acre is still among the highest in the South, and the single gin left in the county in the little village of Drewryville processes each year several thousand bales which are trucked to market down in North Carolina. Lumbering is also very profitable, owing mainly to an abundance of the loblolly pines valuable in the production of kraft wood pulp; and the Union Bag–Camp Paper Company's plant on the Blackwater River in Franklin is a huge enterprise employing over 1,600 people. But it is peanuts—the harvested vines in autumn piled up mile after mile in dumpy brown stacks like hay—which have brought money to Southampton, and a sheen of prosperity that can be seen in the freshly painted farmhouses along the monotonously flat state highway which leads into Franklin, and the new-model Dodges and Buicks parked slantwise against the curb of some crossroads hamlet, and the gaudy, eye-catching signs that advise the wisdom of a bank savings account for all those surplus funds.

The county has very much the look of the New South about it, with its airport and its shiny new motels, its insistent billboards advertising space for industrial sites, the sprinkling of housing developments with television antennas gleaming from every rooftop, its supermarkets and shopping centers and its flavor of go-getting commercialism. This is the New South, where agriculture still prevails but has joined in a vigorous union with industry, so that even the peanut when it goes to market is ground up in some rumbling engine of commerce and becomes metamorphosed into wood stain or soap or cattle feed. The Negroes, too, have partaken of this abundance—some of it, at least—for they own television sets also, and if not new-model Buicks (the Southern white man's strictures against Negro ostentation remain intimidating), then decent late-model used Fords; while in the streets of Franklin the Negro women shopping seemed on the day of my visit very proud and well-dressed compared to the shabby stooped figures I recalled from the Depression years when I was a boy. It would certainly appear that Negroes deserve some of this abundance, if only because they make up so large a part of the work force. Since Nat Turner's day the balance of population in Southampton—almost 60 percent Negro—has hardly altered by a hair.

"I don't know anywhere that a Negro is treated better than around here," Mr. Seward was saying to the three of us, on the spring morning I visited him with my wife and my father. "You take your average person from up North, he just doesn't *know* the Negro like we do. Now for instance I have a Negro who's worked for me for years, name of Ernest. He knows if he breaks his arm—like he did a while ago, fell off a tractor—he knows he can come to me and I'll see that he's taken care of, hospital expenses and all, and I'll take care of him and his family while he's unable to work, right on down the line. I don't ask him to pay back a cent, either, that's for sure. We have a wonderful relationship, that Negro and myself. By God, I'd die for that Negro and he knows it, and he'd do the same for me. But Ernest doesn't want to sit down at my table, here in this house, and have supper with me—and he wouldn't want me in *his* house. And Ernest's got kids like I do, and he doesn't want them to go to school with my Bobby, any more than Bobby wants to go to school with *his* kids. It works both ways. People up North don't seem to be able to understand a simple fact like that."

Mr. Seward was a solidly fleshed, somewhat rangy, big-shouldered man in his early forties with an open, cheerful manner which surely did nothing to betray the friendliness with which he had spoken on the telephone. He had greeted us—total strangers, really—with an animation and uncomplicated good will that would have shamed an Eskimo; and for a moment I realized that, after years amid the granite outcroppings of New England, I had forgotten that this *was* the passionate, generous, outgoing nature of the South, no artificial display but a social gesture as natural as breathing.

Mr. Seward had just finished rebuilding his farmhouse on the outskirts of town, and he had shown us around with a pride I found understandable: there was a sparkling electric kitchen worthy of an advertisement in *Life* magazine, some handsome modern furniture, and several downstairs rooms paneled beautifully in the prodigal and lustrous hardwood of the region. It was altogether a fine, tasteful house, resembling more one of the prettier medium-priced homes in the Long Island suburbs than the house one might contemplate for a Tidewater farmer. Upstairs, we had inspected his son Bobby's room, a kid's room with books like *Pinocchio* and *The Black Arrow* and *The Swiss Family Robinson,* and here there was a huge paper banner spread across one entire wall with the crayon inscription: *"Two . . . four . . . six . . . eight! We don't want to integrate!"* It was a sign which so overwhelmingly dominated the room that it could not help provoking comment, and it was this that eventually had led to Mr. Seward's reflections about *knowing* Negroes.

There might have been something vaguely defensive in his remarks but not a trace of hostility. His tone was matter-of-fact and good-natured, and he pronounced the word Negro as *nigra,* which most Southerners do with utter naturalness while intending no disrespect whatsoever, in fact quite the opposite—the mean epithet, of course, is *nigger.* I had the feeling that Mr. Seward had begun amiably to regard us as sympathetic but ill-informed outsiders, non-Southern, despite his knowledge of my Tidewater background and my father's own accent, which is thick as grits. Moreover, the fact that I had admitted to having lived in the North for fifteen years caused me, I fear, to appear alien in his eyes, *déraciné,* especially when my acculturation to Northern ways has made me adopt the long "e" and say Negro. The racial misery, at any rate, is within inches of driving us mad: how can I explain that, with all my silent disagreement with Mr. Seward's paternalism, I knew that when he said, "By God, I'd die for that Negro," he meant it?

Perhaps I should not have been surprised that Mr. Seward seemed to know very little about Nat Turner. When we got around to the subject, it developed that he had always thought that the insurrection occurred way back in the eighteenth century. Affably, he described seeing in his boyhood the "Hanging Tree," the live oak from which Nat had been executed in Courtland (Jerusalem had undergone this change of name after the Civil War), and which had died and been cut down some thirty years ago; as for any other landmarks, he regretted that he did not know of a single one. No, so far as he knew, there just wasn't anything.

For me, it was the beginning of disappointments which grew with every hour. Had I really been so ingenuous as to believe that I would unearth some shrine, some home preserved after the manner of Colonial Williamsburg, a relic of the insurrection at whose portal I would discover a lady in billowing satin and crinoline, who for fifty cents would shepherd me about the rooms with a gentle drawl indicating the spot where a good mistress fell at the hands of the murderous darky? The native Virginian, despite himself, is cursed with a suffocating sense of history, and I do not think it impossible that I actually suspected some such monument. Nevertheless, confident that there would be something to look at, I took heart when Mr. Seward suggested that after lunch we all drive over to Courtland, ten miles to the west. He had already spoken to a friend of his, the Sheriff of the county, who knew all the obscure byways and odd corners of Southampton, mainly because of his endless search for illegal stills; if there was a solitary person alive who might be able to locate some landmark, or could help retrace part of Nat Turner's march, it was the Sheriff. This gave me hope. For I had brought along Drewry's book and its map which showed the general route of the uprising, marking the houses by name. In the sixty years since Drewry, there would have been many changes in the landscape. But with this map oriented against the Sheriff's detailed county map, I should easily be able to pick up the trail and thus experience, however briefly, a sense of the light and shadow that played over that scene of slaughter and retribution 134 years ago.

Yet it was as if Nat Turner had never existed, and as the day lengthened and afternoon wore on, and as we searched Nat's part of the county—five of us now, riding in the Sheriff's car with its huge star emblazoned on the doors, and its radio blatting out hoarse intermittent messages, and its riot gun protectively nuzzling the backs of our necks over the edge of the rear seat—I had the sensation from time to time that this Negro, who had so long occupied my thoughts, who indeed had so obsessed my imagination that he had acquired larger spirit and flesh than most of the living people I encountered day in and day out, had been merely a crazy figment of my mind, a phantom no more real than some half-recollected image from a fairy tale. For here in the back country, this horizontal land of woods and meadows where he had roamed, only a few people had heard of Nat Turner, and of those who had—among the people we stopped to make inquiries of, both white and black, along dusty country roads, at farms, at filling stations, at crossroad stores—most of them confused him, I think, with something spectral, mythic, a black Paul Bunyan who had perpetrated mysterious and nameless deeds in millennia past. They were neither facetious nor evasive, simply unaware. Others confounded him with the Civil War—a Negro general. One young Negro field hand, lounging at an Esso station, figured he was a white man. A white man, heavy-lidded and paunchy, slow-witted, an idler at a rickety store, thought him an illustrious racehorse of bygone days.

The Sheriff, a smallish, soft-speaking ruminative man, with the whisper of a smile frozen on his face as if he were perpetually enjoying a good joke, knew full well who Nat Turner was, and I could tell he relished our frustrating charade. He was a shrewd person, quick and sharp with countrified wisdom, and he soon became quite as fascinated as I with the idea of tracking down some relic of the uprising (although he said that Drewry's map was hopelessly out of date, the roads of that time now abandoned to the fields and woods, the homes burnt down or gone to ruin); the country people's ignorance he found irresistible and I think it tickled him to perplex their foolish heads, white or black, with the same old leading question: "You heard about old Nat Turner, ain't you?" But few of them had heard, even though I was sure that many had plowed the same fields that Nat had crossed, lived on land that he had passed by; and as for dwellings still standing which might have been connected with the rebellion, not one of these back-country people could offer the faintest hint or clue. As effectively as a monstrous and unbearable dream, Nat had been erased from memory.

It was late afternoon when, with a sense of deep fatigue and frustration, I suggested to Mr. Seward and the Sheriff that maybe we had better go back to Courtland and call it a day. They were agreeable—relieved, I felt, to be freed of this tedious and fruitless search—and as we headed east down a straight unpaved road, the conversation became desultory, general. We spoke of the North. The Sheriff was interested to learn that I often traveled to New York. He went there occasionally himself, he said; indeed, he had been there only the month before—"to pick up a nigger," a fugitive from custody who had been awaiting trial for killing his wife. New York was a fine place to spend the night, said the Sheriff, but he wouldn't want to live there.

As he spoke, I had been gazing out of the window, and now suddenly something caught my eye—something familiar, a brief flickering passage of a distant outline, a silhouette against the sun-splashed woods—and I asked the Sheriff to stop the car. He did, and as we backed up slowly through a cloud of dust, I recognized a house standing perhaps a quarter of a mile off the road, from this distance only a lopsided oblong sheltered by an enormous oak, but the whole tableau—the house and the glorious hovering tree and the stretch of woods beyond—so familiar to me that it might have been some home I passed every day. And of course now as recognition came flooding back, I knew whose house it was. For in *The Southampton Insurrection*, the indefatigable Drewry had included many photographs—amateurish, doubtless taken by himself, and suffering from the fuzzy offset reproduction of 1900. But they were clear enough to provide an unmistakable guide to the dwellings in question, and now as I again consulted the book I could see that this house—the monumental oak above it grown scant inches it seemed in sixty years—was the one referred to by Drewry as having belonged to Mrs. Catherine Whitehead. From this distance, in the soft clear light of a spring afternoon, it seemed most tranquil, but few houses have come to know such a multitude of violent deaths. There in the late afternoon of Monday, August 22, Nat Turner and his band had appeared, and they set upon and killed "Mrs. Catherine Whitehead, son Richard, and four daughters, and grandchild."

The approach to the house was by a rutted lane long ago abandoned and overgrown with lush weeds which made a soft, crushed, rasping sound as we rolled over them. Dogwood, white and pink, grew on either side of the lane, quite wild and wanton in lovely pastel splashes. Not far from the house a pole fence interrupted our way; the Sheriff stopped the car and we got out and stood there for a moment, looking at the place. It was quiet and still—so quiet that the sudden chant of a mockingbird in the woods was almost frightening—and we realized then that no one lived in the house. Scoured by weather, paintless, worn down to the wintry gray of bone and with all the old mortar gone from between the timbers, it stood alone and desolate above its blasted, sagging front porch, the ancient door ajar like an open wound. Although never a manor house, it had once been a spacious and comfortable country home; now in near-ruin it sagged, finished, a shell, possessing only the most fragile profile of itself. As we drew closer still we could see that the entire house, from its upper story to the cellar, was filled with thousands of shucked ears of corn— feed for the malevolent-looking little razorback pigs which suddenly appeared in a tribe at the edge of the house, eyeing us, grunting. Mr. Seward sent them scampering with a shied stick and a farmer's sharp "Whoo!" I looked up at the house, trying to recollect its particular role in Nat's destiny, and then I remembered.

There was something baffling, secret, irrational about Nat's own participation in the uprising. He was unable to kill. Time and time again in his confession one discovers him saying (in an offhand tone; one must dig for the implications): "I could not give the death blow, the hatchet glanced from his head," or, "I struck her several blows over the head, but I was unable to kill her, as the sword was dull . . ." It is too much to believe, over and over again: the glancing hatchet, the dull sword. It smacks rather, as in *Hamlet,* of rationalization, ghastly fear, an access of guilt, a shrinking from violence, and fatal irresolution. Alone here at this house, turned now into a huge corncrib around which pigs rooted and snorted in the silence of a spring afternoon, here alone was Nat finally able—or was he forced?—to commit a murder, and this upon a girl of eighteen named Margaret Whitehead, described by Drewry in terms perhaps not so romantic or farfetched after all, as "the belle of the county." The scene is apocalyptic—afternoon bedlam in wild harsh sunlight and August heat.

"I returned to commence the work of death, but those whom I left had not been idle; all the family were already murdered but Mrs. Whitehead and her daughter Margaret. As I came round the door I saw Will pulling Mrs. Whitehead out of the house and at the step he nearly severed her head from her body with his axe. Miss Margaret, when I discovered her, had concealed herself in the corner formed by the projection of the cellar cap from the house; on my approach she fled into the field but was soon overtaken and after repeated blows with a sword, I killed her by a blow on the head with a fence rail."

It is Nat's only murder. Why, from this point on, does the momentum of the uprising diminish, the drive and tension sag? Why, from this moment in the *Confessions,* does one sense in Nat something dispirited, listless, as if all life and juice had been drained from him, so that never again through the course of the rebellion is he even on the scene when a murder is committed? What happened to Nat in this place? Did he discover his humanity here, or did he lose it?

I lifted myself up into the house, clambering through a doorway without steps, pushing myself over the crumbling sill. The house had a faint yeasty fragrance, like flat beer. Dust from the mountains of corn lay everywhere in the deserted rooms, years and decades of dust, dust an inch thick in some places, lying in a fine gray powder like

25

sooty fallen snow. Off in some room amid the piles of corn I could hear a delicate scrabbling and a plaintive squeaking of mice. Again it was very still, the shadow of the prodigious old oak casting a dark pattern of leaves, checkered with bright sunlight, aslant through the gaping door. As in those chilling lines of Emily Dickinson, even this lustrous and golden day seemed to find its only resonance in the memory, and perhaps a premonition, of death.

> This quiet Dust was Gentlemen and Ladies,
>   And Lads and Girls;
> Was laughter and ability and sighing,
>   And frocks and curls.

Outside, the Sheriff was calling in on his car radio, his voice blurred and indistinct; then the return call from the county seat, loud, a dozen incomprehensible words in an uproar of static. Suddenly it was quiet again, the only sound my father's soft voice as he chatted with Mr. Seward.

I leaned past the rotting frame of the door, gazing out past the great tree and into that far meadow where Nat had brought down and slain Miss Margaret Whitehead. For an instant, in the silence, I thought I could hear a mad rustle of taffeta, and rushing feet, and a shrill girlish piping of terror; then that day and this day seemed to meet and melt together, becoming almost one, and for a long moment indistinguishable.

MY WHITE FATHER

(NOVEMBER 1989)

Priscilla Butler

I WAS BORN in Escambia County, Alabama, on the old Clinton plantation. My mother was— You know, it's the funniest thing—I can't find no record that she ever was born or that I was ever born. I tried to trace it back, when I got my Social Security.

I guess it might have been some mix-up or because my mother, she was nothing but a child when I was born. And so they all felt it was best that I be with my grandmother. I don't know why exactly. It had to do with me being born out of wedlock and everyone knowing I was the child of one of those Clinton boys—the white people that owned the plantation.

My mother never even told my aunt who my father was. I don't know why. We didn't know who he was for sure until my mother died. I was nine years old then. But see, when the time come to come out from the cloud and say who was my father, they all come out, him and his brothers. After she died, they all come out.

See, everybody that lived on that plantation, well, whenever one of them died and they got word, well, you didn't have no expenses about the burial. You just go over there and tell the one who had the coffin

27

house, Harry Clinton. He had a houseful of coffins, all kinds and all sizes, and he'd bring the peach tree switch down, and they measured the body and then brought the coffin.

So when my mother died, my father told his youngest brother, Andrew, to come see about me. All through my life, Andrew played a major role. He always came for my father. See, my father was old enough to be my daddy, and Andrew wasn't. If my daddy had come, that would have kind of pointed to him. My daddy was the lawyer one in the family. He was considered more professional than the rest of them. They had a lot of boys, and everybody knew I was cross-breeded but nobody could lay their fingers on just who it was.

Anyway, the day my mother died, Andrew said to my aunt, "We want you to take Priscilla because we don't want her to nurse nobody's babies until she's nursed her own." My aunt said my mother had asked them for that promise. "And she is never to get out in the field. And whenever she needs something, you come over to the store and knock and you'll wake me up and we'll let her father know." Andrew ran one of the stores on the plantation where you could buy different things.

So after that, I was raised with the best of everything. But I never did want anything to do with my daddy. My husband had to blow on me cold to make me be nice to him. A long time after I was grown and gone, he and his chauffeur came here once the day after Christmas. That was the first time. Before that, he always sent Andrew home whenever I needed anything or he thought I needed anything. He started the habit that year: if he came, he'd always come the day after Christmas. And he'd bring a great big old box with apples and oranges.

My daughter was at the door that first time he came. He said, "Is your mother home?" And she said, "Yes sir, Mister." He said, "Don't you ever call me 'Mister.' " He says, "I am your grandfather, and always when I come here, you call me Grandfather."

He ended up giving us all some money. Sometimes he gave my husband as much as fifty dollars and each one of the children ten dollars. And I always got my share all through the year. But I still didn't like him. I didn't really hate him, but I didn't cultivate a friendship for him to think that he was on the same level of society as me or that I was on the same level of society with him.

I just don't know why. I didn't feel he was better than me or I was better than him. I felt that the society that I lived in and around didn't want anything to do with me. On account of I was a mulatto, and I guess I blamed him for that.

Once, I remember—I guess I just won't let it die—I was standing up on one of the store porches one Saturday. And my aunt used to dress me up. She would make me the beautifulest clothes. 'Cause my daddy paid for it.

Well, I was standing there on the porch—look like to me it was drizzling rain—waiting for it to stop. And somebody said, "Oh, who's that little girl?" I used to have long plaits coming down to my belt line. If I had on a little red checkerdy gingham dress, well, then I had a big red bow on my hair, a great big one. If I had on a pink checkerdy dress, a pink bow.

So, anyway, they said, "Who's that little girl?" This old woman—I can't remember what her name was. But I hope she done served the time in hell and out by now, 'cause she was an old devil. She said, "Don't you know?" Said, "That's Aunt Grace's old Elizabeth's baby." My grandmother was Grace, and my mother was Elizabeth. She said it in a mean way, like there was something horrible about me. I can remember they said, "Well, that's a beautiful child." She said, "Well, don't think too much of that," say, "because when she grows up, so's the mammy, so's the child."

I went home to my aunt and I cried and cried. It was something terrible with me, I thought, for her to say such a thing. I had that stigma in me. "So is the mammy, so is the child." I just won't let that die.

Well, I don't know if it was rape or money or lust or affection or what that caused the mingling-up. I never talked to no one about it in those terms. In my mother's case, I don't know. I've spent a lot of my life trying to know, but I don't. My father felt something to keep up with me, but I don't know why he felt it—duty or guilt or what. I just don't know.

My mother protected me by making them promise I wouldn't have to nurse no babies until I'd nursed my own. Maybe the trouble came in when you were so young and went into the white homes. I don't know.

After I married, see, I moved to Mississippi and was glad to go, and my husband worked there in a paper mill. He made good money and we had two children. But one of the supervisors there told him he'd been up North and saw the Depression coming, and said they were gonna start laying off soon. And said we should move to Mobile, because in the city, women could always work in white homes.

So we moved to Mobile in 1930. We moved and stayed with another aunt of mine, Aunt Caroline. We stayed there until we built our own home. I went to work for Lawyer Scott, and they paid you ten a week, and oh, that was a lot of money then. But darling! You stayed there. If they wanted to have a conversation around the table, you didn't act sour, didn't rattle those pots and pans. And maybe it be nine-thirty before you'd get out of the kitchen. And oh, my dear, you'd been there since six-thirty in the morning.

I was glad when I didn't have to work there more. And why I didn't work more was on account of we had a run-in. Because my aunt, she needed help getting insurance money from her son dying. They wouldn't pay, and finally Lawyer Scott got them to pay. He put the money in the bank in his name, though. He said he was just taking his 4 percent out slow. My aunt, she accepted that. She was raised up where Negroes were supposed to do whatever boss told you, you accept that. She thought she'd get it in time.

Well, a year went by and no money for my aunt. I quit there. And I called on Miz Lucy Meyers. She was a white lady, and she would do all she could for the Negroes because the white people didn't recognize her husband altogether as being white. His mother had had two colored children before she married his father, and the white people, for that, wouldn't let those children go to school. So she got in touch with Andrew, my daddy's brother. And Andrew called on Lawyer Scott and fixed it.

He was stealing her money! And some of those whites, I don't know! I never felt quite like I could trust any of them. Not even

Andrew, who played the dear one, always coming for my father. No, I didn't trust the ones that were family or the ones I worked for, neither one. Now Andrew, he died not long ago. He'd been down sick. His cook was named Willie Bell, and Willie Bell let me know about it. She called and said he's been asking for you and asking for you. I kept on avoiding it, till finally my husband said, "Why don't you go?"

So he carried me there one Sunday, and when I got there, that doctor had just given him some kind of sedative. I was on the porch, and his wife asked me, "What's your name?" I said, "Priscilla." She said, "You waited a mighty long time to come." I say, "I admit that." And pecans began falling on the house, on the roof. I told her I'd better go so she could close the door and he wouldn't hear the noise of the pecans on the roof. He was right down the hall there.

So I left, and he died that week. Well, I didn't see him, so I never knew for sure if I would have trusted him in the end. We knew each other most all our lives. And I later heard through the grapevine that I cheated myself out of something, some money or some land, by not going earlier. But you know, some days I care and some days I don't.

WHY I RETURNED

(APRIL 1965)

Arna Bontemps

THE LAST TIME I visited Louisiana, the house in which I was born was freshly painted. To my surprise, it seemed almost attractive. The present occupants, I learned, were a Negro minister and his family. Why I expected the place to be run-down and the neighborhood decayed is not clear, but somewhere in my subconscious the notion that rapid deterioration was inevitable where Negroes live had been planted and allowed to grow. Moreover, familiar as I am with the gloomier aspects of living Jim Crow, this assumption did not appall me. I could reject the snide inferences. Seeing my birthplace again, however, after many years, I felt apologetic on other grounds.

Mine had not been a varmint-infested childhood so often the hallmark of Negro American autobiography. My parents and grandparents had been well-fed, well-clothed, and well-housed, although in my earliest recollections of the corner at Ninth and Winn in Alexandria both streets were rutted and sloppy. On Winn there was an abominable ditch where water settled for weeks at a time. I can remember Crazy George, the town idiot, following a flock of geese with the bough of a tree in his hand, standing in slush while the geese paddled

33

about or probed into the muck. So fascinated was I, in fact, I did not hear my grandmother calling from the kitchen door. It was after I felt her hand on my shoulder shaking me out of my daydream that I said something that made her laugh. "You called me Arna," I protested, when she insisted on knowing why I had not answered. "My name is George." But I became Arna for the rest of her years.

I had already become aware of nicknames among the people we regarded as members of the family. Teel, Mousie, Buddy, Pinkie, Ya-ya, Mat, and Pig all had other names which one heard occasionally. I got the impression that to be loved intensely one needed a nickname. I was glad my grandmother, whose love mattered so much, had found one she liked for me.

As I recall, my hand was in my grandmother's a good part of the time. If we were not standing outside the picket gate waiting for my young uncles to come home from school, we were under the tree in the front yard picking up pecans after one of the boys had climbed up and shaken the branches. If we were not decorating a backyard bush with eggshells, we were driving in our buggy across the bridge to Pineville on the other side of the Red River.

This idyll came to a sudden, senseless end at a time when everything about it seemed flawless. One afternoon my mother and her several sisters had come out of their sewing room with thimbles still on their fingers, needles and thread stuck to their tiny aprons, to fill their pockets with pecans. Next, it seemed, we were at the railroad station catching a train to California, my mother, sister, and I, with a young woman named Susy.

The story behind it, I learned, concerned my father. When he was not away working at brick or stone construction, other things occupied his time. He had come from a family of builders. His oldest brother had married into the Metoyer family on Cane River, descendants of the free Negroes who were the original builders of the famous Melrose plantation mansion. Another brother older than my father went down to New Orleans, where his daughter married one of the prominent jazzmen. My father was a bandman himself and, when he was not working too far away, the chances were he would be blowing his horn under the direction of Claiborne Williams, whose passion for band music awakened the impulse that worked its way up the river and helped to quicken American popular music.

My father was one of those dark Negroes with "good" hair, meaning almost straight. This did not bother anybody in Avoyelles Parish, where the type was common and "broken French" accents expected, but later in California people who had traveled in the Far East wondered if he were not a Ceylonese or something equally exotic. In Alexandria his looks, good clothes, and hauteur were something of a disadvantage in the first decade of this century.

He was walking on Lee Street one night when two white men wavered out of a saloon and blocked his path. One of them muttered, "Let's walk over the big nigger." My father was capable of fury, and he might have reasoned differently at another time, but that night he calmly stepped aside, allowing the pair to have the walk to themselves. The decision he made as he walked on home changed everything for all of us.

My first clear memory of my father as a person is of him waiting for us outside the Southern Pacific Depot in Los Angeles. He was shy about showing emotion, and he greeted us quickly on our arrival and let us know this was the place he had chosen for us to end our journey. We had tickets to San Francisco and were prepared to continue beyond if necessary.

We moved into a house in a neighborhood where we were the only colored family. The people next door and up and down the block were friendly and talkative, the weather was perfect, there wasn't a mud puddle anywhere, and my mother seemed to float about on the clean air. When my grandmother and a host of others followed us to this refreshing new country, I began to pick up comment about the place we had left, comment which had been withheld from me while we were still in Louisiana.

They talked mainly about my grandmother's younger brother, nicknamed Buddy. I could not remember seeing him in Louisiana, and I now learned he had been down at the Keeley Institute in New Orleans taking a cure for alcoholism. A framed portrait of Uncle Buddy was placed in my grandmother's living room in California, a young mulatto dandy in elegant cravat and jeweled stickpin. All the talk about him gave me an impression of style, grace, éclat.

The impression vanished a few years later, however, when we gathered to wait for him in my grandmother's house; he entered wearing a detachable collar without a tie. His clothes did not fit. They had been slept in for nearly a week on the train. His shoes had come unlaced. His face was pockmarked. Nothing resembled the picture in the living room.

Two things redeemed the occasion, however. He opened his makeshift luggage and brought out jars of syrup, bags of candy my grandmother had said in her letters that she missed, pecans, and filé for making gumbo. He had stuffed his suitcase with these instead of clothes; he had not brought an overcoat or a change of underwear. As we ate the sweets, he began to talk. He was not trying to impress or even entertain us. He was just telling how things were down home, how he had not taken a drink or been locked up since he came back from Keeley the last time, how the family of his employer and benefactor had been scattered or died, how the schoolteacher friend of the family was getting along, how high the Red River had risen along the levee, and such things.

Someone mentioned his white employer's daughter. A rumor persisted that Buddy had once had a dangerous crush on her. This, I took it, had to be back in the days when the picture in the living room was made, but the dim suggestion of interracial romance had an air of unreality. It was all mostly gossip, he commented, with only a shadow of a smile. Never had been much to it, and it was too long ago to talk about now. He did acknowledge, significantly, I thought, that his boss's daughter had been responsible for his enjoyment of poetry and fiction and had taught him perhaps a thousand songs, but neither of these circumstances had undermined his lifelong employment in her father's bakery, where his specialty was fancy cakes. Buddy had never married. Neither had the girl.

When my mother became ill, a year or so after Buddy's arrival, we went to live with my grandmother in the country for a time. Buddy was there. He had acquired a rusticity wholly foreign to his upbringing. He had never before worked out of doors. Smoking a corncob pipe and wearing oversized clothes provided by my uncles, he resembled a scarecrow in the garden, but the dry air and the smell of green vegetables seemed to be good for him. I promptly became his companion and confidant in the corn rows.

At mealtime we were occasionally joined by my father, home from his bricklaying. The two men eyed each other with suspicion, but they did not quarrel immediately. Mostly they reminisced about Louisiana. My father would say, "Sometimes I miss all that. If I was just thinking about myself, I might want to go back and try it again. But I've got the children to think about—their education."

"Folks talk a lot about California," Buddy would reply thoughtfully, "but I'd a heap rather be down home than here, if it wasn't for the *conditions*."

Obviously their remarks made sense to each other, but they left me with a deepening question. Why was this exchange repeated after so many of their conversations? What was it that made the South—excusing what Buddy called the *conditions*—so appealing for them?

There was less accord between them in the attitudes they revealed when each of the men talked to me privately. My father respected Buddy's ability to quote the whole of Thomas Hood's "The Vision of Eugene Aram," praised his reading and spelling ability, but he was concerned, almost troubled, about the possibility of my adopting the old derelict as an example. He was horrified by Buddy's casual and frequent use of the word *nigger*. Buddy even forgot and used it in the presence of white people once or twice that year, and was soundly criticized for it. Buddy's new friends, moreover, were sometimes below the level of polite respect. They were not bad people. They were what my father described as don't-care folk. To top it all, Buddy was still crazy about the minstrel shows and minstrel talk that had been the joy of his young manhood. He loved dialect stories, preacher stories, ghost stories, slave and master stories. He half-believed in signs and charms and mumbo-jumbo, and he believed wholeheartedly in ghosts.

I took it that my father was still endeavoring to counter Buddy's baneful influence when he sent me away to a white boarding school during my high school years, after my mother had died. "Now don't go up there acting colored," he cautioned. I believe I carried out his wish. He sometimes threatened to pull me out of school and let me scuffle for myself the minute I fell short in any one of several ways he indicated. Before I finished college, I had begun to feel that in some large and important areas I was being miseducated, and that perhaps I should have rebelled.

How dare anyone, parent, schoolteacher, or merely literary critic, tell me not to act *colored?* White people have been enjoying the privilege of acting like Negroes for more than a hundred years. The minstrel show, their most popular form of entertainment in America for a whole generation, simply epitomized, while it exaggerated, this privilege. Today nearly everyone who goes on a dance floor starts acting colored immediately, and this had been going on since the cakewalk was picked up from Negroes and became the rage. Why should I be ashamed of such influences? In popular music, as in the music of religious fervor, there is a style that is unmistakable, and its origin is certainly no mystery. On the playing field a Willie Mays could be detected by the way he catches a ball, even if his face were hidden. Should the way some Negroes walk be changed or emulated? Sometimes it is possible to tell whether or not a cook is a Negro without going into the kitchen. How about this?

In their opposing attitudes toward roots my father and my great uncle made me aware of a conflict in which every educated American Negro, and some who are not educated, must somehow take sides. By implication at least, one group advocates embracing the riches of the folk heritage; their opposites demand a clean break with the past and all it represents. Had I not gone home summers and hobnobbed with Negroes, I would have finished college without knowing that any Negro other than Paul Laurence Dunbar ever wrote a poem. I would have come out imagining that the story of the Negro could be told in two short paragraphs: a statement about jungle people in Africa and an equally brief account of the slavery issue in American history.

So what did one do after concluding that for him a break with the past and the shedding of his Negro-ness were not only impossible but unthinkable? First, perhaps, like myself, he went to New York in the twenties, met young Negro writers and intellectuals who were similarly searching, learned poems like Claude McKay's "Harlem Dancer" and Jean Toomer's "Song of the Son," and started writing and publishing things in this vein himself.

My first book was published just after the Depression struck. Buddy was in it, conspicuously, and I sent him a copy, which I imagine he read. In any case, he took the occasion to celebrate. Returning from an evening with his don't-care friends, he wavered along the highway and was hit and killed by an automobile. He was sixty-seven, I believe.

Alfred Harcourt, Sr. was my publisher. When he invited me to the office, I found that he was also to be my editor. He explained with a smile that he was back on the job doing editorial work because of the hard times. I soon found out what he meant. Book business appeared to be as bad as every other kind, and the lively and talented young people I had met in Harlem were scurrying to whatever brier patches they could find. I found one in Alabama.

It was the best of times and the worst of times to run to that state for refuge. Best, because the summer air was so laden with honeysuckle and spiraea it almost drugged the senses at night. I have occasionally returned since then but never at a time when the green of trees, of countryside, or even of swamps seemed so wanton. While paying jobs were harder to find here than in New York, indeed scarcely existed, one did not see evidences of hunger. Negro girls worked in kitchens not for wages but for the toting privilege—permission to take home leftovers.

The men and boys rediscovered woods and swamps and streams with which their ancestors had been intimate a century earlier, and about which their grandparents still talked wistfully. The living critters still abounded. They were as wild and numerous as anybody had ever dreamed, some small, some edible, some monstrous. I made friends with these people and went with them on possum hunts, and I was astonished to learn how much game they could bring home without gunpowder, which they did not have. When the possum was treed by the dogs, a small boy went up and shook him off the limb, and the bigger fellows finished him with sticks. Nets and traps would do for birds and fish. Cottontail rabbits driven into a clearing were actually run down and caught by barefoot boys.

Such carryings-on amused them while it delighted their palates. It also took their minds off the hard times, and they were ready for church when Sunday came. I followed them there, too, and soon began to understand why they enjoyed it so much. The preaching called to mind James Weldon Johnson's "The Creation" and "Go Down Death." The long-meter singing was from another world. The shouting was ecstasy itself. At a primitive Baptist foot washing I saw bench-walking for the first time, and it left me breathless. The young woman who rose from her seat and skimmed from the front of the church to the back, her wet feet lightly touching the tops of the pews, her eyes upward, could have astounded me no more had she walked on water. The members fluttered and wailed, rocked the church with their singing, accepted the miracle for what it was.

It was also the worst times to be in northern Alabama. That was the year, 1931, of the nine Scottsboro boys and their trials in nearby Decatur. Instead of chasing possums at night and swimming in creeks in the daytime, this group of kids without jobs and nothing else to do had taken to riding empty boxcars. When they found themselves in a boxcar with two white girls wearing overalls and traveling the same way, they knew they were in bad trouble. The charge against them was rape, and the usual finding in Alabama, when a Negro man was so much as remotely suspected, was guilty; the usual penalty, death.

To relieve the tension, as we hoped, we drove to Athens one night and listened to a program of music by young people from Negro high schools and colleges in the area. A visitor arrived from Decatur during the intermission and reported shocking developments at the trial that day. One of the girls involved had given testimony about herself which reasonably should have taken the onus from the boys. It had only succeeded in infuriating the crowd around the courthouse. The rumor that reached Athens was that crowds were spilling along the highway, lurking in unseemly places, threatening to vent their anger. After the music was over, someone suggested nervously that those of us from around Huntsville leave at the same time, keep our cars close together as we drove home, be prepared to stand by, possibly help, if anyone met with mischief.

We readily agreed. Though the drive home was actually uneventful, the tension remained, and I began to take stock with a seriousness comparable to my father's when he stepped aside for the Saturday night bullies on Lee Street in Alexandria. I was younger than he had been when he made his move, but my family was already larger by one. Moreover, I had weathered a Northern as well as a Southern exposure. My education was different, and what I was reading in newspapers differed greatly from anything he could have found in the Alexandria *Town Talk* in the first decade of this century.

With Gandhi making world news in India while the Scottsboro case inflamed passions in Alabama and awakened consciences elsewhere, I thought I could sense something beginning to shape up, possibly something on a wide scale. As a matter of fact, I had already written a stanza foreshadowing the application of a nonviolent strategy to the Negro's efforts in the South:

> We are not come to wage a strife
>   With swords upon this hill;
> It is not wise to waste the life
>   Against a stubborn will.
> Yet would we die as some have done:
> Beating a way for the rising sun.

Even so, deliverance did not yet seem imminent, and it was becoming plain that an able-bodied young Negro with a healthy family could not continue to keep friends in that community if he sat around trifling with a typewriter on the shady side of his house when he should have been working or at least trying to raise something for the table. So we moved to Chicago.

Crime seemed to be the principal occupation of the South Side at the time of our arrival. The openness of it so startled us we could scarcely believe what we saw. Twice our small apartment was burglarized. Nearly every week we witnessed a stickup, a purse-snatching, or something equally dismaying on the street. Once I saw two men get out of a car, enter one of those blinded shops around the corner from us, return dragging a resisting victim, slam him into the back seat of the car, and speed away. We had fled from the jungle of Alabama's Scottsboro era to the jungle of Chicago's crime-ridden South Side, and one was as terrifying as the other.

Despite literary encouragement, and the heartiness of a writing clan that adopted me and bolstered my courage, I never felt that I could settle permanently with my family in Chicago. I could not accept the ghetto, and ironclad residential restrictions against Negroes situated as we were made escape impossible, confining us to neighborhoods where we had to fly home each evening before darkness fell and honest people abandoned the streets to predators. Garbage was dumped in alleys around us. Police protection was regarded as a farce. Corruption was everywhere.

When I inquired about transfers for two of our children to integrated schools which were actually more accessible to our address, I was referred to a person not connected with the school system or the city government. He assured me he could arrange the transfers—at an outrageous price. This represented ways in which Negro leadership was operating in the community at that time and by which it had been reduced to impotence.

I did not consider exchanging this way of life for the institutionalized assault on Negro personality one encountered in the Alabama of the Scottsboro trials, but suddenly the campus of a Negro college I had twice visited in Tennessee began to seem attractive. A measure of isolation, a degree of security seemed possible there. If a refuge for the harassed Negro could be found anywhere in the 1930s, it had to be in such a setting.

Fisk University, since its beginnings in surplus barracks provided by a general of the occupying army six months after the close of the Civil War, had always striven to exemplify racial concord. Integration started immediately with children of white teachers and continued till state laws forced segregation after the turn of the century. Even then, a mixed faculty was retained, together with a liberal environment, and these eventually won a truce from an outside community that gradually changed from hostility to indifference to acceptance and perhaps a certain pride. Its founders helped fight the battle for public schools in Nashville, and donated part of the college's property for this purpose. Its students first introduced Negro spirituals to the musical world. The college provided a setting for a continuing dialogue between scholars across barriers and brought to the city before 1943 a pioneering Institute of Race Relations and a Program of African Studies, both firsts in the region. When a nationally known scholar told me in Chicago that he found the atmosphere *yeasty*, I thought I understood what he meant.

We had made the move, and I had become the Librarian at Fisk when a series of train trips during World War II gave me an opportunity for reflections of another kind. I started making notes for an essay to be called "Thoughts in a Jim Crow Car." Before I could finish it, Supreme Court action removed the curtains in the railway diners, and the essay lost its point. While I had been examining my own feelings and trying to understand the need men have for customs like this, the pattern had altered. Compliance followed with what struck me, surprisingly, as an attitude of relief by all concerned. White passengers, some of whom I recognized by their positions in the public life of Nashville, who had been in a habit of maintaining a frozen silence until the train crossed the Ohio River, now nodded and began chatting with Negroes before the train left the Nashville station. I wanted to stand up and cheer. When the Army began to desegregate its units, I was sure I detected a fatal weakness in our enemy. Segregation, the monster that had terrorized my parents and driven them out of the green Eden in which they had been born, was itself vulnerable and could be attacked, possibly destroyed. I felt as if I had witnessed the first act of a spectacular drama. I wanted to stay around for the second.

Without the miseries of segregation, the South as a homeplace for a Negro of my temperament had clear advantages. In deciding to wait and see how things worked out, I was also betting that progress toward this objective in the Southern region would be more rapid, the results more satisfying, than could be expected in the metropolitan centers of the North, where whites were leaving the crumbling central areas to Negroes while they themselves moved into restricted suburbs and began setting up another kind of closed society.

The second act of the spectacular on which I had focused began with the 1954 decision of the Supreme Court. While this was a landmark, it provoked no wild optimism. I had no doubt that the tide would now turn, but it was not until the freedom movement began to express itself that I felt reassured. We were in the middle of it in Nashville. Our little world commenced to sway and rock with the fury of a resurrection. I tried to discover just how the energy was generated. I think I found it. The singing that broke out in the ranks of protest marchers, in the jails where sit-in demonstrations were held, in the mass meetings and boycott rallies, was gloriously appropriate. The only American songs suitable for a resurrection—or a revolution, for that matter—are Negro spirituals. The surge these awakened was so mighty it threatened to change the name of our era from the "space age" to the "age of freedom."

The Southern Negro's link with his past seems to me worth preserving. His greater pride in being himself, I would say, is all to the good, and I think I detect a growing nostalgia for these virtues in the speech of relatives in the North. They talk a great deal about "Soulville" nowadays, when they mean "South." "Soulbrothers" are simply the homefolks. "Soulfood" includes black-eyed peas, chitterlings, grits, and gravy. Aretha Franklin, originally from Memphis, sings, "Soulfood—it'll make you limber; it'll make you quick." Vacations in Soulville by these expatriates in the North tend to become more frequent and to last longer since times began to get better.

Colleagues of mine at Fisk who like me have pondered the question of staying or going have told me their reasons. The effective young Dean of the Chapel, for example, who since has been wooed away by Union Theological Seminary, felt constrained mainly by the opportunities he had here to guide a large number of students and by the privilege of identifying with them. John W. Work, the musicologist and composer, finds the cultural environment more stimulating than any he could discover in the North. Aaron Douglas, an art professor, came down thirty-four years ago to get a "real, concrete experience of the touch and feel of the South." Looking back, he reflects, "If one could discount the sadness, the misery, the near-volcanic intensity of Negro life in most of the South, and concentrate on the mild, almost tropical climate and the beauty of the landscape, one is often tempted to forget the senseless cruelty and inhumanity the strong too often inflict on the weak."

For my own part, I am staying on in the South to write something about the changes I have seen in my lifetime, and about the Negro's awakening and regeneration. That is my theme, and this is where the main action is. There is also the spectacular I am watching. Was a climax reached with the passage of the Civil Rights Act last year? Or was it with Martin Luther King's addressing Lyndon B. Johnson as "my fellow Southerner"? Having stayed this long, it would be absurd not to wait for the third act—and possibly the most dramatic.

HARLEM IS NOWHERE

(AUGUST 1964)

Ralph Ellison

TO LIVE IN Harlem is to dwell in the very bowels of the city; it is to pass a labyrinthine existence among streets that explode monotonously skyward with the spires and crosses of churches and clutter under foot with garbage and decay. Harlem is a ruin—many of its ordinary aspects (its crimes, its casual violence, its crumbling buildings with littered areaways, ill-smelling halls, and vermin-invaded rooms) are indistinguishable from the distorted images that appear in dreams, and which, like muggers haunting a lonely hall, quiver in the waking mind with hidden and threatening significance. Yet this is no dream but the reality of well over four hundred thousand Americans; a reality which for many defines and colors the world. Overcrowded and exploited politically and economically, Harlem is the scene and symbol of the Negro's perpetual alienation in the land of his birth.

But much has been written about the social and economic aspects of Harlem; I am here interested in its psychological character—a character that arises from the impact between urban slum conditions and folk sensibilities. Historically, American Negroes are caught in a vast process of change that has swept them from slavery to the condition of indus-

47

trial man in a space of time so telescoped (a bare eighty-five years) that it is possible literally for them to step from feudalism into the vortex of industrialism simply by moving across the Mason-Dixon Line.

This abruptness of change and the resulting clash of cultural factors within the Negro personality account for some of the extreme contrasts found in Harlem, for both its negative and its positive characteristics. For if Harlem is the scene of the folk-Negro's death agony, it is also the setting of his transcendence. Here it is possible for talented youths to leap through the development of decades in a brief twenty years, while beside them white-haired adults crawl in the feudal darkness of their childhood. Here a former cotton picker develops the sensitive hands of a surgeon, and men whose grandparents still believe in magic prepare optimistically to become atomic scientists. Here the grandchildren of those who possessed no written literature examine their lives through the eyes of Freud and Marx, Kierkegaard and Kafka, Malraux and Sartre. It explains the nature of a world so fluid and shifting that often within the mind the real and the unreal merge, and the marvelous beckons from behind the same sordid reality that denies its existence.

Hence the most surreal fantasies are acted out upon the streets of Harlem; a man ducks in and out of traffic shouting and throwing imaginary grenades that actually exploded during World War I; a boy participates in the rape-robbery of his mother; a man beating his wife in a park uses boxing "science" and observes Marquess of Queensberry rules (no rabbit punching, no blows beneath the belt); two men hold a third while a lesbian slashes him to death with a razor blade; boy gangsters wielding homemade pistols (which in the South of their origin are but toy symbols of adolescent yearning for manhood) shoot down their young rivals. Life becomes a masquerade, exotic costumes are worn every day. Those who cannot afford to hire a horse wear riding habits; others who could not afford a hunting trip or who seldom attend sporting events carry shooting sticks.

For this is a world in which the major energy of the imagination goes not into creating works of art, but to overcome the frustrations of social discrimination. Not quite citizens and yet Americans, full of the tensions of modern man, but regarded as primitives, Negro Americans are in desperate search for an identity. Rejecting the second-class status assigned them, they feel alienated and their whole lives have become a search for answers to the questions: Who am I, What am I, Why am I, and Where? Significantly, in Harlem the reply to the greeting, "How are you?" is very often, "Oh, man, I'm *nowhere*"—a phrase revealing an attitude so common that it has been reduced to a gesture, a seemingly trivial word. Indeed, Negroes are not unaware that the conditions of their lives demand new definitions of terms like *primitive* and *modern, ethical* and *unethical, moral* and *immoral, patriotism* and *treason, tragedy* and *comedy, sanity* and *insanity.*

But for a long time now—despite songs like the "Blow Top Blues" and the eruption of expressions like *frantic, buggy,* and *mad* into Harlem's popular speech, doubtless a word-magic against the states they name—calm in face of the unreality of Negro life becomes increasingly difficult. And while some seek relief in strange hysterical forms of religion, in alcohol and drugs, others learn to analyze the causes for their predicament and join with others to correct them.

In relation to their Southern background, the cultural history of Negroes in the North reads like the legend of some tragic people out of mythology, a people which aspired to escape from its own unhappy homeland to the apparent peace of a distant mountain; but which, in migrating, made some fatal error of judgment and fell into a great chasm of mazelike passages that promise ever to lead to the mountain but end ever against a wall. Not that a Negro is worse off in the North than in the South, but that in the North he surrenders and does not replace certain important supports to his personality. He leaves a relatively static social order in which, having experienced its brutality for hundreds of years—indeed, having been formed within it and by it— he has developed those techniques of survival to which Faulkner refers as "endurance," and an ease of movement within explosive situations which makes Hemingway's definition of courage, "grace under pressure," appear mere swagger. He surrenders the protection of his peasant cynicism—his refusal to hope for the fulfillment of hopeless hopes—and his sense of being "at home in the world" gained from confronting and accepting (for day-to-day living, at least) the obscene absurdity of his predicament. Further, he leaves a still authoritative religion which gives his life a semblance of metaphysical wholeness; a family structure which is relatively stable; and a body of folklore— tested in life-and-death terms against his daily experience with nature and the Southern white man—that serves him as a guide to action.

These are the supports of Southern Negro rationality (and, to an extent, of the internal peace of the United States); humble, but of inestimable psychological value,* they allow Southern Negroes to maintain their almost mystical hope for a future of full democracy—a hope accompanied by an irrepressible belief in some Mecca of equality, located in the North and identified by the magic place names New York, Chicago, Detroit. A belief sustained (as all myth is sustained by ritual) by identifying themselves ritually with the successes of Negro celebrities, by reciting their exploits and enumerating their dollars, and by recounting the swiftness with which they spiral from humble birth to headline fame. And doubtless the blasting of this dream is as damaging to Negro personality as the slum scenes of filth, disorder, and crumbling masonry in which it flies apart.

When Negroes are barred from participating in the main institutional life of society, they lose far more than economic privileges or the satisfaction of saluting the flag with unmixed emotions. They lose one of the bulwarks which men place between themselves and the constant threat of chaos. For whatever the assigned function of social institutions, their psychological function is to protect the citizen against the irrational, incalculable forces that hover about the edges of human life like cosmic destruction lurking within an atomic stockpile.

And it is precisely the denial of this support through segregation and discrimination that leaves the most balanced Negro open to anxiety.

Though caught not only in the tensions arising from his own swift history, but in those conflicts created in modern man by a revolution-

Their political and economic value is the measure of both the positive and negative characteristics of American democracy.

50

ary world, he cannot participate fully in the therapy which the white American achieves through patriotic ceremonies and by identifying himself with American wealth and power. Instead, he is thrown back upon his own "slum-shocked" institutions.

But these, like his folk personality, are caught in a process of chaotic change. His family disintegrates, his church splinters; his folk wisdom is discarded in the mistaken notion that it in no way applies to urban living; and his formal education (never really his own) provides him with neither scientific description nor rounded philosophical interpretation of the profound forces that are transforming his total being. Yet even his art is transformed; the lyrical ritual elements of folk jazz—that artistic projection of the only real individuality possible for him in the South, that embodiment of a superior democracy in which each individual cultivated his uniqueness and yet did not clash with his neighbors—have given way to the near-themeless technical virtuosity of bebop, a further triumph of technology over humanism. His speech hardens; his movements are geared to the time clock; his diet changes; his sensibilities quicken; and his intelligence expands. But without institutions to give him direction, and lacking a clear explanation of his predicament—the religious ones being inadequate, and those offered by political and labor leaders obviously incomplete and opportunistic—the individual feels that his world and his personality are out of key. The phrase "I'm nowhere" expresses the feeling borne in upon many Negroes that they have no stable, recognized place in society. One's identity drifts in a capricious reality in which even the most commonly held assumptions are questionable. One "is" literally, but one is nowhere; one wanders dazed in a ghetto maze, a "displaced person" of American democracy.

And as though all this were not enough of a strain on a people's sense of the rational, the conditions under which it lives are seized upon as proof of its inferiority. Thus the frustrations of Negro life (many of them the frustrations of *all* life during this historical moment) permeate the atmosphere of Harlem with a hostility that bombards the individual from so many directions that he is often unable to identify it with any specific object. Some feel it the punishment of some racial or personal guilt and pray to God; others (called "evil Negroes" in Harlem) become enraged with the world. Sometimes it provokes dramatic mass responses.

And why have these explosive matters—which are now a problem of our foreign policy—been ignored? Because there is an argument in progress between black men and white men as to the true nature of American reality. Following their own interests, whites impose interpretations upon Negro experience that are not only false but, in effect, a denial of Negro humanity. Too weak to shout down these interpretations, Negroes live nevertheless as they have to live, and the concrete conditions of their lives are more real than white men's arguments.

I Know Why the
Caged Bird Sings

(FEBRUARY 1970)

Maya Angelou

"What you looking at me for?
I didn't come to stay . . ."

I HADN'T SO much forgot as I couldn't bring myself to remember.
Other things were more important.

"What you looking at me for?
I didn't come to stay . . ."

Whether I could remember the rest of the poem or not was imma-
terial. The truth of the statement was like a wadded-up handkerchief,
sopping wet in my fists, and the sooner they accepted it the quicker I
could let my hands open and the air would cool my palms.

"What you looking at me for . . . ?"

The children's section of the Colored Methodist Episcopal Church
of Stamps, Arkansas, was wiggling and giggling over my well-known
forgetfulness.

The dress I wore was lavender taffeta, and each time I breathed it rustled, and now that I was sucking in air to breathe out shame it sounded like crepe paper on the back of hearses.

As I'd watched Momma put ruffles on the hem and cute little tucks around the waist, I knew that once I put it on I'd look like a movie star. (It was silk and that made up for the awful color.) I was going to look like one of the sweet little white girls who were everybody's dream of what was right with the world. Hanging softly over the black Singer sewing machine, it looked like magic, and when people saw me wearing it they were going to run up to me and say, "Marguerite [sometimes it was 'dear Marguerite'], forgive us, please, we didn't know who you were," and I would answer generously, "No, you couldn't have known. Of course I forgive you."

Just thinking about it made me go around with angel's dust sprinkled over my face for days. But Easter's early morning sun had shown the dress to be a plain ugly cut-down from a white woman's once-was-purple throwaway. It was old-lady-long too, but it didn't hide my skinny legs, which had been greased with Blue Seal Vaseline and powdered with the Arkansas red clay. The age-faded color made my skin look dirty like mud, and everyone in church was looking at my skinny legs.

Wouldn't they be surprised when one day I woke out of my black ugly dream, and my real hair, which was long and blond, would take the place of the kinky mass that Momma wouldn't let me straighten? My light-blue eyes were going to hypnotize them, after all the things they said about "my daddy must of been a Chinaman" (I thought they meant made out of china, like a cup) because my eyes were so small and squinty. Then they would understand why I had never picked up a Southern accent, or spoken the common slang, and why I had to be forced to eat pigs' tails and snouts. Because I was really white and because a cruel fairy stepmother, who was understandably jealous of my beauty, had turned me into a too-big Negro girl, with nappy black hair, broad feet, and a space between her teeth that would hold a number-two pencil.

"What you looking . . . " The minister's wife leaned toward me, her long yellow face full of sorry. She whispered, "I just come to tell you, it's Easter Day." I repeated, jamming the words together, "IjustcometotellyouitsEasterDay," as low as possible. The giggles hung in the air like melting clouds that were waiting to rain on me. I held up two fingers, close to my chest, which meant that I had to go to the toilet, and tiptoed toward the rear of the church. Dimly, somewhere over my head, I heard ladies saying, "Lord bless the child" and, "Praise God." My head was up and my eyes were open, but I didn't see anything. Halfway down the aisle, the church exploded with, "Were you there when they crucified my Lord?" and I tripped over a foot stuck out from the children's pew. I stumbled and started to say something, or maybe to scream, but a green persimmon, or it could have been a lemon, caught me between the legs and squeezed. I tasted the sour on my tongue and felt it in the back of my mouth. Then before I reached the door, the sting was burning down my legs and into my Sunday socks. I tried to hold, to squeeze it back, to keep it from speeding, but when I reached the church porch I knew I'd have to let it go, or it would probably run right back up to my head and my poor head would burst like a dropped watermelon, and all the brains and spit and tongue and eyes would roll all over the place. So I ran down into the yard and let it go. I ran, peeing and crying, not toward the toilet out back but to our house. I'd get a whipping for it, to be sure, and the nasty children would have something new to tease me about. I laughed anyway, partially for the sweet release; still, the greater joy came not from being liberated from the silly church but from the knowledge that I wouldn't die from a busted head.

If growing up is painful for the Southern Black girl, being aware of her displacement is the rust on the razor that threatens the throat. It is an unnecessary insult.

1.

My brother Bailey and I had come to the musty little town of Stamps when I was three and he four. We had arrived wearing tags on our wrists which instructed—"To Whom It May Concern"—that we were Marguerite and Bailey Johnson, Jr., from Long Beach,

55

California, en route to Stamps, Arkansas, c/o Mrs. Annie Henderson.

Our parents had decided to put an end to their calamitous marriage, and Father shipped us home to his mother. A porter had been charged with our welfare—he got off the train the next day in Arizona—and our tickets were pinned to my brother's inside coat pocket.

I don't remember much of the trip, but after we reached the segregated Southern part of the journey, things must have looked up. Negro passengers, who always traveled with loaded lunch boxes, felt sorry for "the poor little motherless darlings" and plied us with cold fried chicken and potato salad. Years later I discovered that the United States had been crossed thousands of times by frightened Black children traveling alone to their newly affluent parents in Northern cities, or back to grandmothers in Southern towns when the urban North reneged on its economic promises.

The town reacted to us as its inhabitants had reacted to all things new before our coming. It regarded us awhile without curiosity but with caution, and after we were seen to be harmless (and children) it closed in around us, as a real mother embraces a stranger's child. Warmly, but not too familiarly.

We lived with our grandmother and uncle in the rear of the Store (it was always spoken of with a capital *s*), which she had owned some twenty-five years. Early in the century, Momma (we soon stopped called her Grandmother) sold lunches to the sawmen in the lumberyard (east Stamps) and the seedmen at the cotton gin (west Stamps). Her crisp meat pies and cool lemonade, when joined to her miraculous ability to be in two places at the same time, assured her business success. From having a mobile lunch counter, she set up a stand between the two points of fiscal interest and supplied the workers' needs for a few years. Then she had the Store built in the heart of the Negro area. Over the years it became the lay center of activities in town. On Saturdays, barbers sat their customers in the shade on the porch of the Store, and troubadours on their ceaseless crawlings through the South leaned across its benches and sang their sad songs of The Brazos while they played juice harps and cigar-box guitars.

The formal name of the Store was the Wm. Johnson General Merchandise Store. Customers could find food staples, a good variety of colored thread, mash for hogs, corn for chickens, coal oil for lamps, light bulbs for the wealthy, shoestrings, hair dressing, balloons, and flower seeds. Anything not visible had only to be ordered. Until we became familiar enough to belong to the Store and it to us, we were locked up in a Fun House of Things where the attendant had gone home for life.

Each year I watched the field across from the Store turn caterpillar green, then gradually frosty white. I knew exactly how long it would be before the big wagons would pull into the front yard and load on the cotton pickers at daybreak to carry them to the remains of slavery's plantations.

During the picking season my grandmother would get out of bed at four o'clock (she never used an alarm clock) and creak down to her knees and chant in a sleep-filled voice, "Our Father, thank you for letting me see this New Day. Thank you that you didn't allow the bed I lay on last to be my cooling board, nor my blanket my winding sheet. Guide my feet this day along the straight and narrow, and help me to put a bridle on my tongue. Bless this house, and everybody in it. Thank you, in the name of your Son, Jesus Christ, Amen." Before she had quite arisen, she called our names and issued orders, and pushed her large feet into home slippers and across the bare lye-washed wooden floor to light the coal-oil lamp.

The lamplight in the Store gave a soft make-believe feeling to our world which made me want to whisper and walk about on tiptoe. The odors of onions and oranges and kerosene had been mixing all night and wouldn't be disturbed until the wooded slat was removed from the door and the early morning air forced its way in with the bodies of people who had walked miles to reach the pickup place.

"Sister, I'll have two cans of sardines."

"I'm gonna work so fast today I'm gonna make you look like you standing still."

"Lemme have a hunk uh cheese and some sody crackers."

"Just gimme a coupla them fat peanut paddies." That would be from a picker who was taking his lunch. The greasy brown-paper sack was stuck behind the bib of his overalls. He'd use the candy as a snack before the noon sun called the workers to rest.

In those tender mornings the Store was full of laughing, joking, boasting, and bragging. One man was going to pick two hundred pounds of cotton, and another three hundred. Even the children were promising to bring home fo' bits and six bits. The champion picker of the day before was the hero of the dawn. If he prophesied that the cotton in today's field was going to be sparse and stick to the bolls like glue, every listener would grunt a hearty agreement. The sound of the empty cotton sacks dragging over the floor and the murmurs of waking people were sliced by the cash register as we rang up the five-cent sales.

If the morning sounds and smells were touched with the supernatural, the late afternoon had all the features of the normal Arkansas life. In the dying sunlight the people dragged, rather than their empty cotton sacks. Brought back to the Store, the pickers would step out of the backs of trucks and fold down, dirt-disappointed, to the ground. No matter how much they had picked, it wasn't enough. Their wages wouldn't even get them out of debt to my grandmother, not to mention the staggering bill that waited on them at the white commissary downtown.

The sounds of the new morning had been replaced with grumbles about cheating houses, weighted scales, snakes, skimpy cotton, and dusty rows. In later years I was to confront the stereotyped picture of gay song-singing cotton pickers with such inordinate rage that I was told even by fellow Blacks that my paranoia was embarrassing. But I had seen the fingers cut by the mean little cotton bolls, and I had witnessed the backs and shoulders and arms and legs resisting any further demands.

Some of the workers would leave their sacks at the Store to be picked up the following morning, but a few had to take them home for repairs. I winced to picture them sewing the coarse material under a coal-oil lamp with fingers stiffening from the day's work. In too few hours they would have to walk back to Sister Henderson's Store, get vittles, and load, again, onto the trucks. Then they would face another day of trying to earn enough for the whole year with the heavy knowledge that they were going to end the season as they started it. Without the money or credit necessary to sustain a family for three months. In cotton-picking time the late afternoons revealed the harshness of Black Southern life, which in the early morning had been softened by nature's blessing of grogginess, forgetfulness, and the soft lamplight.

2.

When Bailey was six and I a year younger, we used to rattle off the times tables with the speed I was later to see Chinese children in San Francisco employ on their abacuses. Our summer-gray potbellied stove bloomed rosy red during winter, and became a severe disciplinarian threat if we were so foolish as to indulge in making mistakes.

Uncle Willie used to sit, like a giant black Z (he had been crippled as a child), and hear us testify to the Lafayette County Training School's abilities. His face pulled down on the left side, as if a pulley had been attached to his lower teeth, and his left hand was only a mite bigger than Bailey's, but on the second mistake or on the third hesitation his big overgrown right hand would catch one of us behind the collar, and in the same moment would thrust the culprit toward the dull red heater, which throbbed like a devil's toothache. We were never burned, although once I might have been when I was so terrified I tried to jump onto the stove to remove the possibility of its remaining a threat. Like most children, I thought if I could face the worst danger voluntarily, and *triumph,* I would forever have power over it. But in my case of sacrificial effort I was thwarted. Uncle Willie held tight to my dress and I only got close enough to smell the clean dry scent of hot iron. We learned the times tables without understanding their grand principle, simply because we had the capacity and no alternative.

The tragedy of lameness seems so unfair to children that they are embarrassed in its presence. And they, most recently off nature's mold, sense that they have only narrowly missed being another of her jokes. In relief at the narrow escape, they vent their emotions in impatience and criticism of the unlucky cripple.

59

Momma related times without end, and without any show of emotion, how Uncle Willie had been dropped when he was three years old by a woman who was minding him. She seemed to hold no rancor against the baby-sitter, nor for her just God who allowed the accident. She felt it necessary to explain over and over again to those who knew the story by heart that he wasn't "born that way."

In our society, where two-legged, two-armed strong Black men were able at best to eke out only the necessities of life, Uncle Willie, with his starched shirts, shined shoes, and shelves full of food, was the whipping boy and butt of jokes of the underemployed and underpaid. Fate not only disabled him but laid a double-tiered barrier in his path. He was also proud and sensitive. Therefore he couldn't pretend that he wasn't crippled, nor could he deceive himself that people were not repelled by his defect.

Only once in all the years of trying not to watch him, I saw him pretend to himself and others that he wasn't lame. Coming home from school one day, I saw a dark car in our front yard. I rushed in to find a strange man and woman (Uncle Willie said later they were schoolteachers from Little Rock) drinking Dr. Peppers in the cool of the Store. I sensed a wrongness around me, like an alarm clock that had gone off without being set.

I knew it couldn't be the strangers. Not frequently, but often enough, travelers pulled off the main road to buy tobacco or soft drinks in the only Negro store in Stamps. When I looked at Uncle Willie, I knew what was pulling my mind's coattails. He was standing erect behind the counter, not leaning forward or resting on the small shelf that had been built for him. Erect. His eyes seemed to hold me with a mixture of threat and appeal.

I dutifully greeted the strangers and roamed my eyes around for his walking stick. It was nowhere to be seen. He said, "Uh . . . this this . . . this . . . uh, my niece. She's . . . uh . . . just come from school." Then to the couple—"You know . . . how, uh, children are . . . th-th-these days . . . they play all d-d-day at school and c-c-can't wait to get home and pl-play some more."

The people smiled, very friendly.

He added, "Go on out and pl-play, Sister."

The lady laughed in a soft Arkansas voice and said, "Well, you know, Mr. Johnson, they say, You're only a child once. Have you children of your own?"

Uncle Willie looked at me with an impatience I hadn't seen in his face even when he took thirty minutes to loop the laces over his high-topped shoes. "I . . . I thought I told you to go . . . go outside and play."

Before I left I saw him lean back on the shelves of Garret Snuff, Prince Albert, and Spark Plug chewing tobacco.

"No ma'am . . . no ch-children and no wife." He tried a laugh. "I have an old m-m-mother and my brother's t-two children to l-look after."

The couple left after a few minutes, and from the back of the house I watched the red car scare chickens, raise dust, and disappear toward Magnolia.

Uncle Willie was making his way down the long shadowed aisle between the shelves and the counter—hand over hand, like a man climbing out of a dream. I stayed quiet and watched him lurch from one side, bumping to the other, until he reached the coal-oil tank. He put his hand behind that dark recess and took his cane in the strong fist and shifted his weight on the wooden support. He thought he had pulled it off.

I'll never know why it was important to him that the couple (he said later that he'd never seen them before) would take a picture of a whole Mr. Johnson back to Little Rock. He must have tired of being crippled, as prisoners tire of penitentiary bars and the guilty tire of blame. The high-topped shoes and the cane, his uncontrollable muscles and thick tongue, and the looks he suffered of either contempt or pity had simply worn him out, and for one afternoon, one part of an afternoon, he wanted no part of them.

I understood and felt closer to him at the moment than ever before or since.

During these years in Stamps, I met and fell in love with William

61

Shakespeare. He was my first white love. Although I enjoyed and respected Kipling, Poe, Butler, Thackeray, and Henley, I saved my young and loyal passion for Paul Lawrence Dunbar, Langston Hughes, James Weldon Johnson, and W.E.B. Du Bois's "Litany at Atlanta." But it was Shakespeare who said, "When in disgrace with fortune and men's eyes." It was a state with which I felt myself most familiar. I pacified myself about his whiteness by saying that after all he had been dead so long it couldn't matter to anyone anymore.

Bailey and I decided to memorize a scene from *The Merchant of Venice,* but we realized that Momma would question us about the author and that we'd have to tell her that Shakespeare was white, and it wouldn't matter to her whether he was dead or not. So we chose "The Creation" by James Weldon Johnson instead.

3.

Until I was thirteen and left Arkansas for good, the Store was my favorite place to be. Alone and empty in the mornings, it looked like an unopened present from a stranger. Opening the front doors was pulling the ribbon off the unexpected gift. The light would come in softly (we faced north), easing itself over the shelves of mackerel, salmon, tobacco, thread. It fell flat on the big vat of lard and by noontime during the summer the grease had softened to a thick soup. Whenever I walked into the Store in the afternoon, I sensed that it was tired. I alone could hear the slow pulse of its job half done. But just before bedtime, after numerous people had walked in and out, had argued over their bills, or joked about their neighbors, or just dropped in "to give Sister Henderson a 'Hi y'all,' " the promise of magic mornings returned to the Store and spread itself over the family in washed life waves.

Momma opened boxes of crispy crackers and we sat around the meat block at the rear of the Store. I sliced onions, and Bailey opened two or even three cans of sardines and allowed their juice of oil and fishing boats to ooze down and around the sides. That was supper. In the evening, when we were alone like that, Uncle Willie didn't stutter or shake or give any indication that he had an "affliction." It seemed that the peace of a day's ending was an assurance that the covenant God made with children, Negroes, and the crippled was still in effect.

Throwing scoops of corn to the chickens and mixing sour dry mash with leftover food and oily dishwater for the hogs were among our evening chores. Bailey and I sloshed down twilight trails to the pig-pens, and standing on the first fence rungs we poured down the unap-pealing concoctions to our grateful hogs. They mashed their tender pink snouts down into the slop, and rooted and grunted their satisfac-tion. We always grunted a reply only half in jest. We were also grateful that we had concluded the dirtiest of chores and had only gotten the evil-smelling swill on our shoes, stockings, feet, and hands.

Late one day, as we were attending to the pigs, I heard a horse in the front yard (it really should have been called a driveway, except that there was nothing to drive into it), and ran to find out who had come riding up on a Thursday evening. The used-to-be sheriff sat rakishly astraddle his horse. His nonchalance was meant to convey his authori-ty and power over even dumb animals. How much more capable he would be with Negroes, it went without saying.

His twang jogged in the brittle air. From the side of the Store, Bailey and I heard him say to Momma, "Annie, tell Willie he better lay low tonight. A crazy nigger messed with a white lady today. Some of the boys'll be coming over here later." Even after the slow drag of years, I remember the sense of fear which filled my mouth with hot, dry air, and made my body light.

The "boys"? Those cement faces and eyes of hate that burned the clothes off you if they happened to see you lounging on the main street downtown on Saturday. Boys? It seemed that youth had never happened to them. Boys? No, rather men who were covered with graves' dust and age without beauty or learning. The ugliness and rot-tenness of old abominations.

If on Judgment Day I were summoned by St. Peter to give testimo-ny to the used-to-be sheriff's act of kindness, I would be unable to say anything in his behalf. His confidence that my uncle and every other Black man who heard of the Klan's coming ride would scurry under their houses to hide in chicken droppings was too humiliating to hear. Without waiting for Momma's thanks, he rode out of the yard, sure that things were as they should be and that he was a gentle squire, saving those deserving serfs from the laws of the land, which he condoned.

Immediately, while his horse's hoofs were still loudly thudding the ground, Momma blew out the coal-oil lamps. She had a quiet, hard talk with Uncle Willie and called Bailey and me into the Store.

We were told to take the potatoes and onions out of their bins and knock out the dividing walls that kept them apart. Then with a tedious and fearful slowness Uncle Willie gave me his rubber-tipped cane and bent down to get into the now-enlarged empty bin. It took forever before he lay down flat, and then we covered him with potatoes and onions, layer upon layer, like a casserole. Grandmother knelt praying in the darkened Store.

It was fortunate that the "boys" didn't ride into our yard that evening and insist that Momma open the Store. They would have surely found Uncle Willie and just as surely lynched him. He moaned the whole night through as if he had, in fact, been guilty of some heinous crime. The heavy sounds pushed their way up out of the blanket of vegetables and I pictured his mouth pulling down on the right side and his saliva flowing into the eyes of new potatoes and waiting there like dewdrops for the warmth of morning.

4.

Bailey was the greatest person in my world. And the fact that he was my brother, my only brother, and I had no sisters to share him with, was such good fortune that it made me want to live a Christian life just to show God that I was grateful. Where I was big, elbowy, and grating, he was small, graceful, and smooth. When I was described by our playmates as being shit color, he was lauded for his velvet-black skin. His hair fell down in black curls, and my head was covered with black steel wool. And yet he loved me.

When our elders said unkind things about my features (my family was handsome to a point of pain for me), Bailey would wink at me from across the room, and I knew that it was a matter of time before he would take revenge. He would allow the old ladies to finish wondering how on earth I came about, then he would ask, in a voice like cooling bacon grease, "Oh Mizeriz Coleman, how is your son? I saw him the other day, and he looked sick enough to die."

Aghast, the ladies would ask, "Die? From what? He ain't sick."

And in a voice oilier than the one before, he'd answer with a straight face, "From the Uglies."

I would hold my laugh, bite my tongue, grit my teeth, and very seriously erase even the touch of a smile from my face. Later, behind the house by the black-walnut tree, we'd laugh and laugh and howl. Bailey could count on very few punishments for his consistently outrageous behavior, for he was the pride of the Henderson/Johnson family.

His movements, as he was later to describe those of an acquaintance, were activated with oiled precision. He was also able to find more hours in the day than I thought existed. He finished chores, homework, read more books than I, and played the group games on the side of the hill with the best of them. He could even pray out loud in church, and was apt at stealing pickles from the barrel that sat under the fruit counter and Uncle Willie's nose.

After our early chores were done, while Uncle Willie or Momma minded the Store, we were free to play the children's games, as long as we stayed within yelling distance. Playing hide-and-seek, his voice was easily identified, singing, "Last night, night before, twenty-four robbers at my door. Who all is hid? Ask me to let them in, hit 'em in the head with a rolling pin. Who all is hid?" In follow-the-leader, naturally he was the one who created the most daring and interesting things to do. And when he was on the tail of the pop-the-whip, he would twirl off the end like a top, spinning, falling, laughing, finally stopping just before my heart beat its last, and then he was back in the game, still laughing.

Of all the needs (there are none imaginary) a lonely child has, the one that must be satisfied, if there is going to be hope and a hope of wholeness, is the unshaking need for an unshakable God. My pretty Black brother was my Kingdom Come.

In Stamps the segregation was so complete that most Black children didn't really, absolutely know what whites looked like. Other than that they were different, to be dreaded, and in that dread was included the hostility of the powerless against the powerful, the poor against the rich, the worker against the worked-for, and the ragged against the well-dressed. I remember never believing that whites were really real.

Many women who worked in their kitchens traded at our Store, and when they carried their finished laundry back to town they often set the big baskets down on our front porch to pull a singular piece from the starched collection and show either how graceful was their ironing hand or how rich and opulent was the property of their employers.

I looked at the items that weren't on display. I knew, for instance, that white men wore shorts, as Uncle Willie did, and that they had an opening for taking out their "things" and peeing, and that white women's breasts weren't built into their dresses, as people said, because I saw their brassieres in the baskets. But I couldn't force myself to think of them as people. People were Mrs. LaGrone, Mrs. Hendricks, Momma, Reverend Sneed, Lillie B, and Louise and Rex. Whitefolks couldn't be people because their feet were too small, their skin too white and see-throughy, and they didn't walk on the balls of their feet the way people did—they walked on their heels like horses.

People were those who lived on my side of town. I didn't like them all, or, in fact, any of them very much, but they were people. These others, the strange pale creatures that lived in their alien unlife, weren't considered folks. They were whitefolks.

5.

Some families of powhitetrash lived on Momma's farmland behind the school. Sometimes a gaggle of them came to the Store, filling the whole room, chasing out the air, and even changing the well-known scents. The children crawled over the shelves and into the potato and onion bins, twanging all the time in their sharp voices like cigar-box guitars. They took liberties in my Store that I would never dare. Since Momma told us that the less you say to whitefolks (or even powhite-trash) the better, Bailey and I would stand, solemn, quiet, in the displaced air. But if one of the playful apparitions got close to us, I pinched it. Partly out of angry frustration and partly because I didn't believe in its flesh reality.

They called my uncle by his first name and ordered him around the Store. He, to my crying shame, obeyed them in his limping dip-straight-dip fashion. My grandmother, too, followed their orders, except that she didn't seem to be servile because she anticipated their needs.

"Here's sugar, Miz Potter, and here's baking powder. You didn't buy soda last month, you'll probably be needing some."

Momma always directed her statements to the adults, but sometimes, oh painful sometimes, the grimy, snotty-nosed girls would answer her. "Naw, Annie . . ."—to Momma? Who owned the land they lived on? Who forgot more than they would ever learn? If there was any justice in the world, God should strike them dumb at once!— "Just give us some extry sody crackers, and some more mackerel."

At least they never looked in her face, or I never caught them doing so. Nobody with a smidgen of training, not even the worst roustabout, would look right in a grown person's face. It meant the person was trying to take the words out before they were formed. The dirty little children didn't do that, but they threw their orders around the Store like lashes from a cat-o'-nine-tails.

When I was around ten years old, those scruffy children caused me the most painful and confusing experience I had ever had with my grandmother. One summer morning, after I had swept the dirt yard of leaves, spearmint-gum wrappers, and Vienna-sausage labels, I raked the yellow-red dirt, and made half-moons carefully, so that the design stood out clearly and masklike. I put the rake behind the Store and came through the back of the house to find Grandmother on the front porch in her big, wide white apron. The apron was so stiff by virtue of the starch that it could have stood alone. Momma was admiring the yard, so I joined her. It truly looked like a flat redhead that had been raked with a big-toothed comb. Momma didn't say anything but I knew she liked it. She looked around, hoping one of the community pillars would see the design before the day's business wiped it out. Then she looked upward toward the school. My head had swung with hers, so at just about the same time we saw a troop of the powhite-trash kids marching over the hill and down by the side of the school.

I looked to Momma for direction. She did an excellent job of sagging from her waist down, but from the waist up she seemed to be pulling for the top of the oak tree across the road. Then she began to moan a hymn. Maybe not to moan, but the tune was so slow and the meter so strange that she could have been moaning. She didn't look at me again. When the children reached halfway down the hill, halfway to the Store, she said without turning, "Sister, go on inside."

I wanted to beg her, "Momma, don't wait for them. Come on inside with me. If they come in the Store, you go to the bedroom and let me wait on them. They only frighten me if you're around. Alone I know how to handle them," but of course I couldn't say anything, so I went in and stood behind the screen door.

Before the girls got to the porch I heard their laughter crackling and popping like pine logs in a cooking stove. I suppose my lifelong paranoia was born in those cold, molasses-slow minutes. They came finally to stand on the ground in front of Momma. At first they pretended seriousness. Then one of them wrapped her right arm in the crook of her left, pushed out her mouth, and started to hum. I realized that she was aping my grandmother. Another said, "Naw, Helen, you ain't standing like her. This here's it." Then she lifted her chest, folded her arms, and mocked that strange carriage that was Annie Henderson. Another laughed, "Naw, you can't do it. Your mouth ain't pooched out enough. It's like this."

I thought about the rifle behind the door, but I knew I'd never be able to hold it straight, and the .410, our sawed-off shotgun, which stayed loaded and was fired every New Year's night, was locked in the trunk and Uncle Willie had the key on his chain. Through the fly-

specked screen door, I could see that the arms of Momma's apron jiggled from the vibrations of her humming. But her knees seemed to have locked as if they would never bend again.

She sang on. No louder than before, but no softer either. No slower or faster.

The dirt of the girls' cotton dresses continued on their legs, feet, arms, and faces to make them all of a piece. Their greasy uncolored hair hung down, uncombed, with a grim finality. I knelt to see them better, to remember them for all time. The tears that had slipped down my dress left unsurprising dark spots, and made the front yard blurry and even more unreal. The world had taken a deep breath and was having doubts about continuing to revolve.

The girls had tired of mocking Momma and turned to other means of agitation. One crossed her eyes, stuck her thumbs in both sides of her mouth, and said, "Look here, Annie." Grandmother hummed on and the apron strings trembled. I wanted to throw a handful of black pepper in their faces, to throw lye on them, to scream that they were dirty, scummy peckerwoods, but I knew I was as clearly imprisoned behind the scene as the actors outside were confined to their roles.

One of the smaller girls did a kind of puppet dance while her fellow clowns laughed at her. But the tall one, who was almost a woman, said something very quietly, which I couldn't hear. They all moved backward from the porch, still watching Momma. For an awful second I thought they were going to throw a rock at Momma, who seemed (except for the apron strings) to have turned into stone herself. But the big girl turned her back, bent down, and put her hands flat on the ground—she didn't pick up anything. She simply shifted her weight and did a hand stand.

Her dirty bare feet and long legs went straight for the sky. Her dress fell down around her shoulders, and she had on no drawers. The slick pubic hair made a brown triangle where her legs came together. She hung in the vacuum of that lifeless morning for only a few seconds, then wavered and tumbled. The other girls clapped her on the back and slapped their hands.

"Momma changed her song to "Bread of Heaven, bread of Heaven, feed me till I want no more."

I found that I was praying too. How long could Momma hold out? What new indignity would they think of to subject her to? Would I be able to stay out of it? What would Momma really like me to do?

Then they were moving out of the yard, on their way to town. They bobbed their heads and shook their slack behinds and turned, one at a time:

" 'Bye, Annie."

" 'Bye, Annie."

" 'Bye, Annie."

Momma never turned her head or unfolded her arms, but she stopped singing and said, " 'Bye, Miz Helen, 'bye, Miz Ruth, 'bye, Miz Eloise."

I burst. A firecracker July-the-Fourth burst. How could Momma call them Miz? The mean nasty things. Why couldn't she have come inside the sweet, cold Store when we saw them breasting the hill? What did she prove? And then if they were dirty, mean, and impudent, why did Momma have to call them Miz?

She stood another whole song through and then opened the screen door to look down on me crying in rage. She looked until I looked up. Her face was a brown moon that shone on me. She was beautiful. Something had happened out there, which I couldn't completely understand, but I could see that she was happy. Then she bent down and touched me as mothers of the church "lay hands on the sick and afflicted" and I quieted.

"Go wash your face, Sister." And she went behind the candy counter and hummed, "Glory, glory, hallelujah, when I lay my burden down." I threw the well water on my face and used the weekday handkerchief to blow my nose. Whatever the contest had been out front, I knew Momma had won.

I took the rake back to the front yard. The smudged footprints were easy to erase. I worked for a long time on my new design and laid the rake behind the wash pot. When I came back in the Store, I took Momma's hand and we both walked outside to look at the pattern.

It was a large heart with lots of hearts growing smaller inside, and piercing from the outside rim to the smallest heart was an arrow. Momma said, "Sister, that's right pretty." Then she turned back to the Store and resumed, "Glory, glory hallelujah, when I lay my burden down."

My Daughter Married a Negro

(July 1951)

Anonymous

BOTH WEDDINGS IN our family since the war were at distant points. Announcements and the notices to the papers were in the usual form, without mention of the races to which the principals belonged. In one of them was a pertinent item. Late in August of 1949 our daughter married a member of her college class who is a Negro.

Friends and relatives were notified. The news got around quickly and in the field of race relations our education has been expanding ever since. People are friendly and understanding, even neighbors who still contrive to avoid the subject of our youngest daughter. I forget when it was that we stopped dividing people into those who knew and those we were not sure about. It was a time when seating arrangements at dinners, encounters on the street, and even phone calls were adventures with the laws of probability. One friend phoned me at the office with what he called "a weekend sleuthing assignment. A girl out

73

your way has married a 'jig' and is coming home with a sprout." He wanted the family's name and thought I might have some fun getting it. Sometimes it was possible to straighten things out by telling the truth. Often I let them find out for themselves. There are no good shortcuts for telling the story of the marriage of one's daughter to a Negro. The easiest to talk to are Anne's contemporaries. Her schoolmates are loyal. I have business friends who, I hope, will never hear about it. With knights of the white supremacy I keep my mouth shut and calculate the explosive effect, in their company, of a few words dropped from our annals.

Now and then I found a sympathetic audience. After a committee meeting one of the group told of her appointment to a county interracial board. She wanted suggestions and said she hoped to be spared the question about how she would like her daughter marrying a colored man. It was a large committee. She was the only person in the room who did not know about Anne and I told her the story. I am on the board of governors of a country club. Nearly a year ago at one of our meetings, I made my report and left early to keep another engagement. A few days later a copy of the minutes of the meeting arrived. Its last long paragraph read, in part: "The question of admitting members of the Jewish faith and Negro race was discussed at great length. It was decided finally that each applicant be considered, and accepted or rejected upon his or her merits as a person. No rejections shall be made solely on the basis of race or religion." This was a stunning surprise. Nothing like it was mentioned in my presence nor had I ever talked with any of the board about my daughter and her husband. It is quite unlikely that Negroes will apply for membership for some time and when they do, the screening by any membership chairman now in view will be close.

We were a long way from the Christmas vacation when Anne first talked to us of her serious interest in a colored classmate. During that holiday, except when the part-time girl worked upstairs, his picture was on her bureau. It was a good face with fine eyes and the cabinet-size photograph spoiled our Christmas just as completely as the

German offensive in the Ardennes had done four years earlier. That one we waited out. This time the urgent thing was to keep close to Anne and try to find our way in a new situation. Neither of our parents would have conceded, as we did at once, that a mixed marriage is neither immoral nor biologically wrong. When a girl was granted the final word in the choice of a husband, the color scheme was taken for granted. An alarming list of complications, facing a white girl who marries a Negro, began to grow rankly in my head. It was endless and finally I wrote them down to get the wheels stopped. The appalling collection made us miserable and from it Anne would have learned, under many headings and subheadings, that we did not want a Negro in the family; that we were certain a mixed marriage must fail.

Naturally there was little relaxation in the household during the following months. Some calculated effort to find and advance a white suitor or two, for competition, missed fire and left us feeling like conspirators. We became more deeply involved as selected uncles, aunts, and friends were told of the problem and added to our team. It was on the theory that other people's children, in this case one of our own, might inspire their wisdom. Every parent, at times when away from the family, is touched with vision. Results were mixed. Some were less sure than we that the right of parental rule, unlimited, should stop with college years. Certainly it would have taken more than our trace of adolescence for us to attempt to bully our way through the problem.

Others thought psychiatry was needed. They reasoned that a good-looking girl who passed up members of her own race for a colored boy was mentally ill. While not professional it seemed a plausible diagnosis; what to do about it in our dealings with Anne was the problem. Doubtless my wife and I needed a psychiatrist. We might have picked up some ideas on ways to convince our daughter that she needed professional advice. "When ill, go to a doctor; when mentally ill or emotionally upset, see a psychiatrist." That sounds simple enough and I believe there must be a way to put it on the line, even within a family, without breaking up the game or losing contact with the one needing help. We tried and failed. Months later Anne did go to a psychiatrist but that was after her mind was made up about the marriage. The report was confidential. What we know of it convinced us that, although there were things he did not understand, the doctor was sure she was not a mental case; was capable of making her own decisions.

It is plain now that our daughter knew clearly from the first how her contemplated marriage must affect all of us. I imagine her going over that ground, again and again, until it was familiar and hateful. Perhaps the only advice which had a chance with her was what she finally followed: "Go ahead with it; find out." Yet all along we hoped for the miracle; first for a clean break; later for a long engagement. I wrote to the wisest men and women I knew and to some strangers. Replies came from a philosopher, a writer, headmasters, teachers, and a social worker. All of the letters were wise and kind, but we failed to bring any of the writers face to face with Anne.

Children's problems thrive in most families. Why it is that ours include a mixed marriage is not clear. The records of as much as two decades are not too hard to follow, even with some of our mistakes thrown in. It might be useful, though difficult to arrange, for a father and a daughter to collaborate sometime on the family's annals. From the two versions, they might learn what it was that set up a strange pattern and perhaps made all the difference.

Anne came home at the end of the college year. We tried to believe that a firm case for a long engagement already was made. Letters to the boy were careful efforts to encourage a postponement of serious plans. They may have been too clear. His replies were not, and perhaps that should have made us call off the vacation, for in the middle of it was the only weekend John could take off for a visit. We passed up that chance for what might have been a showdown. The vacation was needed, nor were we prepared for the ordeal of having a colored boy ask for our daughter's hand. The weeks passed like a wartime furlough; everything ran against the clock and the calendar. At night, the thought of her asleep in the room across the hall always set in motion a calculation of how many more nights she would be there. There was a month of that.

We did things together, usually avoiding the subject which was closest to all of us and, for our part, most of the ugly signs of a family ganging up to have its way. Anne bought us *Color Blind* by Margaret Halsey. It was read and I suppose each of us found in the excellent book matter to support our several views. On the day she left I drove her to town and it was like seeing her brother off during the war. She sat on the steps in the hall with the dachshund in her lap while I loaded the bags. At the end of the drive when I stopped for traffic, Anne twisted around and looked at the house. I had done that too, at other special times, for luck, and because the house where I have lived over half my life is one of the knots which holds.

Three weeks later Anne got through to us by phone at our little boarding place and announced their plans for the marriage. That night two friendly boarders drove me the thirty miles to the railroad. Later, in a deserted pine-paneled grill, the three of us drank beer to the success of my mission, on a "family matter." The following morning I was on a plane and that afternoon, just before six, I rode a hot crowded trolley toward my destination. Close to me in the crush near the conductor a girl dropped an immense box of chocolates. She recovered a few and then passengers, pushing for the door, got the rest under foot; soon all of us were standing in a sticky mess. I pulled free from the stuff at my street and was picked up by a forlorn mongrel which licked the blobs of candy where I touched the pavement. I was the last white passenger off the car. The neighborhood seemed wholly colored; at my heels, the dog was a link between our two races, while I hunted for the number and the sweetness on my shoes lasted.

The woman at the apartment door was John's mother. Anne and he were out for dinner. The rest of his family were in the apartment and we had some friendly talk. At nine I rang the bell again. In the lower hall, after the latch was released, I heard Anne's voice calling me from the landing above. We faced each other in her room. She was beautiful, very white and calm. For that moment, memorable to both of us, there may have been words, free of design and of a father's abiding selfishness, which would have served our turn. They were beyond me. She was in love and I was a suppliant, asking for a postponement. My distress made her unhappy but she was sure it would be just the same a year later, if they waited. Probably she was right.

Afterward, in the living room, I met the boy. He was very attractive, a trifle darker than I expected after seeing his photograph. The Indian strain which Anne had spoken about was present in all of them. He was quite equal to the situation, yet not too much so; his conversation was much better than his letters. When we were seated, with Anne next to me on a davenport, John's mother switched off the lights. She was a good stage manager. Darkness helped all of us in the hour which followed. I faced the boy's chair, talking to him and the dark room, now and then touching Anne's hand at my side. They were good listeners. I continued a suppliant, but emotion nearly got the better of me and probably gave rise to an illusion that I was succeeding. Late that night I phoned my hopes to the waiting family.

In the morning they were to give me their answer. I found them seated together in the lobby of the hotel. The change of scene from the night before was startling, more difficult surely for all three of us, yet in the crowded lobby I alone was the novice. Nobody appeared to notice us. I never have seen John ill at ease, with his race or with ours. Anne, in the most difficult role, was natural and oblivious to her surroundings. It was not quite real. We went out to the street, walking three abreast with Anne in the middle. At a crossing both of us reached for her arm and John gave way to me. After that I guided her through traffic and talked. We walked for a long time. I was afraid to stop talking. Finally we came to a park bench. I left them there and walked over to a big buttonwood, trying to pray, over and over again, for the miracle. I had done that so many times before. When I returned to them I could see that there was to be no miracle, on my terms. I had failed. They did not want to hurt me but they were going ahead. In a taxi on the way to the station the thought of taking Anne with me by force or even appealing to the police did cross my mind. It was as quickly gone. She was of age and force would have changed nothing. John carried my bag to the gate. We shook hands and I kissed Anne. There were only a few minutes to train time. Through the barrier I watched them cross the station, shoulder to shoulder.

They walked faster than when the three of us were together on the street; in a moment they were gone in the crowd.

We received a cheerful letter describing the wedding. A number of the guests were members of her class and she took some pains to be amusing. Racial proportions were not mentioned but evidently whites were well represented. Apparently Anne thought the solemnity of the event was felt deeply enough by us without further emphasis. One sentence seemed to be especially for me. I used the tough little word now and then and she must have heard it. "You do admit, don't you, that I have guts?" During the following months Anne worked and her husband returned to college. A couple which should have had most of the breaks got along with very few, and without any help from us. Mail was scarce and we spent an uncomfortable time getting used to the fact that we were not needed. One of Anne's jobs in the early winter stopped short on the day she fainted and her employers learned that she was pregnant. Afterward she found another, which kept her off her feet, and held that until she began "to get in people's way." A baby girl was born in June.

Two weeks later at the airport, a tall pilot carried the small bundle down the landing steps, followed by Anne. The town started to call, mostly women, from Brownie Scouts to great-grandmothers. All of them were friendly in satisfying natural curiosity: the baby girl was very light, with straight hair. When not howling she was as charming as new babies can be. Anne and she put on a long run of late summer afternoon circuses, which may become historic in the town's annals as its first showings, to all attenders, of the offspring of a mixed marriage. It was a happy summer, free of tension. In his own home town John was working. He earned enough to pay the doctor bills and Anne's fare back. By that time he had started the long apartment hunt for a mixed couple with a baby. There often is news in that quarter but most of it is discouraging.

They keep their troubles to themselves. Letters are too few but none of them are bitter. "Finding an apartment for a mixed couple," Anne wrote recently, "is tough as the devil. Sometimes I blush for my own race." We think of her, with John away at college, moving from room to apartment to room of college friends, around and across boundaries which run along a city's streets and through men's minds. With the baby and clothes goes her small library: dictionary, anthologies of verse and plays, and among others perhaps the *Pickwick* I sent winter before last. With her cramped quarters in mind I have to resist the impulse to send more. In my own life they have been weapons against insecurity and despair. It is difficult not to believe that in her adventure, books will serve Anne's turn as well.

Differences in backgrounds mean more to us than to their generation. A colored boy, with the help of an outstanding mother, learned a lot about people, of his race and ours, by the time he entered college. The Navy in wartime helped. The hard effective ways in which John came by this experience are not often duplicated outside his race. An intelligent Negro must find introductory courses in sociology dull going. It cannot mean much to him yet that Anne, her mother, and I grew up among books: a less exacting way to improve one's knowledge of the human race. Each of us made different discoveries, and Anne's daughter, our grandchild, with her mixed racial background, before very long will be exploring on her own. Against that day and the time when John gets his degree and a job, and they set up a home, we will help them build a library. The list grows. If, in the years just ahead, television continues to be the popular dish, we expect to expose this pioneer family to richer fare. If John and his daughter discover *Alice in Wonderland* together, so much the better. He and his race, the best of them, are on the make. After the fallow years they are catching up, with intense and moving energy. We are lifted in spirit with their successes and cast down by their failures. A Brooklyn second baseman, a Yale football captain, and a Nobel Prize winner join the family's gallery of greats and near greats.

We were told a while ago by a mother, whose daughter and son married their own kind and color, that we must find it exciting to be pioneers. Of course we are not the pioneers; we did our best to break things up. However, as the parents of one of the principals, we do have our share of excitement, some of it anxious. The lives of friends whose children did the regular thing sometimes look ecstatically peaceful. I overhear reports to my wife from these quiet fronts—about some snug little house built in an orchard, or a lucky stroke with an apartment lease. A woman takes this sensibly and is enthusiastic. I tighten up and find myself thinking of Anne's situation, which is stupid, because she knew what she was getting into. Somewhere we have a letter describing her sensations when she walked on the street with John at the beginning of their friendship. It was detailed and vivid. She wants no sympathy.

A few continue to greet us as though we had a death in the family. Time will help them. Once we felt the same way, nor are we yet as adaptable as Anne's generation. "Color Blindness" in the Margaret Halsey sense takes time and cultivation and there is not likely to be any at hand to give us an assist: to "switch off the lights" as John's mother did. During his last term at college Anne and the baby live in the apartment where I first saw him. It must be lonely. Yet she writes: "The baby is delightful company, keeps trying to talk in a most touching way. The other day we counted seven teeth. One weekend John and I went to a party, and with no baby sitter available, we took her along. She slept like a lamb in a bureau drawer upstairs while we played games and square-danced. She is standing up, is syllable-conscious."

We crowd the mails. Now and then I mark a *New Yorker* where hilarity gets a good play. It is a help at this end to think of these reaching her, between the cooking and washing, brightening up a dull day. Two years ago all which we were wise enough to offer Anne was our sometime benevolent opposition. We thought we knew best, perhaps we did. Now, it is not so clear. What is very clear is her tough cheerful courage which grows with use and meets all demands upon it. The miracle, for which we prayed so many times, Anne seems to find within herself.

RACE AND FEAR

(JUNE 1956)

William Faulkner

IMMEDIATELY AFTER THE Supreme Court decision abolishing segregation in schools, the talk began in Mississippi of ways and means to increase taxes to raise the standard of the Negro schools to match the white ones. I wrote the following letter to the open forum page of our most widely read Memphis paper:

> We Mississippians already know that our present schools are not good enough. Our young men and women themselves prove that to us every year by the fact that, when the best of them want the best of education which they are entitled to and competent for, not only in the humanities but in the professions and crafts— law and medicine and engineering—too, they must go out of the state to get it. And quite often, too often, they don't come back.
>
> So our present schools are not even good enough for white people; our present state reservoir of education is not of high enough quality to assuage the thirst of even our white young men and women. In which case, how can it possibly assuage the thirst and need of the Negro, who obviously is thirstier, needs it worse, else the federal government would not have had to pass a law compelling Mississippi (among others of course) to make the best of our education available to him.
>
> That is, our present schools are not even good enough for white people. So what do we do? Make them good enough, improve them to the best possible? No. We beat the bushes, rake and scrape to raise additional taxes to establish another system at best only equal to that one which is already not good enough,

which therefore won't be good enough for Negroes either; we will have two identical systems neither of which are good enough for anybody.

A few days after my letter was printed in the paper, I received by post the carbon copy of a letter addressed to the same forum page of the Memphis paper. It read as follows:

When Weeping Willie Faulkner splashes his tears about the inadequacy of Mississippi schools . . . we question his gumption in these respects, etc.

From there it went on to cite certain facts of which all Southerners are justly proud: that the seed-stock of education in our land was preserved through the evil times following the Civil War when our land was a defeated and occupied country, by dedicated teachers who got little in return for their dedication. Then, after a brief sneer at the quality of my writing and the profit motive which was the obvious reason why I was a writer, he closed by saying: "I suggest that Weeping Willie dry his tears and work up a little thirst for knowledge about the basic economy of his state."

Later, after this letter was printed in the Memphis paper in its turn, I received from the writer of it a letter addressed to him by a correspondent in another small Mississippi town, consisting in general of a sneer at the Nobel Prize which was awarded me, and commending the Weeping Willie writer for his promptness in taking to task anyone traitorous enough to hold education more important than the color of the educatee's skin. Attached to it was the Weeping Willie writer's reply. It said in effect:

In my opinion Faulkner is the most capable commentator on Southern facts of life to date. . . . If we could insult him into acquiring an insight into the basic economy of our region, he could [sic] do us a hell of a lot of good in our fight against integration.

My answer was that I didn't believe that insult is a very sound method of teaching anybody anything, of persuading anyone to think or act as the insulter believes they should. I repeated that what we needed in Mississippi was the best possible schools, to make the best possible use of the men and women we produced, regardless of what color they were. And even if we could not have a school system which would do that, at least let us have one which would make no distinction among pupils except that of simple ability, since our principal and perhaps desperate need in America today was that all Americans at least should be on the side of America; that if all Americans were on the same side, we would not need to fear that other nations and ideologies would doubt us when we talked of human freedom.

But this is beside the point. The point is, what is behind this. The tragedy is not the impasse, but what is behind the impasse—the impasse of the two apparently irreconcilable facts which we are faced with in the South: the one being the decree of our national government that there be absolute equality in education among all citizens, the other being the white people in the South who say that white and Negro pupils shall never sit in the same classroom. Only apparently irreconcilable, because they must be reconciled since the only alternative to change is death. In fact, there are people in the South, Southerners born, who not only believe they can be reconciled but who love our land—not love white people specifically nor love Negroes specifically, but our land, our country: our climate and geography, the qualities in our people, white and Negro too, for honesty and fairness, the splendors in our traditions, the glories in our past—enough to try to reconcile them, even at the cost of displeasing both sides. These people are willing to face the contempt of the Northern radicals who believe we don't do enough, and the contumely and threats of our own Southern reactionaries who are convinced that anything we do is already too much.

The tragedy is the reason behind the fact, the fear behind the fact that some of the white people in the South—people who otherwise are rational, cultured, gentle, generous, and kindly—will—must—fight against every inch which the Negro gains in social betterment. It is the fear behind the desperation which could drive rational and successful men (my correspondent, the Weeping Willie one, is a banker, perhaps president of a—perhaps the—bank in another small Mississippi town like my own) to grasp at such straws for weapons as contumely and threat and insult, to change the views or anyway the voice which dares to suggest that betterment of the Negro's condition does not necessarily presage the doom of the white race.

Nor is the tragedy the fear so much as the tawdry quality of the fear—fear not of the Negro as an individual Negro nor even as a race, but as an economic class or stratum or factor, since what the Negro threatens is not the Southern white man's social system but the Southern white man's economic system—that economic system which the white man knows and dares not admit to himself is established on an obsolescence—the artificial inequality of man—and so is itself already obsolete and hence doomed. He knows that only three hundred years ago the Negro's naked grandfather was eating rotten elephant or hippo meat in an African rain forest, yet in only three hundred years the Negro produced Dr. Ralph Bunche and George Washington Carver and Booker T. Washington. The white man knows that only ninety years ago not one percent of the Negro race could own a deed to land, let alone read that deed; yet in only ninety years, although his only contact with a county courthouse is the window through which he pays the taxes for which he has no representation, he can own his land and farm it with inferior stock and worn-out tools and gear—equipment which any white man would starve with—and raise children and feed and clothe them and send them North where they can have equal scholastic opportunity, and end his life holding his head up because he owes no man, with even enough over to pay for his coffin and funeral.

That's what the white man in the South is afraid of: that the Negro, who has done so much with no chance, might do so much more with an equal one that he might take the white man's economy away from him, the Negro now the banker or the merchant or the planter and the white man the sharecropper or the tenant. That's why the Negro can gain our country's highest decoration for valor beyond all call of duty for saving or defending or preserving white lives on foreign battlefields, yet the Southern white man dares not let that Negro's children learn their ABC's in the same classroom with the children of the white lives he saved or defended.

Now the Supreme Court has defined exactly what it meant by what it said: that by "equality" it meant, simply, equality, without qualifying or conditional adjectives: not "separate but equal" nor "equally separate," but simply, equal; and now the Mississippi voices are talking of something which does not even exist anymore.

In the first half of the nineteenth century, before slavery was abolished by law in the United States, Thomas Jefferson and Abraham Lincoln both held that the Negro was not yet competent for equality.

That was more than ninety years ago, and nobody can say whether their opinions would be different now or not.

But assume that they would not have changed their belief, and that that opinion is right. Assume that the Negro is still not competent for equality, which is something which neither he nor the white man knows until we try it.

But we do know that, with the support of the federal government, the Negro is going to gain the right to try and see if he is fit or not for equality. And if the Southern white man cannot trust him with something as mild as equality, what is the Southern white man going to do when he has power—the power of his own fifteen millions of unanimity backed by the federal government—when the only check on that power will be that federal government which is already the Negro's ally?

In 1849, Senator John C. Calhoun made his address in favor of secession if the Wilmot Proviso was ever adopted. On October 12 of that year, Senator Jefferson Davis wrote a public letter to the South, saying:

> The generation which avoids its responsibility on this subject sows the wind and leaves the whirlwind as a harvest to its children. Let us get together and build manufactories, enter upon industrial pursuits, and prepare for our own self-sustenance.

At that time the Constitution guaranteed the Negro as property along with all other property, and Senator Calhoun and Senator Davis had the then undisputed validity of States' Rights to back their position. Now the Constitution guarantees the Negro equal right to equality, and the States' Rights which the Mississippi voices are talking about do not exist anymore. We—Mississippi—sold our state's rights back to the federal government when we accepted the first cotton price-support subsidy twenty years ago. Our economy is not agricultural any longer. Our economy is the federal government. We no longer farm in Mississippi cotton fields. We farm now in Washington corridors and Congressional committee rooms.

We—the South—didn't heed Senator Davis's words then. But we had better do it now. If we are to watch our native land wrecked and ruined twice in less than a hundred years over the Negro question, let us be sure this time that we know where we are going afterward.

There are many voices in Mississippi. There is that of one of our United States Senators, who, although he is not speaking for the United States Senate and what he advocates does not quite match the oath he took when he entered into his high office several years ago, at least has made no attempt to hide his identity and his condition. And there is the voice of one of our circuit judges, who, although he is not now speaking from the Bench and what he advocates also stands a little awry to his oath that before the law all men are equal and the weak shall be succored and defended, makes no attempt either to conceal his identity and condition. And there are the voices of the ordinary citizens who, although they do not claim to speak specifically for the white Citizens' Councils and the NAACP, do not try to hide their sentiments and their convictions; not to mention those of the schoolmen—teachers and professors and pupils—though, since most Mississippi schools are state-owned or -supported, they don't always dare to sign their names to the open letters.

There are all the voices in fact, except one. That one voice which would adumbrate them all to silence, being the superior of all since it is the living articulation of the glory and the sovereignty of God and the hope and aspiration of man. The Church, which is the strongest unified force in our Southern life since all Southerners are not white and are not democrats, but all Southerners are religious and all religions serve the same single God, no matter by what name He is called. Where is that voice now? The only reference to it which I have seen was in an open forum letter to our Memphis paper which said that to his (the writer's) knowledge, none of the people who begged leave to doubt that one segment of the human race was forever doomed to be inferior to all the other segments, just because the Old Testament five thousand years ago said it was, were communicants of any church.

Where is that voice now, which should have propounded perhaps two but certainly one of these still-unanswered questions?

(1) The Constitution of the U.S. says: Before the Law, there shall be no artificial inequality—race, creed, or money—among citizens of the United States.

(2) Morality says: Do unto others as you would have others do unto you.

(3) Christianity says: I am the only distinction among men since whosoever believeth in Me shall never die.

Where is this voice now, in our time of trouble and indecision? Is it trying by its silence to tell us that it has no validity and wants none outside the sanctuary behind its symbolical spire?

If the facts as stated in the *Look* magazine account of the Till affair are correct, this is what ineradicably remains: two adults, armed, in the dark, kidnap a fourteen-year-old boy and take him away to frighten him. Instead of which, the fourteen-year-old boy not only refuses to be frightened, but, unarmed, alone, in the dark so frightens the two armed adults that they must destroy him.

What are we Mississippians afraid of? Why do we have so low an opinion of ourselves that we are afraid of people who by all our standards are our inferiors?—economically: *i.e.*, they have so much less than we have that they must work for us not on their terms but on ours; educationally: *i.e.*, their schools are so much worse than ours that the federal government has to threaten to intervene to give them equal conditions; politically: *i.e.*, they have no recourse in law for protection from nor restitution for injustice and violence.

Why do we have so low an opinion of our blood and traditions as to fear that, as soon as the Negro enters our house by the front door, he will propose marriage to our daughter and she will immediately accept him?

Our ancestors were not afraid like this—our grandfathers who fought at First and Second Manassas and Sharpsburg and Shiloh and Franklin and Chickamauga and Chancellorsville and the Wilderness; let alone those who survived that and had the additional and even greater courage and endurance to resist and survive Reconstruction, and so preserved to us something of our present heritage. Why are we, descendants of that blood and inheritors of that courage, afraid? What are we afraid of? What has happened to us in only a hundred years?

For the sake of argument, let us agree that all white Southerners (all white Americans maybe) curse the day when the first Briton or Yankee sailed the first shipload of manacled Negroes across the Middle Passage and auctioned them into American slavery. Because that doesn't matter now. To live anywhere in the world today and be against equality because of race or color, is like living in Alaska and being against snow. We have already got snow. And as with the Alaskan, merely to live in armistice with it is not enough. Like the Alaskan, we had better use it.

Suddenly about five years ago and with no warning to myself, I adopted the habit of travel. Since then I have seen (a little of some, a little more of others) the Far and Middle East, North Africa, Europe, and Scandinavia. The countries I saw were not Communist (then) of course, but they were more: they were not even Communist-inclined, where it seemed to me they should have been. And I wondered why. Then suddenly I said to myself with a kind of amazement: It's because of America. These people still believe in the American dream; they do not know yet that something happened to it. They believe in us and are willing to trust and follow us not because of our material power: Russia has that: but because of the idea of individual human freedom and liberty and equality on which our nation was founded, which our founding fathers postulated the word "America" to mean.

And, five years later, the countries which are still free of Communism are still free simply because of that: that belief in individual liberty and equality and freedom which is the one idea powerful enough to stalemate the idea of Communism. And we can thank our gods for that, since we have no other weapon to fight Communism with; in diplomacy we are children to Communist diplomats, and production in a free country can always suffer because under monolithic government all production can go to the aggrandizement of the state. But then, we don't need anything more since that simple belief of man that he can be free is the strongest force on earth and all we need to do is use it.

Because it makes a glib and simple picture, we like to think of the world situation today as a precarious and explosive balance of two irreconcilable ideologies confronting each other: which precarious balance, once it totters, will drag the whole universe into the abyss along with it. That's not so. Only one of the opposed forces is an ideology. The other one is that simple fact of Man: that simple belief of individual man that he can and should and will be free. And if we who are still free want to continue so, all of us who are still free had better confederate, and confederate fast, with all others who still have a choice to be free—confederate not as black people nor white people nor blue or pink or green people, but as people who still are free, with all other people who are still free; confederate together and stick together too, if we want a world or even a part of a world in which individual man can be free, to continue to endure.

And we had better take in with us as many as we can get of the nonwhite peoples of the earth who are not completely free yet but who want and intend to be, before that other force which is opposed to individual freedom, befools and gets them. Time was when the nonwhite man was content to—anyway, did—accept his instinct for freedom as an unrealizable dream. But not any more; the white man himself taught him different with that phase of his—the white man's—own culture which took the form of colonial expansion and exploitation based and morally condoned on the premise of inequality, not because of individual incompetence but of mass race or color. As a result of which, in only ten years we have watched the non-white peoples expel, by bloody violence when necessary, the white man from all the portions of the Middle East and Asia which he once dominated, into which vacuum has already begun to move that other and inimical power which people who believe in freedom are at war with—that power which says to the non-white man:

"We don't offer you freedom because there is no such thing as freedom; your white overlords whom you have just thrown out have already proved that to you. But we offer you equality, at least equality in slavedom; if you are to be slaves, at least you can be slaves to your own color and race and religion."

We, the Western white man who does believe that there exists an individual freedom above and beyond this mere equality of slavedom, must teach the non-white peoples this while there is yet a little time left. We, America, who are the strongest national force opposing Communism and monolithicism, must teach all other peoples, white and non-white, slave or (for a little while yet) still free. We, America, have the best opportunity to do this because we can begin here, at home; we will not need to send costly freedom task forces into alien and inimical non-white places which are already convinced that there is no such thing as freedom and liberty and equality and peace for non-white people too, or we would practice it at home. Because our non-white minority is already on our side; we don't need to sell the Negro on America and freedom because he is already sold; even when ignorant from inferior or no education, even despite the record of his history of inequality, he still believes in our concepts of freedom and democracy.

That is what America has done for the Negro in only three hundred years. Not done *to* them: done *for* them, because to our shame we have made little effort so far to teach them to be Americans, let alone to use their capacities and capabilities to make us a stronger and more unified America. These are the people who only three hundred years ago lived beside one of the largest bodies of inland water on earth and never thought of sail, who yearly had to move by whole villages and tribes from famine and pestilence and enemies without once thinking of the wheel; yet in three hundred years they have become skilled artisans and craftsmen capable of holding their own in a culture of technocracy. The people who only three hundred years ago were eating the carrion in the tropical jungles have produced the Phi Beta Kappas and the Doctor Bunches and the Carvers and the Booker Washingtons and the poets and musicians. They have yet to produce a Fuchs or Rosenberg or Gold or Burgess or Maclean or Hiss, and for every Negro Communist or fellow traveler there are a thousand white ones.

The Bunches and Washingtons and Carvers and the musicians and the poets, who were not just good men and women but good teachers too, taught him—the Negro—by precept and example what a lot of our white people have not learned yet: that to gain equality, one must deserve it, and to deserve equality, one must understand what it is: that there is no such thing as equality *per se*, but only equality *to*: equal right and opportunity to make the best one can of one's life within one's capacity and capability, without fear of injustice or oppression or violence. If we had given him this equality ninety or fifty or even ten years ago, there would have been no Supreme Court ruling about segregation in 1954.

But we didn't. We dared not; it is our Southern white man's shame that in our present economy the Negro must not have economic equality; our double shame that we fear that giving him more social equality will jeopardize his present economic status; our triple shame that even then, to justify our stand, we must becloud the issue with the bugaboo of miscegenation. What a commentary that the one remaining place on earth where the white man can flee and have his uncorrupted blood protected and defended by law, is in Africa— Africa: the source and origin of the threat whose present presence in America will have driven the white man to flee it.

Soon now all of us—not just Southerners nor even just Americans, but all people who are still free and want to remain so—are going to have to make a choice, lest the next (and last) confrontation we face will be, not Communists against anti-Communists, but simply the remaining handful of white people against the massed myriads of all the people on earth who are not white. We will have to choose not between color nor race nor religion nor between East and West either, but simply between being slaves and being free. And we will have to choose completely and for good; the time is already past now when we can choose a little of each, a little of both. We can choose a state of slavedom, and if we are powerful enough to be among the top two or three or ten, we can have a certain amount of license—until someone more powerful rises and has us machine-gunned against a cellar wall.

But we cannot choose freedom established on a hierarchy of degrees of freedom, on a caste system of equality like military rank. We must be free not because we claim freedom, but because we practice it; our freedom must be buttressed by a homogeny equally and unchallengeably free, no matter what color they are, so that all the other inimical forces everywhere—systems political or religious or racial or national—will not just respect us because we practice freedom, they will fear us because we do.

WHEN MORPHEUS HELD HIM

(JANUARY 1990)

Itabari Njeri

DADDY WORE BOXER shorts when he worked; that's all. He'd sit
for hours reading and writing at a long, rectangular table covered with
neat stacks of *I. F. Stone's Weekly, The Nation, The New Republic,* and
the handwritten pages of his book in progress, *The Tolono Station and
Beyond.* A Mott's applesauce jar filled with Teacher's scotch was a constant, and his own forerunner of today's wine coolers was the ever-
present chaser: ginger ale and Manischewitz Concord grape wine in a
tall, green iced-tea glass.

  As he sat there, his beer belly weighing down the waistband of his
shorts, I'd watch. I don't know if he ever saw me. I hid from him at
right angles. From the bend of the hallway, at the end of a long, dark,
L-shaped corridor in our Harlem apartment, it was at least thirty feet
to the living room where my father worked, framed by the doorway. I
sat cross-legged on the cold linoleum floor and inspected his seated,
six-foot-plus figure through a telescope formed by my forefinger and
thumb: bare feet in thonged sandals, long hairy legs that rose toward
the notorious shorts (I hated those shorts, wouldn't bring my girl-
friends home because of those shorts), breasts that could fill a B cup,

and a long neck on which a balding head rested. Viewed in isolation, I thought perhaps I'd see him clearer, know him better.

Daddy was a philosopher, a Marxist historian, an exceptional teacher, and a fine tenor. He had a good enough voice to be as great a concert artist as John McCormack, one of his favorites. The obstacles to that career couldn't have been much greater than the ones he actually overcame.

The state of Georgia, where my father grew up, established its version of the literacy test in 1908, the year he was born. If you substituted Georgia for Mississippi in the story that Lerone Bennett, Jr., relates in *Before the Mayflower: A History of Black America*, the main character could easily have been my father: A black teacher, a graduate of Eton and Harvard, presents himself to a Mississippi registrar. The teacher is told to read the state constitution and several books. He does. The registrar produces a passage in Greek, which the teacher reads. Then another in Latin. Then other passages in French, German, and Spanish, all of which the teacher reads. The registrar finally holds up a page of Chinese characters and asks: "What does this mean?" The teacher replies: "It means you don't want me to vote."

Apocryphal, perhaps, but the tale exemplified enough collective experience that I heard my father tell virtually the same story about a former Morehouse College classmate to a buddy over the phone one afternoon. At the punch line, he fell into a fit of laughter, chuckling hard into a balled fist he held at his mouth. Finally, he said, "Fred, I'll have to call you back," then fell back on the bed, in his boxer shorts, laughing at the ceiling.

He claimed he burst out laughing like this once in a class at Harvard. A law professor, discussing some constitutional issue in class, singled out my father and said, "In this matter, regarding men of your race—"

"Which race is that?" my father boomed, cutting him off, "the 50 yard or the 100?" But it seemed to me he always related that particular tale with a sneer on his lips.

He'd been at Harvard studying law on a postdoctoral scholarship from 1942 to 1943. After receiving his Ph.D. in philosophy from the University of Toronto ten years earlier, he had headed toward the dust bowls others were escaping in the mid-1930s and became the editor of a black newspaper, the *Oklahoma Eagle*, in Tulsa. He eventually returned to academia and by 1949 was the head of the philosophy department at Morgan State University in Baltimore. That's where he met my mother, a nurse many years his junior.

My mother—who commits nothing to paper, speaks of the past cryptically, and believes all unpleasantries are best kept under a rug— once leaked the fact that she and my father took me to a parade in Brooklyn when I was about three. We were standing near the arch at Grand Army Plaza when he suddenly hauled off and punched her in the mouth, with me in her arms. My mother, a very gentle and naive woman, said the whole thing left her in a state of shock. My father had never been violent before.

They separated, and I seldom saw my father again until my parents reunited when I was seven. We moved into my father's six-room apartment on 129th Street, between Convent Avenue and St. Nicholas Terrace. It was certainly far more spacious than the apartment I'd lived in with my mother on St. James Place in Brooklyn. The immediate neighborhood was an attractive, hilly section of Harlem, just a few blocks from City College. All things considered, I hated it. More precisely, I hated my father, so I hated it all.

Because of his past leftist political affiliations, Daddy had lost his government and university jobs. Now, out of necessity but also desire, he decided to devote his time to teaching younger people. He wanted to reach them at a stage in their lives when he felt he could make a difference. He joined the faculty of a Jersey City high school and began teaching journalism, history, and English. He also taught English at night to foreign-born students at City College. His students, I came to learn, loved him; his daughter found it hard to. I made the mistake of calling him Pop—once. He said, "Don't ever call me that again. If you don't like calling me Daddy, you can call me Dr. Moreland."

Once, my mother deserted me, leaving me alone with him. She went to Atlanta for several weeks with my baby brother to tend my ailing Grandma Hattie, my father's mother. Since I hadn't known this man most of my seven years on the planet, and didn't like him much now that I did, I asked him if I could stay around the corner with a family friend, Aunt Pearl. "If she asks you to stay, fine. But don't ask her," he told me. Naturally I asked her.

When he asked me if I had asked her, I hesitated. But I was not a child inclined to lie. So I said, "I don't want to lie. I asked her." I got a beating for that, a brutal beating with a belt that left welts and bruises on my legs for months.

My father felt children should be hit for any infraction. Further, they should be seen and not heard, speak only when spoken to, etc. From the day he hit me, the latter became my philosophy, too. I never consciously decided to stop speaking to my father, but for the next ten years, I rarely initiated a conversation with him. Later he would tell me, "You were a very strange child."

But if I would not accept him as a father, my curiosity would not let me deny him as a teacher. One day, a question about the nature of truth compelled a thaw in my emotional cold war—nothing less could have. Truth changes, a classmate in the seventh grade had insisted that day. It is constant, I argued, and went to my father for confirmation.

People's perceptions change, I explained. New information debunks the lies of the past, but the truth was always there. And I told my father what I had told my mostly white classmates in a Bronx junior high school at the height of the civil rights movement: Black people were always human beings worthy of the same rights other Americans enjoyed, but it took hundreds of years of a slave system that dehumanized the master as well as the slave and a social revolution before most white Americans would accept that truth.

My father turned from his worktable, took off his glasses, with their broken right temple piece, and released a long and resonant "Yesssss." And then he spoke to me of a rational cosmos and what Lincoln had to do with Plato. When our philosophical discussion ended, we each went to our separate corners.

My father had a beaten, black upright piano in the parlor, badly out of tune. But its bench was a treasure of ancient sheet music: Vincent

Youman's "Through the Years," with a picture of Gladys Swarthout on the frayed cover. And I loved the chord changes to "Spring Is Here."

I ventured from the sanctuary of my blue-walled room one summer afternoon, walking down the long hallway toward the kitchen, then stopped abruptly. I heard my father in the kitchen several feet away; he was making an ice-cream soda, something as forbidden to him as alcohol since he was a diabetic. I heard the clink of a metal spoon against a glass as he sang, "For I lately took a notion for to cross the briny ocean, and I'm off to Philadelphia in the morning." It was an Irish folk song made famous by John McCormack. I backed up. Too late. He danced across the kitchen threshold in his boxer shorts, stopped when he spotted me in the shadows, then shook his head. He smiled, lifted one leg and both arms in a Jackie Gleason "and away we go" motion, then slid off.

Minutes later he called me. "Jill the Pill, you know this song?" I knew all the songs and wrote down the words to "Moon River" for him. Then he asked me to sing it. I was always ready to sing, even for my father.

He sat on the edge of his bed with the lyrics in his hand as I sang. When I finished the phrase "We're after the same rainbow's end, waitin' round the bend, my huckleberry friend," my daddy looked at me and said what others would tell me years later but with far less poetry: "My girl, you have the celestial vibration." And then he asked me to sing it again and told me it was "wonderful." Then I left him.

For days, maybe weeks, a tense calm would reign in the apartment. Then, without warning, the hall would fill with harsh voices. My father stood in the narrow, shadowy space hitting my mother. "Put it down," he yelled. "Put it down or I'll . . ."

My mother had picked up a lamp in a lame effort to ward off his blows. His shouting had awakened me. I'd been sick in bed with the flu and a high fever. When he saw me open my bedroom door he yelled, "Get back in your room." I did, my body overtaken by tremors and the image of my mother branded on my eyeballs. I swore that I would never let anyone do that to me or to anyone else I had the power to help. I had no power to help my mother. It was an oath with terrible consequences, one I'd have to disavow to permit myself the vulnerability of being human.

I know my father's fury was fueled by his sense of insignificance. He felt himself to be an intellectual giant boxed in by mental midgets. Unlike Ralph Ellison, Paul Robeson, or Richard Wright—all contemporaries and acquaintances of my father's—he was never acknowledged by the dominant culture whose recognition he sought. He could be found, Ellison once told me, pontificating in Harlem barbershops, elucidating the dialogues of Plato for a captive audience of draped men, held prone, each with a straight-edge razor pressed against his cheek.

My father's unreconciled identities—the classic schizophrenia of being black and an American, the contradictions of internalizing whole the cultural values of a society that sees you, when it sees you at all, as life in one of its lower forms—stoked his alcoholism. And since my father at once critiqued the society that denied him and longed for its approbation, he lived with the pain-filled consciousness of one who knows he is a joke. I think sometimes he laughed the hardest, so often did I stumble upon him alone, chuckling into his balled fist at some silent, invisible comedian.

When his drunken rages ended, he slept for days, spread out on the bed wearing only his boxer shorts. I watched him on those days, too, daring to come closer, safe with the knowledge that Morpheus held him. I examined his face, wondering who he was and why he was. As I watched, he'd lift his head off the pillow, then fall back muttering: "Truth and justice will prevail."

In Search of
Martin Luther King, Jr.

(FEBRUARY 1961)

James Baldwin

I FIRST MET Martin Luther King, Jr., nearly three years ago now, in Atlanta, Georgia. He was there on a visit from his home in Montgomery. He was "holed up," he was seeing no one, he was busy writing a book—so I was informed by the friend who, mercilessly, at my urgent request, was taking me to King's hotel. I felt terribly guilty about interrupting him but not guilty enough to let the opportunity pass. Still, having been raised among preachers, I would not have been surprised if King had cursed out the friend, refused to speak to me, and slammed the door in our faces. Nor would I have blamed him if he had, since I knew that by this time he must have been forced to suffer many an admiring fool.

But the Reverend King is not like any preacher I have ever met before. For one thing, to state it baldly, I liked him. It is rare that one *likes* a world-famous man—by the time they become world-famous they rarely like themselves, which may account for this antipathy. Yet King is immediately and tremendously winning, there is really no other word for it; and there he stood, with an inquiring and genuine smile on his face, in the open door of his hotel room. Behind him, on a desk, was a wilderness of paper. He looked at his friend, he looked at me, I was introduced; he smiled and shook my hand and we entered the room.

I do not remember much about that first meeting because I was too overwhelmed by the fact that I was meeting him at all. There were millions of questions that I wanted to ask him, but I feared to begin. Besides, his friend had warned me not to "bug" him, I was not there in a professional capacity, and the questions I wanted to ask him had less to do with his public role than with his private life. When I say "private life" I am not referring to those maliciously juicy tidbits, those meaningless details, which clutter up the gossip columns and muddy everybody's mind and obliterate the humanity of the subject as well as that of the reader. I wanted to ask him how it felt to be standing where he stood, how he bore it, what complex of miracles had prepared him for it. But such questions can scarcely be asked, they can scarcely be answered.

And King does not like to talk about himself. I have described him as winning, but he does not give the impression of being particularly outgoing or warm. His restraint is not, on the other hand, of that icily uneasy, nerve-racking kind to be encountered in so many famous Negroes who have allowed their aspirations and notoriety to destroy their identities and who always seem to be giving uncertain imitation of some extremely improbable white man. No, King impressed me then and he impresses me now as a man solidly anchored in those spiritual realities concerning which he can be so eloquent. This divests him of the hideous piety which is so prevalent in his profession, and it also saves him from the ghastly self-importance which until recently was all that allowed one to be certain one was addressing a Negro leader. King cannot be considered a chauvinist at all, not even incidentally, or part of the time, or under stress, or subconsciously. What he says to Negroes he will say to whites; and what he says to whites he will say to Negroes. He is the first Negro leader in my experience, or the first in many generations, of whom this can be said; most of his predecessors were in the extraordinary position of saying to white men, *Hurry*, while saying to black men, *Wait*. This fact is of the utmost importance. It says a great deal about the situation which produced King and in which he operates; and, of course, it tells us a great deal about the man.

"He came through it all," said a friend of his to me, with wonder and not a little envy, "really unscarred. He never went around fighting with himself, like we all did." The "we" to whom this friend refers are all considerably older than King, which may have something to do with this lightly sketched species of schizophrenia; in any case, the fact that King really loves the people he represents and has—*therefore*—no hidden, interior need to hate the white people who oppose him has had and will, I think, continue to have the most far-reaching and unpredictable repercussions on our racial situation. It need scarcely be said that our racial situation is far more complex and dangerous than we are prepared to think of it as being—since our major desire is not to think of it at all—and King's role in it is of an unprecedented difficulty.

He is not, for example, to be confused with Booker T. Washington, whom we gratefully allowed to solve the racial problem singlehandedly. It was Washington who assured us, in 1895, one year before it became the law of the land, that the education of Negroes would not give them any desire to become equals; they would be content to remain—or, rather, after living for generations in the greatest intimacy with whites, to become—separate. It is a measure of the irreality to which the presence of the Negro had already reduced the nation that this utterly fantastic idea, which thoroughly controverts the purpose of education, which has no historical or psychological validity, and which denies all the principles on which the country imagines itself to have been founded, was not only accepted with cheers but became the cornerstone of an entire way of life. And this did not come about, by the way, merely because of the venom or villainy of the South. It could never have come about at all without the tacit consent of the North; and this consent robs the North, historically and actually, of any claim to moral superiority. The failure of the government to make any realistic provision for the education of tens of thousands of illiterate former slaves had the effect of dumping this problem squarely into the lap of one man—who knew, whatever else he may not have known, that the education of Negroes had somehow to be accomplished. Whether or not Washington believed what he said is certainly an interesting question. But he *did* know that he could accomplish his objective by telling white men what they wanted to hear. And it has never been very difficult for a Negro in this country to figure out what white men want to hear: he takes his condition as an echo of their desires.

There will be no more Booker T. Washingtons. And whether we like it or not, and no matter how hard or how long we oppose it, there will be no more segregated schools, there will be no more segregated anything. King is entirely right when he says that segregation is dead. The real question which faces the Republic is just how long, how violent, and how expensive the funeral is going to be; and this question it is up to the Republic to resolve, it is not really in King's hands. The sooner the corpse is buried, the sooner we can get around to the far more taxing and rewarding problems of integration, or what King calls community, and what I think of as the achievement of nationhood, or, more simply and cruelly, the growing up of this dangerously adolescent country.

I saw King again, later that same evening, at a party given by this same friend. He came late, did not stay long. I remember him standing in the shadows of the room, near a bookcase, drinking something nonalcoholic, and being patient with the interlocutor who had trapped him in this spot. He obviously wanted to get away and go to bed. King is somewhat below what is called average height, he is sturdily built, but is not quite as heavy or as stocky as he had seemed to me at first. I remember feeling, rather as though he were a younger, much-loved, and menaced brother, that he seemed very slight and vulnerable to be taking on such tremendous odds.

I was leaving for Montgomery the next day, and I called on King in the morning to ask him to have someone from the Montgomery Improvement Association meet me at the airport. It was he who had volunteered to do this for me, since he knew that I knew no one there, and he also probably realized that I was frightened. He was coming to Montgomery on Sunday to preach in his own church.

Montgomery is the cradle of the Confederacy, an unlucky distinction which no one in Montgomery is allowed to forget. The White House which symbolized and housed that short-lived government is still standing, and "people," one of the Montgomery ministers told me, "walk around in those halls and cry." I do not doubt it, the people of Montgomery having inherited nothing less than an ocean of spilt milk. The boycott had been over for a year by the time I got there, and had been ended by a federal decree outlawing segregation in the buses. Therefore, the atmosphere in Montgomery was extraordinary. I think that I have never been in a town so aimlessly hostile, so baffled and demoralized. Whoever has a stone to fling, and flings it, is then left without any weapons; and this was (and remains) the situation of the white people in Montgomery.

I took a bus ride, for example, solely in order to observe the situation on the buses. As I stepped into the bus, I suddenly remembered that I had neglected to ask anyone the price of a bus ride in Montgomery, and so I asked the driver. He gave me the strangest, most hostile of looks, and turned his face away. I dropped fifteen cents into the box and sat down, placing myself, delicately, just a little forward of the center of the bus. The driver had seemed to feel that my question was but another Negro trick, that I had something up my sleeve, and that to answer my question in any way would be to expose himself to disaster. He could not guess what I was thinking, and he was not going to risk further personal demoralization by trying to. And this spirit was the spirit of the town. The bus pursued its course, picking up white and Negro passengers. Negroes sat where they pleased, none very far back; one large woman, carrying packages, seated herself directly behind the driver. And the whites sat there, ignoring them, in a huffy, offended silence.

This silence made me think of nothing so much as the silence which follows a really serious lovers' quarrel: the whites, beneath their cold hostility, were mystified and deeply hurt. They had been betrayed by the Negroes, not merely because the Negroes had declined to remain in their "place," but because the Negroes had refused to be controlled by the town's image of them. And, without this image, it seemed to me, the whites were abruptly and totally lost. The very foundations of their private and public worlds were being destroyed.

I have never heard King preach, and I went on Sunday to hear him at his church. This church is a red brick structure, with a steeple, and it directly faces, on the other side of the street, a white, domed building. My notes fail to indicate whether this is the actual capitol of the state or merely a courthouse; but the conjunction of the two buildings, the steepled one low and dark and tense, the domed one higher and dead white and forbidding, sums up, with an explicitness a set designer might hesitate to copy, the struggle now going on in Montgomery.

At that time in Montgomery, King was almost surely the most beloved man there. I do not think that one could have entered any of the packed churches at that time, if King was present, and not have felt this. Of course, I think that King would be loved by his congregation in any case, and there is always a large percentage of church women who adore the young male pastor, and not always, or not necessarily, out of those grim, psychic motives concerning which everyone today is so knowledgeable. No, there was a feeling in this church which quite transcended anything I have ever felt in a church before. Here it was, totally familiar and yet completely new, the packed church, glorious with the Sunday finery of the women, solemn with the touching, gleaming sobriety of the men, beautiful with children. Here were the ushers, standing in the aisles in white dresses or in dark suits, with armbands on. People were standing along each wall, beside the windows, and standing in the back. King and his lieutenants were in the pulpit, young Martin—as I was beginning to think of him—in the center chair.

When King rose to speak—to preach—I began to understand how the atmosphere of this church differed from that of all the other churches I have known. At first I thought that the great emotional power and authority of the Negro church was being put to a new use, but this is not exactly the case. The Negro church was playing the same role which it has always played in Negro life, but it had acquired a new power.

Until Montgomery, the Negro church, which has always been the place where protest and condemnation could be most vividly articulated, also operated as a kind of sanctuary. The minister who spoke could not hope to effect any objective change in the lives of his hearers, and the people did not expect him to. All they came to find, and all that he could give them, was the sustenance for another day's journey. Now, King could certainly give his congregation that, but he could also give them something more than that, and he had. It is true that it was *they* who had begun the struggle of which he was now the symbol and the leader; it is true that it had taken all of *their* insistence to overcome in him a grave reluctance to stand where he now stood. But it is also true, and it does not happen often, that once he had accepted the place they had prepared for him, their struggle became absolutely indistinguishable from his own, and took over and controlled his life. He suffered with them and, thus, he helped them to suffer. The joy which filled this church, therefore, was the joy achieved by people who have ceased to delude themselves about an intolerable situation, who have found their prayers for a leader miraculously answered, and who now know that they can change their situation, if they will.

And, surely, very few people had ever spoken to them as King spoke. King is a great speaker. The secret of his greatness does not lie in his voice or his presence or his manner, though it has something to do with all these; nor does it lie in his verbal range or felicity, which are not striking; nor does he have any capacity for those stunning, demagogic flights of the imagination which bring an audience cheering to its feet. The secret lies, I think, in his intimate knowledge of the people he is addressing, be they black or white, and in the forthrightness with which he speaks of those things which hurt and baffle them. He does not offer any easy comfort and this keeps his hearers absolutely tense. He allows them their self-respect—indeed, he insists on it.

"We know," he told them, "that there are many things wrong in the white world. But there are many things wrong in the black world, too.

We can't keep on blaming the white man. There are many things we must do for ourselves."

He suggested what some of these were:

"I know none of you make enough money—but save some of it. And there are some things we've got to face. I know the situation is responsible for a lot of it, but do you know that Negroes are 10 percent of the population of St. Louis and are responsible for 58 percent of its crimes? We've got to face that. And we have to do something about our moral standards. And we've got to stop lying to the white man. Every time you let the white man think *you* think segregation is right, you are cooperating with him in doing *evil.*

"The next time," he said, "the white man asks you what you think of segregation, you tell him, Mr. Charlie, I think it's wrong and I wish you'd do something about it by nine o'clock tomorrow morning!"

This brought a wave of laughter and King smiled, too. But he had meant every word he said, and he expected his hearers to act on them. They also expected this of themselves, which is not the usual effect of a sermon; and that they are living up to their expectations no white man in Montgomery will deny.

There was a dinner in the church basement afterwards, where, for the first time, I met Mrs. King—light brown, delicate, really quite beautiful, with a wonderful laugh—and watched young Martin, circulating among church members and visitors. I overheard him explaining to someone that bigotry was a disease and that the greatest victim of this disease was not the bigot's object, but the bigot himself. And these people could only be saved by love. In liberating oneself, one was also liberating them. I was shown, by someone else, the damage done to the church by bombs. King did not mention the bombing of his own home, and I did not bring it up. Late the next night, after a mass meeting in another church, I flew to Birmingham.

I did not see King again for nearly three years. I saw him in Atlanta, just after his acquittal by a Montgomery court on charges of perjury, tax evasion, and misuse of public funds. He had moved to Atlanta and was co-pastor, with his father, of his father's church. He had made this move, he told me, because the pressures on him took him away from Montgomery for such excessively long periods that he did not feel that he was properly fulfilling his ministerial duties there. An attempt had been made on his life—in the North, by a mysterious and deranged Negro woman; and he was about to receive, in the state of Georgia, for driving without a resident driver's license, a suspended twelve-month sentence.

And, since I had last seen him, the Negro student movement had begun and was irresistibly bringing about great shifts and divisions in the Negro world, and in the nation. In short, by the time we met again, he was more beleaguered than he had ever been before, and not only by his enemies in the white South. Three years earlier, I had not encountered very many people—I am speaking now of Negroes—who were really critical of him. But many more people seemed critical of him now, were bitter, disappointed, skeptical. None of this had anything to do—I want to make this absolutely clear—with his personal character or his integrity. It had to do with his effectiveness as a leader. King has had an extraordinary effect in the Negro world, and therefore in the nation, and is now in the center of an extremely complex cross fire.

He was born in Atlanta in 1929. He has Irish and Indian blood in his veins—Irish from his father's, Indian from his mother's side. His maternal grandfather built Ebenezer Baptist Church, which, as I have said, young Martin now co-pastors with his father. This grandfather seems to have been an extremely active and capable man, having been one of the NAACP leaders in Atlanta thirty or forty years ago, and having been instrumental in bringing about the construction of Atlanta's first Negro high school. The paternal grandfather is something else again, a poor, violent, and illiterate farmer who tried to find refuge from reality in drinking. He clearly had a great influence on the formation of the character of Martin, Sr., who determined, very early, to be as unlike his father as possible.

Martin, Sr. came to Atlanta in 1916, a raw, strapping country boy, determined, in the classic American tradition, to rise above his station. It could not have been easy for him in the Deep South of 1916, but he was, luckily, too young for the Army, and prices and wages rose during the war, and his improvident father had taught him the value of thrift. So he got his start. He studied in evening school, entered Atlanta's Morehouse College in 1925, and graduated in June of 1930, more than a year after Martin was born. (There are two other children, an older girl who now teaches at Spelman College, and a younger boy, pastor of a church in Noonan, Georgia.) By this time, Martin, Sr. had become a preacher, and was pastor of two small churches; and at about this time, his father-in-law asked him to become the assistant pastor of Ebenezer Baptist Church, which he did.

His children have never known poverty, and Martin, Sr. is understandably very proud of this. "My prayer," he told me, "was always: Lord, grant that my children will not have to come the way I did." They didn't, they haven't, the prayers certainly did no harm. But one cannot help feeling that a person as single-minded and determined as the elder Reverend King clearly is would have accomplished anything he set his hand to, anyway.

"I equipped myself to give them the comforts of life," he says. "Not to waste, not to keep up with the Joneses, but just to be comfortable. We've never lived in a rented house—and never ridden *too* long in a car on which payment was due."

He is naturally very proud of Martin, Jr., but he claims to be not at all surprised. "He sacrificed to make himself ready"—ready, that is, for a trial, or a series of trials, which might have been the undoing of a lesser man. Yet, though he is not surprised at the extraordinary nature of his son's eminence, he *was* surprised when, at college, Martin decided that he was called to preach. He had expected him to become a doctor or a lawyer because he always spoke of these professions as though he aspired to them.

As he had; and since, as I have said, King is far from garrulous on the subject of his interior life, it is somewhat difficult to know what led him to make this switch. He had already taken premedical and law courses. But he had been raised by a minister, an extremely strong-minded one at that, and in an extraordinarily peaceful and protected way. "Never," says his father, "has Martin known a fuss or a fight or a strike-back in the home." On the other hand, there are some things from which no Negro can really be protected, for which he can only be prepared; and Martin, Sr. was more successful than most fathers in accomplishing this strenuous and delicate task. "I have never believed," he says, "that anybody was better than I." That this is true would seem to be proved by the career of his son, who *"never went around fighting with himself, like we all did."*

Here, speculation is really on very marshy ground, for the father must certainly have fought in himself some of the battles from which young Martin was protected. We have only to consider the era, especially in the South, to realize that this must be true. And it must have demanded great steadiness of mind, as well as great love, to hide so successfully from his children the evidence of these battles. And, since salvation, humanly speaking, is a two-way street, I suggest that, if the father saved the children, it was, almost equally, the children who saved him. It would seem that he was able, with rare success, to project onto his children, or at least onto one of them, a sense of life as he himself would have liked to live it, and somehow made real in their personalities principles on which he himself must often have found it extremely dangerous and difficult to act. Martin, Sr. is regarded with great ambivalence by both the admirers and detractors of his son, and I shall, alas, shortly have more to say concerning his generation; but I do not think that the enormous achievement sketched above can possibly be taken away from him.

Again, young Martin's decision to become a minister has everything to do with his temperament, for he seems always to have been characterized by his striking mixture of steadiness and peace. He apparently did the normal amount of crying in his childhood, for I am told that his grandmother "couldn't stand to see it." But he seems to have done very little complaining; when he was spanked, "he just stood there and took it"; he seems to have been incapable of carrying grudges; and when he was attacked, he did not strike back.

From King's own account, I can only guess that this decision was aided by the fact that, at Morehouse College, he was asked to lead the devotions. The relationship thus established between himself and his contemporaries, or between himself and himself, or between himself and God, seemed to work for him as no other had. Also, I think it is of the utmost importance to realize that King loves the South; many Negroes do. The ministry seems to afford him the best possible vehicle for the expression of that love. At that time in his life, he was discovering "the beauty of the South"; he sensed in the people "a new determination"; and he felt that there was a need for "a new, courageous witness."

But it could not have occurred to him, of course, that *he* would be, and in such an unprecedented fashion, that witness. When Coretta King—then Coretta Scott—met him in Boston, where he was attending Boston University and she was studying at the New England Conservatory of Music, she found him an earnest, somewhat too carefully dressed young man. He had gone from Morehouse to Crozer Theological Seminary in Pennsylvania; the latter institution was interracial, which may have had something to do with his self-consciousness. He was fighting at that time to free himself from all the stereotypes of the Negro, an endeavor which does not leave much room for spontaneity. Both he and Coretta were rather lonely in Boston, and for similar reasons. They were both very distinguished and promising young people, which means that they were also tense, self-conscious, and insecure. They were inevitably cut off from the bulk of the Negro community and their role among whites had to be somewhat ambiguous, for they were not being judged merely as themselves—or, anyway, they could scarcely afford to think so. They were responsible for the good name of all the Negro people.

Coretta had perhaps had more experience than Martin in this role. The more I spoke to her, the more I realized how her story illuminates that of her husband. She had come from Lincoln High in Marion, Alabama, to Antioch College in Ohio, part of one of the earliest groups of Negro students accepted there. She was thus, in effect, part of an experiment, and though she took it very well and can laugh about it now, she certainly must have had her share of exasperated and lonely moments. The social mobility of a Negro girl, especially in such a setting, is even more severely circumscribed than that of a Negro male, and any lapse or error on her part is far more dangerous. From Antioch, Coretta eventually came to Boston on a scholarship and by this time a certain hoydenish, tomboy quality in her had begun, apparently, to be confirmed. The atmosphere at Antioch had been entirely informal, which pleased Coretta; I gather that at this time in her life she was usually to be seen in sweaters, slacks, and scarves. It was a ferociously formal young man and a ferociously informal young girl who finally got together in Boston.

Martin immediately saw through Coretta's disguise, and informed her on their first or second meeting that she had all the qualities he wanted in a wife. Coretta's understandable tendency was to laugh at this; but this tendency was checked by the rather frightening suspicion that he meant it; if he had not meant it, he would not have said it. But a great deal had been invested in Coretta's career as a singer, and she did not feel that she had the right to fail all the people who had done so much to help her. "And I'd certainly never intended to marry a *minister*. It was true that he didn't seem like any of the ministers I'd met, but—still—I thought of how circumscribed my life might become." By circumscribed, she meant dull; she could not possibly have been more mistaken.

What had really happened, in Coretta's case, as in so many others, was that life had simply refused to recognize her private timetable. She had always intended to marry, but tidily, possibly meeting her husband at the end of a triumphant concert tour. However, here he was now, exasperatingly early, and she had to rearrange herself around this fact. She and Martin were married on June 18, 1953. By now, naturally, it is she whom Martin sometimes accuses of thinking too much about clothes. "People who are doing something don't have time to be worried about all that," he has informed her. Well, he certainly ought to know.

Coretta King told me that from the time she reached Boston and all during Martin's courtship, and her own indecision, she yet could not rid herself of a feeling that all that was happening had been, somehow, preordained. And one does get an impression, until this point in the

King story at least, that inexorable forces which none of us really know anything about were shaping and preparing him for that fateful day in Montgomery. Everything that he will need has been delivered, so to speak, and is waiting to be used. Everything, including the principle of nonviolence. It was in 1950 that Dr. Mordecai W. Johnson of Howard University visited India. King heard one of the speeches Johnson made on his return, and it was from this moment that King became interested in Gandhi as a figure, and in nonviolence as a way of life. Later, in 1957, he would visit India himself.

But, so far, of course, we are speaking after the fact. Plans and patterns are always more easily discernible then. This is not so when we try to deal with the present, or attempt speculations about the future.

Immediately after the failure, last June, of Montgomery's case against him, King returned to Atlanta. I entered, late, on a Sunday morning, the packed Ebenezer Baptist Church, and King was already speaking.

He did not look any older, and yet there was a new note of anguish in his voice. He was speaking of his trial. He described the torment, the spiritual state of people who are committed to a wrong, knowing that it is wrong. He made the trials of these white people far more vivid than anything he himself might have endured. They were not ruled by hatred, but by terror; and, therefore, if community was ever to be achieved, these people, the potential destroyers of the person, must not be hated. It was a terrible plea—to the people; and it was a prayer. In *Varieties of Religious Experience*, William James speaks of vastation—of *being*, as opposed to merely regarding, the monstrous creature which came to him in a vision. It seemed to me, though indeed I may be wrong, that something like this had happened to young Martin Luther—that he had looked on evil a long, hard, lonely time. For evil is in the world: it may be in the world to stay. No creed and no dogma are proof against it, and indeed no person is; it is always the naked person, alone, who, over and over and over again, must wrest his salvation from these black jaws. Perhaps young Martin was finding a new and more somber meaning in the command:

"Overcome evil with good." The command does not suggest that to overcome evil is to eradicate it.

King spoke more candidly than I had ever heard him speak before, of his bitterly assaulted pride, of his shame, when he found himself accused, before all the world, of having used and betrayed the people of Montgomery by stealing the money they had entrusted to him. "I knew it wasn't true—but who would believe me?"

He had canceled a speaking trip to Chicago, for he felt that he could not face anyone. And he prayed; he walked up and down in his study, alone. It was borne in on him, finally, that he had no right *not* to go, no right to hide. "I called the airport and made another reservation and went on to Chicago." He appeared there, then, as an accused man, and gave us no details of his visits, which did not, in any case, matter. For if he had not been able to face Chicago, if he had not won that battle with himself, he would have been defeated long before his entrance into that courtroom in Montgomery.

When I saw him the next day in his office, he was very different, kind and attentive, but far away. A meeting of the Southern Christian Leadership Conference was to begin that day, and I think his mind must have been on that. The beleaguered ministers of the Deep South were coming to Atlanta that day in order to discuss the specific situations which confronted them in their particular towns or cities, and King was their leader. All of them had come under immensely greater local pressure because of the student sit-in movement. Inevitably, they were held responsible for it, even though they might very well not have known until reading it in the papers that the students had carried out another demonstration. I do not mean to suggest that there is any question of their support of the students—they may or may not be responsible *for* them but they certainly consider themselves responsible *to* them. But all this, I think, weighed on King rather heavily.

He talked about his visit to India and its effect on him. He was hideously struck by the poverty, which he talked about in great detail. He was also much impressed by Nehru, who had, he said, extraordinary qualities of "perception and dedication and courage—far more than the average American politician." We talked about the South. "Perhaps 4 or 5 percent of the people are to be found on either end of the racial scale"—either actively for or actively against desegregation; "the rest are passive adherents. The sin of the South is the sin of conformity." And he feels, as I do, that much of the responsibility for the situation in which we have found ourselves since 1954 is due to the failure of President Eisenhower to make any coherent, any guiding statement concerning the nation's greatest moral and social problem.

But we did not discuss the impending conference which, in any case, he could scarcely have discussed with me. And we did not discuss any of the problems which face him now and make his future so problematical. For he could not have discussed these with me, either.

That white men find King dangerous is well known. They can say so. But many Negroes also find King dangerous, but cannot say so, at least not publicly. The reason that the Negroes of whom I speak are trapped in such a stunning silence is that to say what they really feel would be to deny the entire public purpose of their lives.

Now, the problem of Negro leadership in this country has always been extremely delicate, dangerous, and complex. The term itself becomes remarkably difficult to define, the moment one realizes that the real role of the Negro leader, in the eyes of the American Republic, was not to make the Negro a first-class citizen but to keep him content as a second-class one. This sounds extremely harsh, but the record bears me out. And this problem, which it was the responsibility of the entire country to face, was dumped into the laps of a few men. Some of them were real leaders and some of them were false. Many of the greatest have scarcely ever been heard of.

The role of the genuine leadership, in its own eyes, was to destroy the barriers which prevented Negroes from fully participating in American life, to prepare Negroes for first-class citizenship, while at the same time bringing to bear on the Republic every conceivable pressure to make their status a reality. For this reason, the real leadership was to be found everywhere, in law courts, colleges, churches, hobo camps; on picket lines, freight trains, and chain gangs; and in jails. Not everyone who was publicized as a leader really was one. And many leaders who would never have dreamed of applying the term to themselves were considered by the Republic—when it knew of their existence at all—to be criminals. This is, of course, but the old and universal story of poverty in battle with privilege, but we tend not to think of old and universal stories as occurring in our brand-new and still relentlessly parochial land.

The real goal of the Negro leader was nothing less than the total integration of Negroes in all levels of the national life. But this could rarely be stated so baldly; it often could not be stated at all; in order to begin Negro education, for example, Booker Washington had found it necessary to state the exact opposite. The reason for this duplicity is that the goal contains the assumption that Negroes are to be treated, in all respects, exactly like all other citizens of the Republic. This is an idea which has always had extremely rough going in America. For one thing, it attacked, and attacks, a vast complex of special interests which would lose money and power if the situation of the Negro were to change. For another, the idea of freedom necessarily carries with it the idea of sexual freedom: the freedom to meet, sleep with, and marry whom one chooses. It would be fascinating, but I am afraid we must postpone it for the moment, to consider just why so many people appear to be convinced that Negroes would then immediately meet, sleep with, and marry white women; who, remarkably enough, are only protected from such undesirable alliances by the majesty and vigilance of the law.

The duplicity of the Negro leader was more than matched by the duplicity of the people with whom he had to deal. They, and most of the country, felt at the very bottom of their hearts that the Negro was inferior to them and, therefore, merited the treatment that he got. But it was not always politic to say this, either. It certainly could never be said over the bargaining table, where white and black men met.

The Negro leader was there to force from his adversary whatever he could get: new schools, new schoolrooms, new houses, new jobs. He was invested with very little power because the Negro vote had so very little power. (Other Negro leaders were trying to correct *that*.) It was not easy to wring concessions from the people at the bargaining table, who had, after all, no intention of giving their power away. People seldom do give their power away, forces beyond their control take their power from them; and I am afraid that much of the liberal cant about progress is but a sentimental reflection of this implacable fact. (Liberal cant about love and heroism also obscures, not to say blasphemes, the great love and heroism of many white people. Our racial story would be inconceivably more grim if these people, in the teeth of the most fantastic odds, did not continue to appear; but they were almost never, of course, to be found at the bargaining table.) Whatever concession the Negro leader carried away from the bargaining table was won with the tacit understanding that he, in return, would influence the people he represented in the direction that the people in power wished them to be influenced. Very often, in fact, he did not do this at all, but contrived to delude the white men (who are, in this realm, rather easily deluded) into believing that he had. But very often, too, he deluded himself into believing that the aims of white men in power and the desires of Negroes out of power were the same.

It was altogether inevitable, in short, that, by means of the extraordinary tableau I have tried to describe, a class of Negroes should have been created whose loyalty to their class was infinitely greater than their loyalty to the people from whom they had been so cunningly estranged. We must add, for I think it is important, that the Negro leader knew that he, too, was called "nigger" when his back was turned. The great mass of the black people around him were illiterate, demoralized, in want, and incorrigible. It is not hard to see that the Negro leader's personal and public frustrations would almost inevitably be turned against these people, for their misery, which formed the cornerstone of his peculiar power, was also responsible for his humiliation. And in Harlem, now, for example, many prominent Negroes ride to and from work through scenes of the greatest misery. They do not see this misery, though, because they do not want to see it. They defend themselves against an intolerable reality, which menaces them, by despising the people who are trapped in it.

The criticism, therefore, of the publicized Negro leadership—which is not, as I have tried to indicate, always the real leadership—is a criticism leveled, above all, against this class. They are, perhaps, the most unlucky bourgeoisie in the world's entire history, trapped, as they are, in a no-man's-land between black humiliation and white power. They cannot move backwards, and they cannot move forward, either.

One of the greatest vices of the white bourgeoisie on which they have modeled themselves is its reluctance to think, its distrust of the independent mind. Since the Negro bourgeoisie has so many things *not* to think about, it is positively afflicted with this vice. I should like at some other time to embark on a full-length discussion of the honorable and heroic role played by the NAACP in the national life, and point out to what extent its work has helped create the present ferment. But, for the moment, I shall have to confine my remarks to its organ, *The Crisis*, because I think it is incontestable that this magazine reveals the state of mind of the Negro bourgeoisie. *The Crisis* has the most exciting subject matter in the world at its fingertips, and yet manages to be one of the world's dullest magazines. When the Reverend James Lawson—who was expelled from Vanderbilt University for his sit-in activities—said this, or something like it, he caused a great storm of ill feeling. But he was quite right to feel as he does about *The Crisis*, and quite right to say so. And the charge is not answered by referring to the history of the NAACP.

Now, to charge *The Crisis* with dullness may seem to be a very trivial matter. It is not trivial, though, because this dullness is the result of its failure to examine what is really happening in the Negro world—its failure indeed, for that matter, to seize upon what is happening in the world at large. And I have singled it out because this inability is revelatory of the gap which now ominously widens between what we shall now have to call the official leadership and the young people who have begun what is nothing less than a moral revolution.

It is because of this gap that King finds himself in such a difficult position. The pressures on him are tremendous, and they come from above and below. He lost much moral credit, for example, especially in the eyes of the young, when he allowed Adam Clayton Powell to force the resignation of his (King's) extremely able organizer and lieutenant, Bayard Rustin. Rustin, also, has a long and honorable record as a fighter for Negro rights, and is one of the most penetrating and able men around. The techniques used by Powell—we will not speculate as to his motives—were far from sweet; but King was faced with the choice of defending his organizer, who was also his friend, or agreeing with Powell; and he chose the *latter* course. Nor do I know of anyone satisfied with the reasons given for the exclusion of James Lawson from the Southern Christian Leadership Conference. It would seem, certainly, that so able, outspoken, and energetic a man might prove of great value to this organization: why, then, is he not part of it?

And there are many other questions, all of them ominous, and too many to go into here. But they all come, finally, it seems to me, to this tremendous reality: it is the sons and daughters of the beleaguered bourgeoisie—supported, in the most extraordinary fashion, by those old, work-worn men and women who were known, only yesterday, as "the country niggers"—who have begun a revolution in the consciousness of this country which will inexorably destroy nearly all that we now think of as concrete and indisputable. These young people have never believed in the American image of the Negro and have never bargained with the Republic, and now they never will. There is no longer any basis on which to bargain: for the myth of white supremacy is exploding all over the world, from the Congo to New Orleans. Those who have been watched and judged and described for so long are now watching and judging and describing for themselves. And one of the things that this means, to put it far too simply and bluntly, is that the white man on whom the American Negro has modeled himself for so long is vanishing. Because this white man was, himself, very largely a mythical creation: white men have never been, here, what they imagined themselves to be. The liberation of Americans from the racial anguish which has crippled us for so long can only mean, truly, the creation of a new people in this still-new world.

But the battle to achieve this has not ended, it has scarcely begun. Martin Luther King, Jr., by the power of his personality and the force of his beliefs, has injected a new dimension into our ferocious struggle. He has succeeded, in a way no Negro before him has managed to do, to carry the battle into the individual heart and make its resolution the province of the individual will. He has made it a matter, on both sides of the racial fence, of self-examination; and has incurred, therefore, the grave responsibility of continuing to lead in the path he has encouraged so many people to follow. How he will do this I do not know, but I do not see how he can possibly avoid a break, at last, with the habits and attitudes, stratagems and fears of the past.

No one can read the future, but we do know, as James has put it, that "all futures are rough." King's responsibility, and ours, is to that future which is already sending before it so many striking signs and portents. The possibility of liberation which is always real is also always painful, since it involves such an overhauling of all that gave us our identity. The Negro who will emerge out of this present struggle—whoever, indeed, this dark stranger may prove to be—will not be dependent, in any way at all, on any of the many props and crutches which help form our identity now. And neither will the white man. We will need every ounce of moral stamina we can find. For everything is changing, from our notion of politics to our notion of ourselves, and we are certain, as we begin history's strangest metamorphosis, to undergo the torment of being forced to surrender far more than we ever realized we had accepted.

VOICES FROM THE SOUTH: 1965

(APRIL 1965)

Robert Coles

AS A CHILD psychiatrist I have spent much of the last several years in the South studying the effects of desegregation on the human beings involved, trying to learn how individuals manage under severe social pressures. The following paragraphs are the words of some of the people of the South, recorded on tapes or written to others or me during this time:

A Negro boy recollecting his experience as a pioneer in the desegregation of Little Rock's schools: *"It was so bad that we figured it couldn't get worse, so if we could just last out it would have to get better; and then it did."*

A white boy in Atlanta comments on his feelings at the sight of a Negro in his classroom: *"I felt as if our history was crumbling right before our eyes. First I couldn't believe it, and then I didn't think it would last.... Now I think we forget about it most of the time."*

A teacher in a North Carolina mountain school: *"I never thought I'd live to see colored children in this school; but to be truthful, after a while I think we have to remind ourselves that a colored child is colored."*

A segregationist woman telling me why she was just that, and why she had pulled her child out of a New Orleans school when it was desegregated: *"If I didn't believe in segregation my children soon would be forgetting the difference, and they'd play with them in school and sink to their level. . . . Who ever heard of making white and colored mix? If they did that a long time ago you and I wouldn't be white."*

A tall, blond, ruddy-faced former sharecropper now become a migrant worker: *"We never much needed money, but then we couldn't buy clothes for the kids, and the bills came knocking on us . . . so we couldn't keep on the farm, and we decided we'd just go where there was the money, even if we had to keep following it."*

A Negro sharecropper in Mississippi: *"I'd like to get me and my family out of here, but I doesn't know how and I doesn't know where to."*

In Georgia a white child wrote in a Negro classmate's yearbook: *"I hope you will forgive those of us who have been mean and ugly. . . ."*

In Mississippi a policeman said to me after a home had been dynamited and two summer volunteer students working on voter registration injured: *"You're lucky you can treat them this time. Next time they might need the coroner."*

In his home in an Alabama city a doctor talks: *"I think you're studying the wrong people. The Negroes have lasted through slavery, so they're certainly going to survive desegregation. . . . And those segregationists screaming in mobs are just the rabble let loose by a dying, confused society. But what about all the scared well-meaning people of the South? I wonder how our minds survive it . . . the lying we do and the shame we have to live with. . . ."*

Finally, a white woman of Louisiana is trying to explain why—in spite of a mob and a nearly complete boycott—she defied threats on her life and her children's lives in order to keep them in a school that had admitted one little six-year-old Negro child: *". . . my heart is divided, and at the worst of it I thought we'd die, not just from dynamite, but from nervous exhaustion. I wasn't brought up to have nigras at school with me or my children. I just wasn't. . . . If I had to do it over, I wouldn't have made this system, but how many people ever have a say about what kind of world they're going to live in? . . . I guess in a sense I did have my way with those mobs. But I didn't plan to, and we were near scared to death most of the time. . . . People blame the South for the mobs, but that's just part of the South. If I did right, that's part of the South, too. . . . They just don't know how a lot of us down here suffer. We didn't make all this, we just were born to it, and we don't have all the opportunity and money down here that they do in the North. . . I told my children the other day that we're going to live to see the end of this trouble, and when we do I'll bet both races get on better down here than anywhere else in America. . . . Why? Because I think we're quieter down here, and we respect one another, and if we could clear up the race thing, we really would know one another better. . . . We've lived so close for so long. . . . "*

CONFESSIONS OF A
BLUE-CHIP BLACK

(APRIL 1982)

Roger Wilkins

IN 1962, AFTER graduating from the University of Michigan and Michigan Law School, marrying the beautiful daughter of a black lawyer from Cleveland, and practicing international law in New York for several years, I was offered a job as special assistant to the head of the Agency for International Development. The administrator, Fowler Hamilton, suggested that I meet a Negro member of his staff to discuss my qualms about living in Washington, which was still regarded as a Southern town.

Bob Kitchen was a revelation. He was very black, about six feet tall, and almost forty years old. He had a round head, dark-tinged eyeballs, and was dressed with a practiced elegance. Brown, shaggy suit, off-yellow shirt, brown-and-green-patterned silk tie with matching handkerchief flopping casually from breast pocket, and highly polished brown shoes all reeked of money. Kitchen moved into the room with a cool assurance I had rarely seen in any Negro, particularly in the presence of white power.

Kitchen's style, especially his verbal gymnastics, seemed consciously or unconsciously designed to send a message to the white world: "This is not a nigger, but rather a serious, educated man." I had seen other educated Negroes use pretentiously big words and complicated sentence structures, but I had never seen it done by anybody as smart as Kitchen.

I was troubled by what I perceived—a Negro bent out of shape by the power and the callousness of the white world. I figured that the way to handle oneself was the way I did it—straight on, no frills. What I didn't understand was that my particular adaptation to white power was the most grotesque of all. I dressed in Ivy League suits, shirts, and ties. Simple, straight white talk had become my native tongue. I had begun to know how white people operated in the world and had begun to emulate them. I had no aspirations that would have seemed foreign to my white contemporaries. I had abdicated my birthright and had become an ersatz white man.

But, of course, what white people saw was a well-educated, well-bred, sensible Negro who, but for the unfortunate color of his skin, was very much like them. I was just the kind of person they wanted, because I was "ready"—ready to face white people without embarrassing "the race." I was just the kind of safe black person white people were beginning to look for.

I worked at AID for two years. Shortly before I left, for an even better job at the Justice Department (ultimately, assistant attorney general), I found myself in Nairobi, Kenya, with an inspection team. The last two evenings we were there, during the cocktail hour at our hotel, the most beautiful woman I had ever seen sat and drank with friends at another table. She had rich brown skin, huge and luminous dark eyes, lush, thick, dark-brown hair, and a fine figure. I couldn't keep my eyes off her. She was a glory, one of nature's great treasures. We speculated on what she might be—an actress, a model, an heiress, a mulatto, an Indian, or a well-tanned white.

Later, when we boarded our Air India flight to Bombay, we found out. She was a tourist-class flight attendant. I was delighted. I stared at her as she moved about the cabin, all delicate grace. I was so awestruck, I could barely talk to her when she served me. At first she had just given me a warm and beautiful smile. Then—could I be seeing things?—she was flirting with me. Since there wasn't anything else to drink, I asked to buy some whiskey, neat. Then I found I didn't have any East African pounds left.

"Will you take dollars?" I asked.

"Dollars?" she asked. "Where did you get dollars?"

"In the United States," I answered.

"When were you there?" she asked.

"Two weeks ago," I replied.

"How long were you there?"

"Thirty-two years," I said.

Her eyes widened and she exclaimed, "Oh, you're an American. I had no idea."

I was stunned. She had taken a load off my head. This beautiful woman hadn't been talking and flirting with a Negro, a "nigger." She'd just been talking to a man, a man whom she had found attractive. I was thirty-two years old, and I had never thought of myself that way. I had internalized the prevailing white American definition of me as a Negro, something less than a whole man. This woman's unexpected exclamation had ripped a veil off my unconscious mind and had shown me how much America's pervasive racism had crippled me. Thanks to her, I would never be the same. I became a *man* in this world that night.

Much of the new black thought settled inside me during the 1960s, but rested there alongside some lessons from white America that couldn't be purged. The sense of deprivation, the sense of exclusion, would not go away but lingered, like a ghost, from my adolescence. In the late Sixties, I had money, power, and prestige. I certainly didn't want to be white anymore—the movement had touched me deeply enough to get rid of that—but I had a keen sense that something was missing. Perhaps it was the ease and assurance that in so many white people seemed to flow from the absolute knowledge that America was their country.

One tangible aspect of that deprivation was white women. By the time I was thirty-four, I had been with one or two white women, and I knew they weren't magical, but the taboo against interracial sex made it more tempting. Gnawing memories of adolescent deprivation and the powerful images of the white goddesses remained.

And so it was in the summer of 1966 during the riot in Chicago that I invited a tall, slender young white woman with long dark hair to my bed. She was a member of my staff and had long pretty legs that looked wonderful in a miniskirt. We were in Chicago at the same time, in the same hotel, by chance, not by design. Her name was Mary and she was a graduate of Smith College and we mainly talked that first night, but it was a beginning.

Mary meant a lot of things to me. There was wonderful sex, youthful, exuberant, and free. There was her whiteness and the fact that at twenty-two she wasn't all that much older than the inaccessible girls from high school. And she came as close to being a hippie as a government employee could come, so she reminded me of wonderful images I had seen in Greenwich Village many years before—white girls with long flowing hair walking with black men—couples who I imagined had the ripest and most abandoned sex.

By the time Richard Nixon won the 1968 election, I was ready to leave the government. John Gardner, the former president of the Carnegie Foundation and one of Lyndon Johnson's secretaries of Health, Education and Welfare, thought that the Ford Foundation would be a good place for me to explore. He put me in touch with McGeorge Bundy, who by now was president of the foundation, and we talked. The conversation went easily and two jobs were offered. One was in international affairs and the other was to run the foundation's largest domestic program. The program gave money for programs in job training, inner-city education, drug rehabilitation, black economic development, and projects for other American minorities. It sounded just right, and the money sounded fine, so I agreed to take it.

The decision to go to Ford was typical of the pattern of my life; it was a mistake and probably an inevitable one. The Ford Foundation was another way station in the white establishment. At a time when the divisions between black and white and between black and black had never been greater, I chose to work once more with a white institution, a decision that was to do little for my peace of mind.

There were by now a variety of strong and well-developed strains of black ideology, each in its own way suggesting that blacks could survive in America only if they banded together outside, and largely in opposition to, mainstream white American life. Instead of turning away from Africa and slavery in shame as most of the older generations of blacks had done, the younger generation was pulling it out in plain view and almost reveling in it.

The crippling imposition of the white fantasy upon the black psyche most enraged and infuriated me. I hadn't understood until the late Sixties. I had bought the fantasy of white superiority, the notions that my thick lips and kinky hair were somehow inferior to the genetic legacies of Europe. I had been ashamed of my skin, my genes, and myself. Those realizations and the rage that flowed from them impelled me toward a stronger feeling of kinship with other blacks than I had ever experienced before. And yet that closeness was more difficult to realize than ever before, because the new ideology carried with it a new hierarchy of color and social class. Once a white member of my staff asked me where I had lived as a youngster in New York and I replied, "In Harlem." A black staff member interjected, "Shit, he lived above 145th Street, that's Sugar Hill, not Harlem." When I was young, I had heard the older people in my neighborhood insist that they lived in Washington Heights, to distance themselves from the poorer people who had lived in the Harlem Valley. Now it was the style to claim that you had lived in Harlem to distance yourself from the richer people uptown.

My acculturation as an adolescent in a completely white, middle-class neighborhood of Grand Rapids, Michigan, had deprived me of easy access to black street language or the sinuous body movements that would have made me comfortable working day by day in a storefront in San Francisco or Cleveland. I'd been born in a little, segregated hospital in Kansas City, and after my father's death, when I was nine, the family had moved to New York for a few years, but in

October 1943, my mother was remarried—to a bachelor doctor who could have passed for white—and I grew up more Midwestern than Harlemite, more American than black. My parents armed me for life in an integrated America, and now the enraged and romantic part of me didn't want to go there; but I was not equipped culturally or psychically to spend my life in the deepest pools of black America. So I was going to the Ford Foundation instead of a ghetto storefront. I could do things here that people in the storefronts could not do nearly as well. But I couldn't find a spiritual peace that I desperately needed.

In December 1969, a delicate, dark-haired woman with fine features and a striking figure came to interview me for a book on Robert F. Kennedy. She identified herself as the former wife of William Vanden Heuvel, a familiar New York political aspirant and a fairly close associate of Robert Kennedy's. I had never heard of Mrs. Vanden Heuvel, but the breathy rush and jumble of her words on the telephone was appealing.

Mrs. Vanden Heuvel turned out to be even more appealing in person. She kept getting tangled up in the wires of her tape recorder as she tried to find the outlet behind the couch in my office. The tentativeness of her approach produced an impression of the woman's vulnerability that I was later to learn was something less than the whole story.

But it was partly true and enormously effective for an interviewer. To help this woman out, I found myself remembering things that I thought I had long forgotten. Each time I would come up with a new nugget of information to her half-formulated question, she would give me a smile suffused with shy gratitude. When the interview was over and she was stumbling over her mike and her cords, she thanked me profusely. Several days later, I received a warm and effusive note of thanks, expressing the hope that I would review the transcript. I was anxious to see that woman again, and so in January 1970, when the transcript had come back, I went over to her Central Park West apartment early one evening to go over the material and have a drink.

Jean and I had one drink and then another. And then I took her out

to dinner that night, and later another. Her smile was bewitching. It would begin and her head would tuck down and sideways, then the smile would begin to fade as if a cloud of doubt were passing, and then the teeth would show again and the smile would rush to fulfillment, powered by a shy giggle. Jean's bones were as thin as her features were fine. Her hair was very dark and her skin very pale. Her touch on hand or cheek was light, sometimes tentative, always affecting. She had a way of making a man feel strong, capable, protective, supported, and, ultimately, loved and loving.

It was clear from her large apartment overlooking Central Park that Jean was not poor. Her father was Dr. Julius Caesar Stein, usually called Jules, president of the Music Corporation of America and a dominant—some would say *the* dominant—force in the movie industry. Jean had grown up as a princess in the canyons above Los Angeles.

Jean started to introduce me to her impressive circle of friends. There was Gillian, who lived in the building next door. Gillian was Jean's best friend, and though her father had been curator of the National Gallery, Gillian was just Gillian from next door, easy to be with. And then there were Jason and Barbara Epstein, stars of the literary world, he at Random House and she at the *New York Review of Books*. My relationship with Jean often landed me at evenings at the Epsteins' with Stephen Spender or Lillian Hellman or, at the least, Bob Bernstein, the lovely man who heads Random House. One night, Jean said we'd been asked to drop by the home of another editor, Aaron Asher, of Holt, Rinehart and Winston. So we went, and in addition to the Ashers, there were the photographer Inge Morath and her husband, Arthur Miller, and there was also, sitting across from the Millers, Philip Roth.

I was gaining access to artistic and literary circles in New York, not only through Jean, but through my own activism as well. Late in 1969, I was asked to attend a meeting at the home of Lillian Hellman. When I got to the meeting, I recognized Burke Marshall, the head of the Civil Rights Division under Robert F. Kennedy, the writer William Styron and his wife, Rose, Norman Dorsen, a distinguished NYU law professor and civil libertarian, Blair Clark, a writer and former radio journalist, the cartoonist Jules Feiffer, and Robert Silvers, editor of the *New York Review of Books*. That night, Jean and I had dinner with Felicia and Leonard Bernstein at their penthouse apartment on Park Avenue.

There was a strain in all of this. I had known when I left the government that I had to forge a new identity, or at least to consolidate the old one, which in large measure had been based on a charter from a president who was no longer in office and at a time that no longer existed. Now I was getting a new identity from associations with some of the most glittering people in America. But an identity built on association was about as valuable as fool's gold. It became absolutely destructive of the ego of one who doubted the value of what he had already accomplished and was on the way to hating what he was presently working on.

Occasionally, my name would slip into a gossip column. "Roger Wilkins of the Ford Foundation," it would say. That was perfectly respectable in print, but the reality was becoming more and more difficult to live with. One day, for example, a black man and a white woman who had founded a private mini-school for poor black kids in the West Philadelphia ghetto came to have lunch with me at Ford. Theirs was exactly the kind of effort that I loved: innovative, concerned, respectful, and loving without condescension. It was for me the purified essence of the black consciousness movement of the late Sixties.

We had lunch in the dining room on the eleventh floor of the elegant foundation headquarters. Over paté, they began to tell me how they had conceived the school program and why. While we ate our steak and lamb chops, they told me how they had built their curriculum, and over chocolate mousse they told me how they had scrabbled for the funding that had kept them alive so far.

After lunch, I led them back to my office, with its elegant furniture and a glass wall that looked out onto the garden.

"We need $25,000 to get us through this year," the man said.

I sighed. I had seen these people because a good friend of mine had asked me to see them as a favor.

"I'm afraid there's nothing I can do for you," I said, having known what they would ask.

Their faces sagged. I tried to explain. "My program only does education in conjunction with the people here at Ford who specialize in education," I began, attempting the impossible task of making institutional constraints plausible to working idealists. "My counterpart in education already has a number of pilot projects like this. That leaves me powerless to help you."

They looked at me, their faces blank. I looked back at them, trying to keep my face blank.

"Won't you even come to Philadelphia to look at the school before you turn us down?" the white woman asked.

"There's no reason for me to come to Philadelphia except to make myself feel worse than I do now," I said.

I stood up and started moving them toward the elevator. There was no use prolonging this agony. We walked down the corridor on the polished floor and then waited for the elevator in silence.

"I'm really sorry," I finally said.

They just shrugged and looked downcast. When the elevator came, they thanked me and stepped in. As the door was closing, I heard the man say, "We could run our school for three years with just what it cost to build this elevator."

Yet the Ford Foundation was the only place where I had any daily connection with blackness—thinly strained and awkward as the connection often was. The places where I had drifted and where I was building an identity outside working hours were all white. I was spending many of my evenings on Central Park West or joining Jean's friends in the newest cultural trend or artistic fad. Jean's sensitivity, warmth, and perceptive intelligence were enough to keep me involved in our relationship, but she had also given me the keys to the candy store. Instead of standing with my nose pressed to the window, I often found myself inside rooms with people whose names were Mailer, Vidal, Javits, Kennedy, or Bernstein.

Those who were Jean's friends seemed as devoid of racism as any group of whites I had ever encountered. Whatever problems people had about Jean and me they kept to themselves. Once, in Roxbury, Connecticut, at Arthur and Inge Miller's home, at a party celebrating Arthur's birthday, a grande dame of a Russian *émigrée* took me to be the bartender. Everybody thought it was pretty funny and I didn't mind. Once, arriving for a party at the apartment of Marion and Jacob Javits, we ran into Warren Beatty, who was just leaving, in the lobby. Beatty grinned and said, "God, what a swell-looking couple."

Normally, there was simply easy acceptance of me, as if I had earned my way into those drawing rooms just as everyone else had. Yet because my work was not individualistic, creative, or as celebrated as that of most of the people I saw around me, I didn't believe I belonged.

Felicia Bernstein, Leonard's delicate, intelligent, and beautiful wife, was one of my favorites in Jean's circle. Felicia knew about my insecurities, and once, when she heard me say I had been the first black to do this or that, she stopped me.

"You know, Roger," she said, "you sound like you're keeping score."

The company of Miller, Bernstein, *et alii* was all heady stuff; I loved it, but it tore me apart. I was enjoying a kind of life that was far beyond the actual or even the imaginative grasp of the poor blacks to whom the serious efforts of my life were supposed to be committed. This was the life where people escaped even the mundane problems that ordinary white people had. It was as if, by entering that world at night, I was betraying everything I told myself I stood for during the day.

One March day in 1970, I went up to meet a young man in the basement of an Episcopal church on Edgecombe Avenue in Harlem. The young man's name was Sam. Sam and his group were working on housing when I met him, and he didn't want Ford money, just my sense of how he was doing and a connection that would make him feel comfortable when he thought it would be useful to him. Sam was nineteen years old.

It was one of those unusually warm March days, and it was late in the afternoon when Sam and I parted, too late to go back to the office. I was due at Jean's for drinks with friends early in the evening, so I decided to walk the sixty blocks or so from Sam's Harlem church to Jean's Central Park West apartment.

Abandonment of real estate had already begun to afflict Harlem by the spring of 1970, and as I walked over toward Eighth Avenue, I saw a number of buildings that were gutted shells with paneless windows staring like hollow eyes at a street filled with day people, who in an hour or so would become night people, doing the same thing in the dark as they had done in the sunlight—nothing, because there was nothing for them to do. The buildings that had not been burned out or abandoned for some other reason were old and often crumbling. At many of the corners there were stores, with faded signs and tired-looking vegetables. There was litter and garbage everywhere. The sanitation department didn't seem to visit often, and the people didn't seem to care much.

Some men sat on stoops, others on folding chairs that they had brought from small, musty apartments upstairs. Many of them were engaged in the long, seemingly aimless conversations that so often occupy the hours of old men. But not all of these men were old. Some of them, in their scuffed shoes and patched jackets, were no older than I. Many of them drank from containers in brown paper bags.

Farther down, on Eighth Avenue, I came upon the drug center that a young Black Panther friend had shown me months before. The people wore brightly colored old clothes, for the most part. Many of the men wore gaudy, light-colored hats. Some of the movement through the thickness of people was flamboyant, a swinging of hips and a dipping of head that communicated the mover was cool and unapproachable. More of the movement was like quiet gliding, making minimal use of arms and legs, moving lips and jaws imperceptibly, passing things from one to another with quick fingers. Some people went in and out of the dark and shoddy bars on the street. Some people just stayed in one place, bending rhythmically from the waist, apparently hearing and seeing nothing. They were, according to the argot of the street, on the nod.

I went on. Farther down Eighth, I saw some small children playing.

They were very dark, and some of the boys had on short pants even though it was only March. The boys were throwing around a soiled toy rabbit that had once been yellow, trying to keep it from the two girls who had been playing with them. The girls were not happy; it had apparently been their toy before the boys had come. Just as I approached them, the boy who had the rabbit gave the toy a wild heave. It went high in the air, over my head, and into the doorway of one of the buildings from which I had seen some of the children emerge just a few moments earlier. I ducked into the doorway to get it and was struck, almost repulsed, by the powerful and acrid smell of dried urine that filled the place. I picked up the rabbit, tossed the dirty thing to one of the girls, and kept on walking.

A couple of blocks farther down, at 110th Street, Eighth Avenue became Central Park West. It was not the Central Park West of the large and well-preserved buildings in Jean's neighborhood. The buildings up at the black end of the famous street were old and not well kept. But it was not central Harlem anymore. There were no more run-down and exorbitant convenience stores. There were no people sitting on the stoops on folding chairs or milk crates. And later, in the low Nineties, it was better preserved, more like the Central Park West that people knew from movies and literature.

Soon I was passing buildings where I had chatted with Saul Steinberg in a room on one evening, or with Arthur Schlesinger, Jr., on another, or with Lukas Foss on another. All of the rooms where I remembered seeing those people were lovely places, and the evenings were usually charged with intelligence and wit. I was only fifty blocks away from Sam and that church basement on Edgecombe Avenue.

Finally, as the shadows of the large apartment buildings facing east were lying long across the park, I came to Jean's building. The doorman, who knew me well by now, smiled and nodded me in, and I went up. A lawyer I knew and liked and his lovely blond wife were already there. Jean was in the back of the apartment, still getting ready. I greeted my friends, poured a lot of Beefeater gin over ice in a wide, short glass, added two drops of dry vermouth and an olive, and then joined my friends looking out of the window at the play of shadows on the still barren trees in the park and at the white people walking home from midtown.

Jean's parents had heard of our relationship and thunder began rolling east from the hills above Hollywood. I never met Jean's father, a circumstance that neither of us regretted. Dr. Stein was a great philanthropist, having given millions to the Jules Stein eye institute at UCLA, but according to his daughter was given to the vicious and casual use of the word "nigger," as in "What are you doing with that nigger?" Jean told me once that when he heard that I had an estranged wife, he commented, "I hope she has a knife and kills him."

I was amused and endlessly fascinated at how much discomfort our relationship was causing the grand couple out on the Coast. After each of Jean's encounters with her parents, I would do my best to draw details out of her. Finally, though her father would not meet me, her mother could not contain her curiosity and announced one day, when they were visiting New York, that she was coming over for drinks. Jean could have prevented the meeting, but the imp in her was as strong as the curiosity in me.

Mrs. Stein was already sitting on a couch in the blue library when I got there. She must have been nearing seventy by then, and she was a striking woman with thin, beautiful features, exquisitely kept white hair, a strong body in an expensive blue suit. It was clear, looking at her, how Jean had come by such delicate beauty. We were introduced. Mrs. Stein was polite and so was I. Conversation was sporadic, disjointed, aimless, and difficult until Mrs. Stein hit upon a topic that she thought suitable. She began talking about her work for the Hollywood Canteen during World War II.

The Hollywood Canteen was probably the most famous U.S.O. center in the country. But there was a problem at the canteen, according to Mrs. Stein. It was the communists. The canteen, it seemed, was democratic. Its doors were open to servicemen of the United States, regardless of color. But the communists were always pressing for the white girls to dance with the colored servicemen. Now, the white girls were some of the nicest girls who could be found, according to Mrs. Stein, and what the communists proposed was out of the question.

But she and the other powers behind the canteen fought off the communists and kept that rest and rehabilitation center safe for all our servicemen and for the American way, Mrs. Stein informed me triumphantly.

"You know, Mrs. Stein, that reminds me of a story," I replied. "It is said that before World War II, there was an annual cotillion down in Charleston, South Carolina, where the loveliest and the finest young women of the state would be presented. Well, during the war, there was a shortage of men, because so many had gone off to fight. So, one year, the woman who was arbiter of Charleston society and who ran the cotillion called a nearby army base for help.

" 'Captain,' she said, 'I want you to send over fifteen of your finest young men to the cotillion tonight to be with some of our finest young ladies.' The captain agreed and then the woman said, 'And, there's just one more thing. Don't send any Jews.' Again the captain agreed.

"The night of the dance, when everyone was assembled, the arbiter saw before her fifteen of the biggest, blackest buck niggers she had ever seen.

" 'There must be some mistake,' she exclaimed in horror.

" 'No, ma'am,' the leader of the blacks said, 'Cap'n Goldstein, he don't never make no mistakes.' "

Mrs. Stein finished her drink quickly after that, and got up to leave. She told me it had been nice to meet me. I told her that it had been nice to meet her.

Jean howled with laughter until she cried.

Today, after several moves back and forth, and several other romances, I am living in Washington with my third wife. Patricia, who is black, teaches at Georgetown Law School. We were married in February 1981, a month shy of my forty-ninth birthday and four months shy of her thirty-ninth. (My second wife was Mary, to whom I was married briefly in 1977.)

My most recent job was at the *Washington Star*. My title was associate editor, but I was more like a writer in residence. At the *Star*, I made a new friend, a young black reporter named Kenny Walker, who was amused at the reactions of some of the whites there to me. "They ain't never seen no blue-chip nigger like you before," he would say with a laugh.

When I moved back to Washington, I got an apartment in Anacostia, a poor black section of town. After so many years of a thoroughly integrated life, it was curious but comforting to get up in the morning and see only black people in my building and at the places where I went to have my clothes cleaned or my shoes repaired. Some people thought my living there was something of a gimmick or a conceit, but it wasn't. The rent was cheap, the view was fabulous, and the constant proximity to ordinary black people was psychologically nourishing.

A few months after the *Star* folded, Kenny and I had lunch at Mel Krupin's restaurant on Connecticut Avenue. When we finished, I went to get a taxi on the southbound side of the avenue. Kenny told me I ought to go over to the northbound side because cabs didn't often pick up blacks going south for fear they were heading toward the ghetto.

"Aw, man, you're crazy," I said.

"No, I'm not," Kenny said. "An awful lot of cabs have passed me by on this side of the street."

"Well, I'll try this one," I said, throwing up my hand as an empty cab came down the street. It slowed and stopped. As I opened the door and stepped in, I turned and grinned at Kenny and said, "Blue-chip."

A PALENESS OF HEART

(JUNE 1973)

Mary Richie

THE OTHER DAY, a Sunday, I went walking in Central Park. Most of the people walking or sitting in the park were black. Whites rolled by on swift bicycles, as if in another dimension of time. I was walking in a People's Park in an African city. Blacks everywhere, nuggets of color on picnic blankets, grave groups of boys and girls sipping from white paper cups. Even a few years ago, I did not see so many blacks this far down in the park. I felt happy, as if, a traveler, I were being accepted, without stares, by the self-contained natives. Three black boys came down the path. One was wearing a sculpted feather head-piece of gold and red and the flickering colors of the pheasant. His chest was bare, his eyes glittering like a drunken priest's. One of his two companions suddenly turned, waved his hand toward a nearby slope, and said to his friends, "Hey man, let's go climb the mountain." Suddenly I saw a mountain and felt my life expand. I remembered Mt. Tom, where I had run as a child down the smooth stones that never shifted, as I was warned they would, but stayed firm under my commanding feet.

A little while later I saw a white man coming toward me, dressed in casual clothes, preoccupied. It was S. I spoke his name and we fell on each other's shoulders, suddenly more than friends of friends, travelers together.

Late one evening, after a reception at the Museum of Modern Art, I went along with D. and his friends to get a hamburger. We walked along Sixth Avenue, across the street from the Hilton. Three tall handsome black men stood together on the sidewalk, facing each other, as if there were a bonfire or a body between them. They wore large flaring hats, slightly cocked on one side; beautiful trousers tucked into soft, nearly knee-high boots; wide-shouldered jackets. Tall and gleaming, they stood like Spanish princes owning a piece of the New World. I guess I stared at them, for they beckoned to us and smiled, and I was pleased. I did not know then that they were probably pimps.

Sometimes I see white men I know, and know to be homosexual, dressed in a similar style, and I am displeased. It displeases me that they seem to be trying to lie about their lives, claiming both power and evil they do not possess. They are trespassing.

In the freight elevator the black porter asked me why I had not left my typewriter in the repair shop to be fixed. "Because they want too much money for the job," I said. I had decided I disliked the old typewriter too much to have it fixed. "I know how it is," said the porter. "Today in a store window on Madison Avenue I saw a pair of shoes marked $40. Why, if you made a hundred dollars a week you couldn't afford $40 shoes." He laughed wisely, a big older man, kind-looking. I had never known anyone in New York who worked for so little money. Why does he bother working?

L. and I walked together quite a lot that summer, the summer of miniskirts. I do my best, but L. is really very stylish. Whenever we passed by them, white construction workers always said something rude; hats even more than short skirts seemed to arouse their ire. I don't know why; perhaps they think only their women may wear hats. But the few black workers always smiled, and if they liked our getups would say, "Man, that's a look," very softly.

He slipped into the building behind me, before the door could slowly swing shut on its spring. He carried a morning newspaper, and when I asked him whom he was looking for he said, "Dr. Brown. I'm delivering his paper." It was late in the afternoon, and I was carrying blueberries home from Gristede's. I said, "There is no Dr. Brown here," and he thanked me and left; but he kept his finger in the door so that it could not shut completely. I thought, he is only a boy up to mischief, and I went boldly back down the stairs to the door to frighten him away; but he saw me coming through the glass panel and burst in, rushing toward me. "You white bitch, how dare you tell me where I belong. You don't own this building. Do you! White bitch! White bitch!" He strode up the stairs at me, a big man, I saw now, with large biceps under his polo shirt. As he came toward me, he grew more and more excited, now believing his own oratory, now a hero, defender of his race. My key did not fit the lock to my door. I ran up the stairs, calling "Police!" and thought, this is absurd: he really believes I'm the one in the wrong. He was right behind me, grabbing for my ankles. I can run fast, but the building is only five stories high and what would I do when I reached the top floor? Someone in the building heard me screaming and unlatched his door, and at the sound of the bolt snapping, the man fled. The police came very quickly, but he was already gone. At that time I was not afraid, only amazed.

After that I began to feel afraid. I went to a party in midtown and left early, while it was still light. I came down through the empty lobby and saw a black man get up from lounging against a parked car and walk toward me. I fled back through the lobby, jumped into an elevator, shot upstairs, and made someone see me to a taxi. Next to the lobby door was a coffee shop, and the large black man was visible in the window, moving refuse cans. He looked out at me and shook his head sadly.

Even so, for several months I remained timid. R. sent a black employee over to me with the gift of an art book. I did not know him and drew back into my foyer when I saw him coming up the stairs.

Later he said, with pitying reasonableness, "I don't blame you for having been frightened."

Another day, early in the morning, my bell rang unexpectedly. I answered it, and up the stairs came a black boy carrying a very ungainly bundle and making strange incomprehensible noises. I jumped back into my apartment, but the boy continued coming, smiling and gurgling and waving his hands. In front of my chained door he put down his bundle, undid a string, and balloons floated up above a basket of flowers. He was a deaf-mute, a delivery boy, and the flowers were to celebrate the publication of my book.

The two B.s had just begun to live together and had just taken a house. Mr. B. wanted to have a holiday party to celebrate the beginning of their life together and to make the situation clear to all their friends. It was a big party, with many people of importance in the liberal world present. Miss B.'s oldest friend was there with her young son and her black lover, for whom she had left her husband. I don't know why she had brought the child; perhaps it was the will of the black man, for he prided himself on being very severe and good at "disciplining" the little boy. Perhaps to demonstrate his power, the black man cuffed the child and ordered him to stand in the corner. The child began to cry, and a very dignified lady said, "Please, as it is a holiday, don't you think you could overlook the child's fault? He is so unhappy." Whereupon the black man struck the white lady and knocked her to the floor. He had already created a disturbance by ranting at the house and all its guests, saying they were all parasites and living in far too much comfort while others suffered. However, he himself was known to be living on his mistress's money. Mr. B. had fled upstairs, fearing a scandal, and Miss B. had gone up to reassure him. Finally, the black man was dragged from the house by indignant guests.

The next day the mistress, Miss B.'s oldest friend, called and said, "I guess we cannot be friends now." And Miss B. answered, "No, I guess we cannot."

On my way to skate in the Park I passed the sea lions. A young black walked up to me and asked, with great gravity, "What time is it, please?" I answered, returning his gravity, "Ten minutes to noon." "Thank you," he murmured ceremoniously. I knew I was playing his game, there being two large outdoor clocks clearly visible to him over my shoulder. I thought, he is testing himself against whites, that's good. I forgot it was I he was challenging; that whatever I said I was giving him an excuse to scorn me.

SOUL IN SUBURBIA

(JANUARY 1972)

Orde Coombs

IF YOU SPOKE to me on the streets of New York, you would assume that I was middle class, for there is nothing in my speech or mannerisms that assigns me to the despairing underclass of that city. As far as I can remember, my family on the lonely, volcanic island of St. Vincent was never destitute. We knew who we were, and we knew that in the social hierarchy of the island we had a secure place.

My father was a self-made man. In his youth he had emigrated to the prosperous Dutch island of Curaçao, and there he must have nourished his West Indian parsimony; after a few years he returned to St. Vincent with enough money to build a stone house and buy a bus. He was called, then, "Pretty Boy Coombs," for he was a striking figure, six feet four inches, handsome, self-assured, and given to wearing sailor caps and scarves in the tropical sun. He drove his bus with the certain arrogance of a young man who sees how he is going to make his way, and soon he had other buses and drivers to drive them.

By the time I reached puberty, my father and mother operated a retail store and planted arrowroot, sugarcane, and bananas on several acres of fertile land that they owned. As my father prospered, his name changed from "Pretty Boy" to "Big Man," and as his stomach rounded, he assumed the position of town oracle. He would give advice on marriages, land disputes, and illegitimate children; he would counsel cuckold husbands and regale his contemporaries with ribald jokes. The people in the town loved him, I think, because his laughter was like theirs and his pleasures very simple. He once told me that he had no inclination to do what other middle-class West Indians then loved to do, which was to make a grand tour of England. He could dream, he said, whenever he wanted to that he was standing in front of Buckingham Palace, and that dream cost him nothing. His attempts at ostentation were usually the result of my mother's proddings, and even those lacked style. When he bought the first two-toned four-door Chevrolet on our island and hired a chauffeur to drive us around on weekends, he did not hesitate to tell the man to pick up other passengers along the way and to charge them a dollar for the ride.

On that tiny island, middle-class black parents wanted their progeny to do well in school; to become men and women of whom they could be proud. They wanted us to believe in the efficacy of family life, to have respect for our elders and faith in God's ultimate goodwill. They assumed that their children would never marry below their class, and, floating as they did within the Western ambit, many hoped that their children would "marry light."

We were a privileged black group, and we did not have much feeling for the poverty-stricken of our island. We gave them old clothes, or the odd dollar, I suppose, but we could not conceive of them rapidly changing their station. We believed that the poor would always be with us, and we expected their overwhelming gratitude if we noticed them.

In the summer of 1960, a group of Choate students came to St. Vincent. They were on a goodwill trip to extol the decency of American democracy. We had never before entertained American students, although even then we had had our fill of those white American tourists who found our thatched houses "quaint" and our frangipani "fabulous." But these young men had a certain easiness of manner, and because we had been raised under the regimentation of a pseudo-British grammar school, we could not help but admire them. They were brash, spoke back to their teacher, talked about masturbation and abortion, and in four days tried to tell us how to run our school.

When one boy found out that I planned to go the following year to the London School of Economics, he told me that I ought to consider Yale. He was sure that I would enjoy the American university, and that I would be fascinated by America's wealth. "The good life is in the United States," he said. "I've been to England three times, and many people there are underfed." And so, in 1961, I came to America.

Another of the students, the son of a famous television star, invited me to spend a few days with his family at their estate in Rye, New York, before I went to New Haven. The day after I arrived, we went to Harlem. Someone had asked me to deliver a package of West Indian herbs to an ailing cousin, and my host drove me there. It was a hot September day. Children were jumping rope while listless adults sat and stared at us as we parked. We walked up the four flights to the tenement apartment, and when we came down fifteen minutes later, the car's back window had been smashed; my friend's tape recorder and clothes were gone. We asked if anyone had seen the culprit, and were told by everyone sitting in full view of the car not ten feet away that they had seen and heard nothing. I tried to smooth my rage, for I thought I was being made a fool of. With as much dignity as I could muster, I got in the car, as my friend smilingly said: "Now you've seen Rye, and you've seen Harlem. You've *almost* seen America."

I didn't quite know what he meant then, but three days later I was to remember his remark when on our way to New Haven we turned off the Merritt Parkway at the Dixwell Avenue exit. As we got closer to Yale, the black slum got worse until suddenly, a stone's throw away from that fetid, garbage-strewn avenue, the stark and beautiful neo-Gothic towers of Morse and Stiles colleges thrust their way into that autumn sky. Such juxtapositions of white wealth and black poverty I could understand at home, but I could not then quite bring myself to believe that they existed in America, the vehement proselytizer of democracy.

There were four black Americans in my class of more than 1,000, and one invited me to spend the Easter vacation with him in Washington. I had told him that all the blacks I had seen so far had been poor.

"I know all about the rich singers," I had remarked, "and I have seen two slums—what about those in between?" It was in Washington, then, that I first met black middle-class Americans. Right away I began to feel a certain uneasiness, a sense that I had not really escaped the tightness of my own little island. It did not take me long to find out that in the Northeast many of the black bourgeoisie know each other, party together, and spend their summers in the quiet comfort of Highland Beach on Chesapeake Bay, in Oak Bluffs on Martha's Vineyard, and in Sag Harbor, Long Island. Most of the young people I met that spring were going either to Ivy League schools or to Howard University or to Stanford. All were sons and daughters of the black professional class. Everyone had a car. No one had any friends in the black slums, and with the exception of making quick visits to poor relatives or picking up late-night snacks of ribs or chicken, my new friends stayed well away from the sprawling ghettos of Washington.

I began to see, too, that there was a kind of ambivalence on the part of my peers as they faced their poor, uneducated brothers. They did not actually dislike the slum dwellers, but they feared their unpredictability, their refusal to live by "acceptable" codes. One spring night, I sat with my middle-class friends in the backyard of a very comfortable Washington home. We had hamburgers and steaks and a very warm feeling of camaraderie. The nephew of a famous black writer was also a guest in that house. The young man had been reared in comfort, and he took great pride in his uncle's accomplishments. It did not matter to him that most of his uncle's fans were whites who relished his tales of pseudo-chivalry but did not know that their author was black.

The young man had been menaced by four youths when he stopped at a light on 14th and U Streets. They had wanted him to empty his pockets, but he had gunned his car and escaped. Now in the safety of this bourgeois backyard, he vehemently denounced the "hooligans" who were making life difficult for everybody. Was there any way he could help these "hooligans"? I wondered. He said no: "We have nothing in common but a black skin, and mine is not really black. They are barely existing while I am busy living my life." I agreed that there were two distinct modes of behavior between poor blacks—and *his* peers. But, I asked him, did he not see that it was only luck that separated his moneyed existence from that of the despairing people in the noisome ghettos? He couldn't help that, he said. Besides, he was tired of all the sympathy lavished on ghetto people. Nobody ever spoke of how miserable "these people" made his life, since he always had to prove to white people that he was different.

Almost ten years later, after the black pain and tumult and victories of the Sixties, after all the rhetoric of black unity and power, I heard the same sentiment expressed last summer in Oak Bluffs. The speaker, a sixtyish, once-beautiful schoolteacher whose mouth had grown slack from too much Johnny Walker Red with a touch of lemon peel, railed against the poorer blacks who come to Martha's Vineyard for a week-end of revelry. As we sat among the pines and flowers of her garden, she said, "We are very, very down on what I call the rooming-house types. They own nothing, and they come up here with weekend money to upset our equilibrium." There was, I gathered, peace and quiet on her part of the island until these blacks came. And although all the "established" blacks snubbed them, they would doubtless give all black people a bad name. This woman, a charming hostess, lived a life of relative ease, and wanted the whites who gazed on her to know with absolute certainty that she was not like those other people with black skins.

Her venom was not really all that difficult to understand. In the decade since I "became" an American, I have come to realize that it is the charade of integration that sparks these outbursts of indignation from middle-class blacks. The young man and the older woman saw themselves as standard-bearers for the race, and they knew that the poor black with his split infinitives could only be a symbol of equality in white-liberal drawing rooms. They knew that they too were symbols. And this caused their gorges to rise, for in education, money, and achievement they were, perhaps, no different from the whites who so identified them. It was the dichotomy, therefore, of wanting to be released as totems of admiration—yet knowing that until the majority of blacks mirrored their achievement, whites would continue to see them as *extraordinary*—that caused their bile to overflow.

They did not see that they had allowed whites to define them and chart their behavior. They did not understand that the proper measure of themselves could only be taken from their poor black brothers and that only the eyes of the ghetto would truly reflect their humanity. I know all this because I too indulged for a time in the foolish pastime of trying to convince whites of the humanity of blacks. I would be sharp and witty and charming at white cocktail parties. I would become for the evening the Ivy League black buffoon in residence. I considered it my duty to meet as many whites as I could and to overwhelm them with my intelligence. What did it matter if I left with a throbbing headache and stumbled home to Anacin and Alka-Seltzer? What if my mind boggled at asinine questions and vapid assumptions? I was in there slugging, doing my bit for the cause. With little pride I now remember those evenings, and the college nights spent trying to persuade two young men from Macon, Georgia, of the validity of black people's lives.

They were both wealthy, and considered themselves aristocrats. One was in my French class. Every question he missed, I answered. I made sure of this by studying French grammar late into the night. And to what avail? To convince one Southerner that a black man knew more French than he did. And what good did this do? None. For until he went to medical school in the North, he was convinced that his maid, who said she couldn't stand Martin Luther King, Jr., was a true reflection of black Southern sentiment. And he was convinced that learning was a most difficult task for blacks. How I regret those useless energies spent under the banner of integration: how much more fruitful it would have been to test my identification with the ghetto black and to learn that resilience and hardiness from him that no school can teach.

With the onset of black power and the call to black unity, a new kind of black bourgeois duplicity has set in, for the middle-class black can now seem relevant to the black struggle, while remaining aloof from the battle. It has become fashionable for blacks to say that they are involved in helping other blacks. A myriad of organizations understaffed, under-financed, and manned by the black bourgeoisie are indeed trying to rekindle black hope. But I wonder if the past is really past. When I commented recently on the expensive clothes of a colleague who worked with the poor, I was told: "I'm getting mine now. It's not that I'm selling out my soul, it's just that I'm bettering my body."

Last summer, during a weekend in Sag Harbor, I spoke to the bright and pessimistic wife of one of the growing cadre of black bourgeois problem-solvers who traipse from city to state to federal agency talking about "the needs of the people." She felt that they approached the ghetto not as relatives trying to help but as technocrats who take pride in seeing a job done. "They *talk* about helping," she said, "and they feel a bit more guilty than their fathers in being so openly materialistic. But they cannot really identify with poverty. All these young management blacks have become white liberals."

Later she invited me to a beach party. As I sat in a summer night's calm and watched the embers from ten moonlight cookouts glowing along the white beach, my bourgeois friends rapped about how their attempts to help poor blacks had been met with hostility and scorn. The impenetrable communications barrier sapped their energies to the point where they longed to escape from the very people they supposedly wanted to help.

And then someone said: "We're going to have to leave the real work to our children. They are the ones who have always lived with black consciousness, and they will make all black people one." And another, his voice shaking with emotion, said: "We've got to build the economic futures of our children, and with money under their belts, they can take up the fight for all black people." I listened that night as black people pledged their children to the black nation while they remained safe and on the periphery of danger. Did they think they could ever accumulate enough money in America so that their children would be able to spend their lives making philanthropic gestures to other blacks? And what of the present? Must we wait until ten-year-olds grow up before we throw off the crutch of class and move en masse toward real unity? As the chatter died down, I asked a doctor, an old internist, if he thought that his peers should be redirecting their efforts toward the black poor. He said, no, then his face grew somber: "Have you thought about how hard we have had to work for what little we have? We cannot lead, Mr. Coombs, because we are tired people. And no one wants us to lead because we have sold out too often. So we spend our time with each other. We enjoy and respect each other, and we get drunk together. They say the younger guys are closer to their consciences, and that they will work with the poorer Negroes, but I don't believe it. What I do believe is that in this country all middle-class Negroes are fucked up."

At the end of that long weekend there was in me a heaviness that would not go away, a feeling that in a time of challenge and danger these former integrationists are now floundering in their own indecision. They have not yet fully realized that no matter how agonizing the differences of style, a tight coalition with their brothers in the horrible slums is vital to their ultimate security. For there is no security for blacks in individual success; there is no escape from the seething underclass and therefore no way to avoid the political maelstrom.

At no small cost to their psyches, these middle-class men and women have won a measure of American comfort. But the work, the sweat, the numbing effort they have put into their endeavors should have made them rich. And had it not been for the racist crunch of their country, they would have by now tasted wealth. Yet they still find that they must work hard and scrimp on some necessities in order to keep up their posture of wealth, their pretense that they are free from financial stress.

It is not difficult to understand why the black bourgeoisie should seek privacy and each other's company. But if there was ever a time when the black masses—bereft of leadership, dulled by dope, by unemployment, by an official national policy of disregard and disrespect—needed the talented bourgeoisie with their degrees and their expertise, it is now. Many of these gifted people, however, seem to wallow in self-pity; and cursed as Oreos by the militants, they no longer want to fraternize with the white middle class. Today, the middle-class black man is, perhaps, the most disturbed of all black men. He is in limbo, and will remain there until he clearly begins to see that the destiny of blacks in the United States is in his hands.

The material comfort of the Northeastern middle-class black is, in 1972, a direct result of the urban fires of the North and of the black Southerners who marched determinedly along their dustscapes and gave a semblance of change to this country. The thirty- to forty-year-old black who holds down a good job in the North must know that his present success is a direct result of past tumult. All his talent, all his effort would not have otherwise given him a toehold in television, in consulting firms, in brokerage firms, in advertising, and in publishing. If he doubts this, he has only to look around and see how small his numbers are and how quickly the thrust to recruit blacks has abated.

Many of these black men know that they owe their livelihoods to their poorer, more militant brethren. They know, too, that with all the marching, the rioting, and the dying, the relative condition of most black people has not greatly improved. *In fact, only one black group has really benefited from the turbulence; and that is the middle class.* Seizing the moment of noisy change, armed with the education that they had wondered how they would use, they immediately managed to alter their economic status. If this is true, then the middle-class blacks owe a debt to their poor brothers that mere benevolence cannot repay. The only way to cancel this debt is to try to lead the weary, the dispossessed, out of their morass. I can hear the chorus of middle-class outrage: "Oh, but we have tried. We are the ones who bring the lawsuits, who hold the benefits and the Nights of Excellence for the Urban League." I am not impressed. Though some individuals have, at great personal cost, assumed the mantle of black mass leadership, most bourgeois blacks have cloaked themselves in recondite chatter about change and left the hard task of organizing to those less talented than they. They have been seduced by the American myth of individualism and have come to believe that their salvation lies in individual conquests of poverty.

If this were not so, the black middle class would have developed group goals that would have embraced and funded black art, black music, and black institutions. But there seems to be little faith in black excellence or creativity. Witness the fact that the United Negro College Fund, the National Urban League, and the Legal Defense Fund must raise most of their money from white sources. There is no tradition of black philanthropy and, with the exception of the churches, no attempt to sustain through black initiative only, the institutions that serve black people. Everyone decries this, or stresses our lack of wealth, but no one demands that there be sacrificial giving on our part, that we give up another bottle of Cutty Sark and send that money to the National Scholarship Fund for Negro Students.

It seems to me that the black bourgeoisie are now in a more precarious state than they will acknowledge. They can never feel comfortable with the despair and filth of the ghettos; and their poor black brothers, having seen so few examples of middle-class altruism, look with deep suspicion on the current halfhearted attempts to establish blood ties. Therefore, many middle-class blacks, pummeled and maligned by the poor, are retreating from their responsibilities. And so black programs mushroom and die for lack of black support, and we find ourselves fighting each other even as we parrot talk of black unity.

Now, I am not advocating messianic leadership. I think the Moses syndrome has run its course for us. It is simply that the time has come for the affluent blacks to see that we must move toward broadly based collective goals and that the political and economic power of the slums must be harnessed for our collective welfare.

At a party in Oak Bluffs last summer, I asked one lady what she thought of the Black Panthers, and she backed away from me. Eyes blinking, nostrils opening: "Black Panthers? We don't talk about all that up here. We leave those problems in the city, because in this place, all we want to do is relax."

"Yes," chimed in a woman with silver-blue hair. "We go to the beach, we tell dirty jokes, we talk about our suntans, about anything that does not require thought. That is what the summer is all about."

An older friend whose wealth has not diminished his fervor for black liberation said to them: "Think about the man's question. Do you know that you too are in danger? Listen. Since the invention of the electric motor and the internal-combustion engine, there is no longer any need for mules and niggers. They have already destroyed the mule by making glue out of him, and the question of the nigger is, as yet, undecided. Now do you understand your danger—that your very existence is a political question?"

The lady with the blinking eyes poured herself another jigger of gin, and the lady with the silver-blue hair said: "I want things to change. Quickly. But I also want some peace and quiet."

Nothing, unfortunately, will give her that peace, for the sands under our foundation are shifting, and will shift until the ghetto black can add some gravel to the mix. Yet I understand her ambiguity, for I too am affected with the black middle-class disease. I crave change, but I am afraid to face the fire; I indulge myself in writing harangues, but stay removed from rent strikes; I wince when I read of another black baby bitten in his crib, but I do nothing to make sure that child will never again feel the tooth of a rat.

It is the translation, then, from sensibility to action that the black bourgeois most urgently needs to make. For in the Northeast he has proved the indestructibility of the human spirit. He has carved out of the granite of white hostility and arrogance a semblance of independence. But it is now up to him to offer his talent to the black ghettos, because there can be no relaxation for him while his brother gazes at the world from a garbage can.

In Sag Harbor last summer, I could not help but think how as ado-

159

lescents in St. Vincent we would wait until Carnival to shout in broken English to our poor black brothers that "all of we is one." Those of us who were light-skinned and educated trumpeted that phrase only once a year, for in that splurge of fantasy and color the wretched of our island could believe us, and we could afford our magnanimity because tomorrow the status quo would remain. It did not seem to us, then, that we were responsible for the black poor, and that we should do more than glimpse their enervating misery. But for the middle-class black American, such mirages of separation are no longer possible.

Portraits in Black

(June 1976)

Henry Louis Gates, Jr.

"I say dere, Brother Andy!"
"Yeah, Brother Kingfish?"
"Let us simonize our watches."

NOT TOO LONG ago, a black face on television gathered a black audience larger than even the regular, pre-dawn assortment congregated to discover what the day's daily double had been. I can remember as a child sitting upstairs in my back bedroom and hearing my mother shout at the top of her voice that someone *"colored . . . colored!"* was on the screen and we'd all best come down right away. And we would. As we ran down the stairs, momma shot to the front porch to let all the neighbors know, while daddy let the folks downtown know by way of the telephone. *"Colored, colored, on channel five!"* he'd shout to be heard over the commercial, while momma's echo sounded from the street: *"Colored, colored."* We were so starved for images of ourselves that we'd all sit in that living room, nervous, expectant, praying that our home boy would not let the race down.

That, of course, was a while ago; a lot has changed since then. Today, there are as many blacks and "black shows" on TV as all of us combined then would ever have dreamed of, back in the late Fifties in Piedmont, West Virginia. Then the tension, the awful terror we felt as we watched and waited for our immediate symbol of racial equality to save the day, made us susceptible to an acute embarrassment should our hero not prevail. More often than not our heroes did *not* prevail. Yet, there was ample occasion when embarrassment for a fallen hero was not an uncomfortable embarrassment, projected onto ourselves; frequently, it was sympathetic, projected onto a duped character whom we managed, quite nicely, to avoid confusing with the race or with our living room. Into this category fell the misadventures of Andy Brown (Spencer Williams), the perennial victim of that urban Br'er Fox, George "Kingfish" Stevens (Tim Moore), who managed to convince Andy that Central Park was Yosemite, that a stage set was a "railroad apartment" (after Andy asked incredulously why his just-rented house had no middle or back), and that little white rabbits would make Andy's fortune in the "rare chinchilla trade"—all this three weeks in a row!

There were, however, embarrassing occasions, when our representative of the race, we were convinced, had set back by at least two centuries our quest to be regarded as equal. There was the night when Joe Louis, one of the two guest celebrities of *Name That Tune* (Sugar Ray Robinson was the other), unable all evening to identify correctly even *one* song title despite loud cues from our living room, hauled all 200-plus bronze pounds down that narrow alleyway (leaving an alarmed Robinson, mouth open, aghast, far in his tracks), only to shout out in a huffing, puffing voice with all the strength of his and our frustrations that the name of *"Tweedlee Dee"* was *"Tiddly Winks"!* The stopper, I suppose, was the night when *Imitation of Life* (1934) was televised. Aunt Delilah (Louise Beavers) was informed by her employer and friend, Miss Bea (Claudette Colbert), that her remarkable pancake mix (long a secret, passed down through untold generations from matriarch to matriarch) was to bring both of them fortune. "Now, Delilah," Claudette Colbert said, "you're going to be rich. You'll be able to move away and buy yourself a nice house." "My own house?" a confused Louise Beavers asked. "You gonna send me away? Don't do that to me. How I gonna take care of you and Miss Jesse if I's away? I's yo' cook. You kin have it. I makes you a present of it." To which Ned Sparks could only reply deadpan, and much to our agreement: "Once a pancake, always a pancake."

We accepted Tarzan as King of the Jungle without too many doubts. It was not until much, much later that anything even remotely "political" about Tarzan ever crossed our greased-down, stocking-capped minds. But the *National Geographic*–type documentaries, with bare-chested black women and grass-skirted tribesmen who spoke funny mumbo-jumbo talk, were the source of *real* embarrassment, and I'm sure that we all silently thanked some nameless Dutch sea captain for carting us up and out of the Heart of Darkness into the good ole U.S.A.

Our feelings, as subconscious and undeveloped as they were then, have characterized black aesthetic arguments for the past hundred years. The novels of Charles Chestnutt, for instance, abound with "refined Afro-American doctors" who could understand why white people kept most blacks confined to Jim Crow sections on trains, but who couldn't for the life of them understand why these same white folks couldn't see *they* were *different* from the herd. Further, the aesthetic arguments of the Harlem Renaissance during the 1920s centered on the controversy "How Shall the Negro Be Portrayed?" and fierce debates raged over the projection of the proper "elevating" cultural images, which would ameliorate the social conditions of the race. This confusion of the realms of art and propaganda was a mutation of Matthew Arnold's notions of culture and anarchy, simplified thirty years later into Booker T. Washington's "toothbrush and a bar of soap" as supremely pressing concerns for the reconstructed black man.

The "New Negro" movement, which contained the Harlem Renaissance, was the logical extension not only of Washington's ideas on social mobility but also of W.E.B. Du Bois's notion of a "talented tenth," the intellectual and professional "natural" aristocracy, whose prime task was to lead the sheltered masses up and out of the psychological effects of slavery. Every artistic creation by the black men of the

1920s was held to be a "revelation"; through art, the black man would be free. Heywood Broun told the New York Urban League on January 25, 1925, that "a supremely great negro artist, who could catch the imagination of the world, would do more than any other agency to remove the disabilities against which the negro now labors." Broun went on to say that this artist-redeemer could come at any time, and asked his audience to remain silent for ten seconds to imagine his coming. Du Bois summarized this line of thinking. "We want," he said, "everything that is said about us to tell of the best and highest and noblest in us. We insist that our Art and Propaganda be one. We fear that evil in us will be called racial while in others it is viewed as individual. We fear that our shortcomings are not merely human but foreshadowings and threatenings of disaster and failure." If the "truth," or even an aspect of the "truth," about black people was held to be in any manner pejorative, then it must be censored, for images of "the lowly life" would hamper the quest for civil rights.

By the mid-Sixties, this kind of thinking had been displaced by a much more sophisticated analysis of black images as projected by the news media. The image, it was held, is not only message but massage. Control of the American news media, for instance, allows for control of projected images of spontaneous events, and these images, in turn, control response to the original event. Thus the image itself becomes the event, as far as millions of media consumers are concerned. Shadow becomes substance; the reflection of reality is taken to be reality itself.

This process gives the media the power to mold perceptions. Reality assumes secondary significance to its reporting, and what is "true" is to be found somewhere between the pages of *Time* and *Reader's Digest*, for the bulk of American readers.

Black Americans contribute very little to the reporting of an event of their own making, and thus white reporters are forced to conjure up their own perceptions of a "black" event. Often this distance allows for a certain objectivity; but more often cultural and social gaps prevail against it. Since white reporters write for a white audience, a black

event is reflected in a gray image to be consumed by white Americans. Reality as perceived replaces reality as experienced. What's more, should that reality, subsequently encountered, fail to conform with its image, it is not recognized as "valid." Suspicious, both blacks and whites disavow these "imitations."

Not only through its capacity for emphasis, but (and often more significantly) through its powers of deletion, the media can make a non-event meaningful or a significant event insignificant. "Black power," for instance, with all its concomitant negative associations, was largely a phenomenon of the white press.

Black power was "born" during the James Meredith march through Mississippi in June 1966. Suddenly, literally overnight, a symbolic march was transformed into the handwriting on the wall: black people, it was said, were at long last giving vent to a new-found militancy and hate, based on reverse racism. In a few hours, black power became a vicious, violent, and sinister focus of the shared hate of blacks for whites.

Black militants, sensing the tremendous energy dormant in this slogan, played upon the media-created, media-reinforced fears of the whites. Rhetorical threats of annihilation and retaliation became prerequisites for "validity" (and adequate press coverage). But means became ends: the rhetoric remained in people's minds, while its deeper aspects were underreported, if reported at all. A slogan that had invoked social development through individual and collective pride came to mean a coming orgy of violence, blacks against whites.

About a year and a half after the Meredith march, the white press gave black power a face-lift. After the November 1967 elections, the radio commentator Paul Harvey, for one, said that the validity of black power lay in the electoral process. Joseph Alsop uncharacteristically exclaimed that "Mayors-elect Stokes and Hatcher represent 'Black Power' in the best American tradition—and thank God for it." *Time* entitled its cover story on Carl Stokes "The Real Black Power." As Columbus discovered America, so did the press discover the political aspect of black power.

The paragon of journalistic reversal in image creation was the *New*

York Times's treatment of black power between July and November 1967. On July 22, a *Times* editorial, "Black Phoenix," suggested that a phoenix of an expanded conception of black power could arise from the ashes of Newark. "The words 'black power' suggest chauvinism and militancy for some dark purpose," the editorial said. "They need not."

Two days later, the *Times* changed its mind. The ongoing conference on black power in Newark was characterized as "racist." Then, on November 12, black power and the *Times* reconciled their differences. In a lead editorial entitled "Black Power and the Elections," the *Times* argued that, at long last, the election of black officials in Cleveland, Gary, and throughout the South had miraculously transformed black power—"that mischievous and opaque slogan"—into "the only meaningful terms it can have: political success achieved through democratic process." By this time, nature had been made to imitate art, and art to imitate nature, much to the detriment of whatever it was "black power" was intended to be. Many black-power advocates had become what they beheld, in the same way that the Panthers would.

Since 1967, much has changed in the relationship between blacks and the media, at least on the surface. In part because of governmental pressures, as well as a growing black consumer market for white media, blacks in major cities are just as likely as women to be announcers and reporters. More blacks are writing under their own by-lines than ever before. And all major newspapers, network news programs, and magazines claim at least a "representative influence" on their editorial boards. On occasion, this "representative influence" is telling: Walter Cronkite just this past spring eulogized Elijah Muhammad as the man who made of the term "black" a description suggesting dignity and self-respect. Yet, fifteen or so years ago, it had been Mike Wallace, in a documentary called *The Hate That Hate Produced*, who had done so much to create a false picture of the Nation of Islam as a violence-prone group of ex-convicts and lower-class blacks.

Prime-time television, too, is replete with situation comedies that depict black people who laugh and cry, who share middle-class aspirations and harbor middle-class prejudices, who live on the East Side of New York and the South Side of Chicago. Blacks fill other TV slots and polka-dot just about every program from soap operas and soap commercials to the Sammy Davis, Jr., show.

Against this background we must place the death of the civil rights era, and the financial demise of those organizations whose *raison d'être* was the integration of American institutions, in the style of Martin Luther King, Jr. This collapse is partly due to the lack of public and private funding; but it is also a result of the failure of these organizations to adapt their strategies and ideologies (where there *are* ideologies) to the new world, which they, ironically, helped to create. The disease from which these groups suffer—the lack of an incisive, coherent approach—can be seen in the pattern of protest that recently arose against Ralph Bakshi's satiric fable, *Coonskin*, and Lars Ulvenstam and Tomas Dillen's documentary, *Harlem: Voices, Faces.*

While the projection of the images of black people was to have become the preoccupation of the major networks, the "quality" of these reflections has become the preoccupation of a tiny coterie of "concerned" black people, determined to protect the black community from images of itself. In part, this loose federation consists of exhausted civil rights leaders searching for that simple answer to social problems that will, overnight, elevate them to national prominence and national funding. To this group of politicos add a dash of black media types, scorned for years by white media and anxious to substitute their view of the black man not only for the white man's view but often for the view of blacks who have infiltrated the white media.

The collective veto of this motley band has such a prescriptive right that to air a program despite their protests is not merely to ignore their opinion but to reject it. This veto was supposed to be a tool to argue the supremacy of a new media elite. However, after a plethora of polemics and pressures over image projection and the black community, it has become patently clear that our Black Oracle is fallible. Sometimes it has been dumb, and sometimes it has lied.

Harlem: Voices, Faces is a three-hour documentary shot in the summer of 1973 by Lars Ulvenstam and Tomas Dillen of the state-controlled Swedish broadcasting system. Shown in its original version in Sweden, East Germany, Canada, Finland, Denmark, and Norway, it won a prestigious prize in Sweden as the best TV documentary of 1974.

About a year and a half ago, Robert Kotlowitz, WNET's vice president of programming, saw the film and liked it. It was approved by nine members each of the programming staffs and the Corporation for Public Broadcasting, including one black viewer on each staff, and CPB provided $23,000 for WNET to buy the film.

Bernette Golden, a young black producer at WNET, assembled a panel of blacks who would appear at the end of the screening to comment on its assumptions. When the station put out a press release on April 23, however, its inept and unfortunate wording ("In Harlem, children learn to use the needle at age 9 or 10. It is considered normal and, to some, a mark of adulthood, which comes early in the ghetto") caused an unprecedented roar of protest, mostly from people who had not seen the film.

Tony Brown, producer and host of the PBS series *Black Journal*, protested formally in two letters to Hartford Gunn, president of PBS; Irma Norris, WNET's engineering coordination manager, circulated a petition calling for the film's suppression, signed by forty-three of the station's seventy-one blacks; Emma Bowen, president of the Black Citizens for Fair Media, sent hundreds of photocopies of the press release to black elected officials and similar organizations around the country; and pressure mounted from the National Urban League, Operation Breadbasket, the National Black Media Coalition, and the Harlem Congress on Racial Equality. One objector, Bill Cherry, national director of communications for Jesse Jackson's PUSH, "writing on behalf of Reverend Jesse Jackson," urged suppression of "the type of interviews it is alleged you have in this film." The original panel resigned; Percy Sutton decided, after seeing the film, that he didn't like it, and on May 13 WNET president John Jay Iselin canceled the film. A few months later, after a postmortem panel had been assembled, the film finally was approved.

I sat through *Harlem: Voices, Faces* twice at New Haven, and found it one of the most remarkable documentaries done to date on black Americans. In fact, I am only sorry that black filmmakers didn't do it first. David Denby, writing in the *Times,* summarized it this way: "The Swedes see America as a cruelly competitive capitalist system, a consumption-happy nightmare-land in which blacks have been defined and maintained as the losers by a racist white majority. Their environment a shambles, their homes disorderly and unsupportive, Harlem's children barely stand a chance at school and are seen as doomed to suffer the crushing disappointments of America's outsiders; the people of Harlem are further trapped by a series of destructive illusions: TV advertising, Shaft-Superfly fantasies, get-rich-quick schemes, and the false consolations of religion. The way out is booze and dope." Denby's summary is correct, and so is the documentary's analysis of Harlem's pathology. Two separate groups of black people— a group of children from Harlem, and a group of older Harlem residents for whom Hilton Clark (the only Harlem resident on the original panel) screened the film—recognized this, and opposed the film's cancellation. "Calling the film detrimental to blacks," an ad hoc committee formed by Clark wrote to the station, "is much akin to blaming the messenger for the bad news he brings."

If the attempt to censor *Harlem: Voices, Faces* was lame, the panel discussion after its showing was pathetic. Marjorie Henderson, of the NAACP in New York, protested loudly about showing "the sinned against, not the sinners," about "exploiting the misery of blacks," and "projecting all the vices in the world on us," and about showing the "perpetrators and purveyors."

James McCullen, of the National Black Media Coalition, called the film "racially inflammatory," and said that it "attacks and assaults black intelligence, dignity, integrity, and self-respect." McCullen said that he urged censorship before he even saw the film. He wanted "to show who was responsible" for the conditions depicted in the film. Yet the whole film showed *precisely* who, and what was responsible: slum landlords, police graft, corruption, and other systemic ills, not whores and winos. Only Hilton Clark made sense. It was, he said slowly, "an

169

aspect we so often try to sweep under the rug."

The protest against *Harlem: Voices, Faces* is as significant as the documentary itself. What emerges from the polemics, once the smoke has cleared, is this: we are no longer an organic community. Stratification accompanying the economic advances for the few, for which we fought so hard for so long, has created separate and distinct black groups, each with its own ideological and economic interests to protect.

Coonskin is Ralph Bakshi's best film. (His previous films were *Fritz the Cat* and *Heavy Traffic*.) It is a satiric fable about the American city as hell. Bakshi uses straight animation mixed with photography to embody an old convict's fantasy. The story he tells is of three Southern rural black men who go to New York, become leaders of black organized crime, then destroy the white gangsters who control Harlem. Although nearly everyone in the film is the object of satire, Bakshi's real targets are those he holds responsible for ghetto life; his most telling blows are aimed at a white policeman and an Italian Mafia family. Again, I wish a black filmmaker had done this. I hope it makes impossible the one-dimensional portrayals of black people found in such films as *Shaft*, *Superfly*, and *Cleopatra Jones*.

This time, censorship cries came largely form CORE, East Coast and West. Elaine Parker, former chairman of the Harlem chapter of CORE, said after a screening, "It depicts blacks as slaves, hustlers, and whores." CORE picketed the New York headquarters of Gulf and Western, which owns Paramount and which had put up the money for *Coonskin*. Paramount, after much pressure, decided not to distribute the film. Fortunately, Bryanston Films, a small independent distributor, worked out an agreement with Albert S. Ruddy, and now the film has been released, much to the protests of Charles Cook, the Los Angeles regional chairman of CORE, who said, in rhetoric reminiscent of the Panthers', "We hold Bakshi, Ruddy, and Bryanston responsible for what happens. We charge them with high crimes against black people—stereotyping and degrading blacks." Cook went on to say that "the black community does not need people like Bakshi who want to make clowns out of us. Every movie and TV show depicts blacks as comics, whores, pushers, or pimps," he said, hyperbolically. Gene Garvin, director of the Los Angeles chapter of CORE, agreed. "We consider the black actors who appeared in this film as traitors to their race." To which Charles Gordone, who plays the preacher in the film (and wrote the Pulitzer Prize–winning *No Place to Be Somebody*), responded, "These organizations like CORE make me angry. If they didn't have something to bitch about, they'd be out of business."

If this sort of analysis is what the Congress of Racial Equality and the NAACP stand for, then it is time for us to hold the mirror to their nostrils and perform the postmortem.

I do not mean to imply that the media have no racist tendencies, or even that I am happy with the way they project black images. But I am saying that the CORE-NAACP arguments outlined above are not adequate anymore, if they ever were. The effect of image distortion on "the black psyche" is complex, and black people can no longer be content to call something "racist" without being able to defend that view, in all its complexity. For what we are speaking of is *censorship*, a practice almost as abhorrent to art as lynching is to justice. Ubiquitous cries of racism serve no real purpose, other than to mask complex problems. Indeed, racism is the opiate of the black elite.

There are, however, questions we can demand answers to. We must oppose the sort of censorship that precludes access to the media by black filmmakers. We must ask ourselves why it is easier to see, say, *The Harder They Come* at Harvard than in Harlem. Just as we must defend the rights of Ulvenstam and Dillen to make a Marxist analysis of Harlem, we must also defend and demand the right of black filmmakers to produce documentaries full of positive black images, as well as to analyze, say, a day in the life of the residents of Scarsdale. We must question the admissions procedures of film and journalism schools, and must continue to press for more and more black editors and reporters on white publications and networks. We must demand equal access to financing and distribution of films and articles. Our voices must be heard beyond the situation comedy and the one-hour talk show.

But there is an even more urgent consideration. We must begin to understand why public outrage over the ghetto as a place of exile, as a living hell in the national imagination, has diminished since the ghetto situation comedies appeared. This sort of thinking is very subtle, and our own black oracle has yet to make its subtleties of thought public. By making ghetto life palatable, TV is defusing its sheer *horror*. Ironically, the decision to portray ghetto life in this way in large measure stems from the standard, simple-minded criticisms that only our seamy side is emphasized publicly. So Harlem and the South Side of Chicago become livable.

We must come to understand that all the "violence" in the "blaxploitation" films only serves to create another form of escapism. Real violence shapes reality; it limits our choices almost as much as do economic pressures. To see what makes people act, what makes them not act, and what creates different value systems—these are the educative functions of black films and TV programs. These could increase understanding between ethnic groups, where only confusion, hate, and distrust reign. One wonders how many whites in South Boston, for example, watch *The Jeffersons*, *Good Times*, or *Sanford and Son*.

By projecting the semblances of motivating social forces, the media encourage the dehumanization of our society. We are allowed to escape reality. This problem must become the preoccupation of those who work in the media, and of black media-watchers concerned with the effects of images on "the black psyche."

If this happened, then the simple-mindedness of protest against the old stereotypes, such as *Amos 'n' Andy*, would be unnecessary. For there is enough of *Amos 'n' Andy* that is "true" for black folks from Harlem to Harvard to crack Kingfish jokes with instant empathy and humor the result. In the exaggerated chorus of American stereotypes and satire is found a remarkable amount of observation that is accurate. We must learn to laugh at ourselves again, without the worry of the nouveau riche, black or white, who long to forget even a satiric rendition of the land from whence they came. We cannot simply toss Mantan Moreland and Stepin Fetchit into the garbage can of history. Is the portrayal of these awkward or ignorant stock characters to be censored entirely, now that we are Black? Did these caricatures have a more insidious or harmful effect on our lives than Pearl Bailey did, when she played the fool on a recent session of *Meet the Press*? No one laughed when Miss Bailey argued (demonstrating as she explained) that African delegates "strutted" down the aisles at the U.N. and hence weren't to be taken seriously. Do these stereotypes injure us as much as the censorship Motown has long practiced over its artists (which Stevie Wonder broke only by threatening to sign a new contract with another, *white* recording company)? We must begin the systematic criticism of our own institutions, and develop sophisticated criticisms of "white" media.

Ultimately, we must return to Du Bois's final word on censorship of the "lowly" side of black life. "The more highly trained we become, the less we can laugh at Negro comedy," he wrote in 1921. "We will have it all tragedy and the triumph of dark Right over pale villains." I hope that we are sophisticated enough to realize that to laugh at *Amos 'n' Andy* is not to believe that all black people fit into one of the stereotypes it portrays. I would like to be able to laugh at the antics of the Kingfish again.

WHAT CAN GOVERNMENT DO?

A Conversation Between
Jesse Jackson and Charles Murray

(APRIL 1986)

CHARLES MURRAY: How can government help the poor? The problem is that, so far, we haven't been very good at it. During the late 1960s and early 1970s, we began a major effort to bring people out of poverty, to educate the uneducated, to employ the unemployable. We have to confront the fact that the effort to help the poor did not have the desired effect. In terms of education, crime, family stability, the lives of poor people have gotten worse since the 1960s, and we have to explain why.

During those years we, in effect, changed the rules of the game for poor people. Essentially we said, in a variety of ways: "It's not your fault. If you are not learning in school, it is because the educational system is biased; if you are committing crimes, it is because the environment is poor; if you have a baby that you can't care for, it's because your own upbringing was bad." Having absolved everybody of responsibility, we then said: "You can get along without holding a job. You can get along if you have a baby but have no husband and no income. You can survive without participating in society the way your parents had to." And lots of young people took the bait. So the question remains: What, if anything, does the government owe the poor?

JESSE JACKSON: I'm as unimpressed with boundless liberalism as I am with heartless conservatism. Creative thinking has to take place. But to begin to think creatively, we have to be realistic: about the role of government, for example.

We cannot be blindly anti-government. The government has made significant interventions in many, many areas for the common good. Without public schools, most Americans would not be educated. Without land-grant colleges, the United States would not have the number one agricultural system in the world. Without federal transit programs, we would not have an interstate highway system. Without subsidized hospitals, most Americans could not afford decent medical care. And the government has played a significant role in providing a base for many American industries. The defense industries, for example, may be considered private, part of the market, but many of them are almost wholly supported by government contracts.

Now, we consider spending the public's money toward these ends to be in our national interest. When we saw the devastation in Europe after World War II, we devised the Marshall Plan—a comprehensive, long-term program. Had the Marshall Plan been a five-year investment program—as the War on Poverty essentially was—Europe would have collapsed. But we determined that the redevelopment of Europe was in our national interest. That's an instance where a vigorous government investment made something positive happen.

But when we shift from the notion of subsidy as something that serves our national interest, to that of welfare, the attitudes suddenly shift from positive to negative. In this country there is a negative predisposition toward the poor. We must learn to see the *development* of people who are poor as in our national interest, as cost-efficient, as an investment that can bring an enormous return to every American. The government definitely has a big role to play.

MURRAY: I agree it has a role. There are some things government *can* do, and one of them is to ensure that a whole range of opportunities is available to everyone. For example, in my ideal world, whether a child lived in the inner city or in the suburbs, everything from preschool to graduate school would be available to him—free. In this ideal world, if someone really looked for a job and just couldn't find one, perhaps because of a downturn in the economy, some minimal unemployment insurance would be in place to help him.

Opportunity should be assured, but attempts at achieving equal outcome abandoned. What would happen if you took away all other government-supported welfare, if the system were dismantled? Well, believe it or not, a lot of good things would begin to happen.

JACKSON: The notion of "opportunity" is more complicated than it sounds. For example, some people are poor *because* of government. When a nation is 51 percent female yet can't get an equal rights amendment passed; when many women still cannot borrow money with the same freedom men can, cannot pursue their ideas and aspirations in the marketplace because they are not equally protected—that amounts to government interference, too, but on the side of the status quo. Many blacks and Hispanics cannot borrow money from banks, on subjective grounds—because some bank official doesn't like their color, or because whole neighborhoods are redlined so that money will not be loaned to anyone living there. Government must be committed to the vigorous enforcement of equal protection under the law and other basic principles; without that enforcement, it is not a government handout that's the issue as much as it is the government's shoving people into a hole and not *letting* them out. When Legal Aid is cut, and the poor no longer have access to the courts, that's an example of government playing a role in *perpetuating* poverty.

MURRAY: If you try to rent an inexpensive apartment in my hometown of Newton, Iowa, even if you're white, you may very well not be able to rent that apartment, on "subjective grounds." I mean, you come to the door, and because of the way you act or the way you look or whatever, the landlord says to himself: "My apartment's going to get trashed." These subjective grounds often have a basis in fact. And it's real tough for people renting out apartments—and maybe even for banks—to operate in ways that enable them to make money if they aren't permitted to make these kinds of subjective judgments.

JACKSON: Dr. Murray, the farmer wearing his bib overalls who walks up to that apartment door and is rejected for the way he looks is not a victim of racial prejudgment. That man could put on a suit and get the apartment. Blacks can't change color. The idea is that bankers choose not to make loans to blacks *institutionally.*

Now, I'm not just throwing around a charge here. John H. Johnson, the president of Johnson Publishing Company, which publishes *Ebony,* is perhaps the most established black business-man in the country. Yet several banks turned down his loan application to build in downtown Chicago. Maybe the most established black businessman in the country was turned down for a loan simply because of the institutional racism of banks. And so we need laws enforced, we need the government to protect people who are black or Hispanic or Asian or Indian or female, from the bankers' ability to do that.

A lot of people, to this day, are simply locked out. Until 1967, there had never been more than a couple of black car dealerships, because the automobile industry's policy was not to allow a black to invest in a car dealership or to learn to run one in any neighborhood, black or white. So blacks now have fewer than 240 dealerships out of the 22,050 in this country. Blacks always had the ability, but they were locked out by race, even if they had the money. Operation PUSH confronted Ford as late as July 1982, when there were fewer than 40 black automobile dealerships out of 5,600. Ford finally agreed to grant thirty new black dealerships in one year, which they had previously claimed was impossible. Well, those thirty dealerships are still operating, employing an average of more than fifty people each, and those jobs represent the alternative to welfare and despair.

MURRAY: If you say that in 1960 blacks as a people were locked out, well, I have no problem with that. But that is no longer accurate. Let's talk about black youth unemployment. Are you saying that America's black youth are marching resolutely from door to door, interviewing for jobs, and that they are getting turned down because they're black? If so, then a jobs programs ought to do wonders. CETA ought to have done wonders. But it didn't.

JACKSON: The private economy, by being so closed for so long, has pushed many people into the public economy. There's just no reason why, in a population of 30 million blacks, there are only two black beverage-bottling franchises. You can't explain it by lack of ambition or an unwillingness to take risks, because for the past twenty years blacks have been the top salesmen in that industry. A lot of people got locked into poverty because of the government's failure to enforce equal protection under the law. Until the Civil Rights Act of 1964 and Lyndon Johnson's executive order of 1965, beverage companies could get lucrative government contracts to operate on U.S. military bases around the world, even though they locked out a significant body of Americans.

MURRAY: I'm not in a position to argue with you about wholesalers and franchises. But I don't think we can assume that if blacks gain more access to entrepreneurial business positions—which I'm all in favor of—it will have a fundamental effect on poverty and the underclass.

JACKSON: If there is an artificial ceiling limiting the growth of the so-called talented 10 percent—I use the term advisedly—then it compounds the problem of the disinherited 90 percent. If where we live our money won't "spend" because of redlining, which becomes a de facto law; if where we live our money cannot buy a car franchise or a beer franchise or a soft-drink franchise—which are some of the great American ways out of poverty—then blacks are effectively locked out of the private economy. And so, just as the political grandfather clause locked blacks out of the political system, economic grandfather clauses have effectively locked

179

blacks out of the economic system. Blacks today can take over a town politically, because its population is almost entirely black. But the economic territory—the entrepreneurial opportunities, beyond mom-and-pop businesses, which allow a people to develop a leadership class in the private economy, which in turn begins to lift others as it hires them and trains them—is still closed. Blacks who worked as salesmen and saleswomen for the first generation of black entrepreneurs now have franchises of their own, because they have access to the franchise head. But that has not happened historically.

MURRAY: Why is it that the Koreans and Vietnamese and all sorts of other people who come here with very few resources do well, including West Indian blacks? They come here, start businesses, and manage to earn a median income which rivals or surpasses that of whites. I'm not trying to say racism doesn't exist. I'm saying it doesn't explain nearly as much as it ought to.

JACKSON: Do not underestimate the impact of 250 years of legal slavery followed by a hundred years of legal segregation. The damage it did to the minds of the oppressor and the oppressed must not be played down. When I grew up in South Carolina, I could caddy but I couldn't play golf. That's why I can't play golf now; I could have been arrested for hitting a golf ball at the Greenville Country Club. I could shag balls, but I couldn't play tennis. I could shine shoes, but I couldn't sit on the stand and couldn't own a stand at the train station. I could wait tables, but I couldn't sit at them; and I could not borrow money to build a competing establishment.

The other groups you mentioned have not known that level of degradation. The Cubans came to Miami as beneficiaries of a cold war between this country and Cuba; we used money and subsidies to induce them to come here, and those who came were in large measure from a class that had some history of business acumen. Many of the Vietnamese were beneficiaries of the same kind of cold war policy.

Now, shagging balls and not playing tennis, caddying and not playing golf, not voting and seeing others vote—all of this had the cumulative effect of lowering people's ambitions and limiting their horizons. Let me give an example. I saw a story in *USA Today* last summer headlined "More Blacks Graduating from High School, Fewer Going to College." A young lady from Chicago was quoted in the story, and I decided to meet with her and her mother. It turned out she had a B+ average, was a member of the National Honor Society—the whole business. I said to the girl, "Do you want to go to college?" She said she did. I said, "Well, have you taken the SAT tests?" She said she hadn't. "Why not?" "Well, the counselor told me that since I couldn't afford to go to college, that stuff was a waste of time." In other words, she was being programmed for failure, taught to be mediocre, programmed downward.

Once I discovered what was happening, I went on the radio and asked any high school student—black, white, brown—who had every college qualification except money to come to Operation PUSH. Seven hundred fifty young people came with their parents; we have placed 250 of them in colleges, including that young lady. But if that young lady hadn't gone to college, she would have been written off three or four years later: people would have said the family was subsidized, dependent; she didn't go to college; now she's pregnant; and the whole cycle begins again. She was programmed into lower ambition, programmed away from college. Yet many schools, especially the better ones like Harvard and Columbia, provide scholarship money. But so many students don't know this; it's a well-kept secret. Those who have, know; the circle remains essentially closed.

MURRAY: Getting that information out would serve as an *incentive*. I know how I'd spend money on educational programs. I'd put up a bunch of posters saying that anybody who gets such-and-such a score on the SATs will get a free ride through college. I'm willing to bet that I'd get more results from my program than the government would get by trying directly to improve the schools.

JACKSON: There's a role for that kind of motivation. There's also a role for increasing opportunity. Often it's not lack of ability or ambition that locks people out, but lack of information.

MURRAY: I'm worried, because I'm starting to agree with you too much!

JACKSON: Just give me time, you'll be all right.

MURRAY: Oh, I think we'll find some things to disagree on. I come from an all-white town. I went back to visit this Christmas, and I said to myself, "I wonder what poverty is like here in Newton, Iowa." So I got in touch with the human services people and spent some time riding around with a caseworker. And as I listened to this caseworker describe what her problems were, I realized that if I closed my eyes, I could have been listening to a caseworker in the South Bronx. The problems were indistinguishable from what are usually considered "black problems."

JACKSON: Yes, we must whiten the face of poverty. It's an *American* problem, not a black problem. But the face of poverty in this country is portrayed as a black face, and that reinforces certain attitudes. I mean, John Kennedy holds up a sick black baby in his arms and people say, "Gee, he's a nice guy." He holds up a sick white baby in West Virginia and people say, "We've got to *do* something about this."

Of the 34 million people living in poverty in America, 23 million are white. The poor are mostly white and female and young. Most poor people work every day. They're not on welfare; they're changing beds in hospitals and hotels and mopping floors and driving cabs and raising other people's children. And there is no basis for taking a few people who cheat the system as examples, and using them to smear millions of people who by and large work very hard.

MURRAY: The welfare queen is not the problem. And the dynamics of dependency operate pretty much the same for both blacks and whites. For example, I did some checking on what the out-of-wedlock birthrate is among poor whites. Guess what? Middle-class blacks don't have much of a problem with out-of-wedlock births, just as middle-class whites don't; but poor blacks *and* poor whites alike have a big problem with it.

Now, when I visit a school in inner-city Washington, I see a couple of different kinds of kids. A lot of kids are sent out of their houses every morning by their moms and dads, who tell them, "Get that education. Study hard. Do what the teacher says." And these youngsters go off to school and study hard, do exactly what the teacher says, and still graduate a couple of years behind grade level—not because they're stupid, but because of what has happened to the school systems during the past twenty years. A great deal of energy and attention has been spent catering to the kind of kid who, for whatever reason, makes it real hard for the first set of kids to learn.

So I think we need to reintroduce a notion which has a disreputable recent history in America: the notion of class. A good part of our problem can be characterized as one of "lower-class behavior," which is distinct from the behavior of poor people.

JACKSON: In other words, the Watergate burglars, though white, male, and rich, were engaging in "lower-class behavior."

MURRAY: No, but if you talk about the danger posed by the increase in crime, it so happens that it is not the rich white folks who are suffering.

JACKSON: Back up now, back up. You introduced a phenomenon there, Dr. Murray, about "lower-class behavior." I suppose that means low morals.

MURRAY: You added that.

JACKSON: Well, I *guessed* that's what it means. What does "lower-class behavior" mean?

MURRAY: The syndrome was identified long ago, although the term is more recent. People in the nineteenth and early twentieth centuries would simply talk about "trash," for example, and later there was the concept of the "undeserving poor." The sociologist who did the Elmstown study certainly recognized the syndrome, as did Edward Banfield. It is characterized by chronic unemployment due to people working for a while and then dropping out, unstable family life, and so on.

183

JACKSON: But you know, Dr. Murray, you made a distinction here on this "lower-class behavior," and I was trying to get a definition of it, but I did not get it. I'm sorry, I haven't read all those books you mentioned. But I suppose it means *immoral* behavior.

MURRAY: I'm not using words like "moral" and "immoral."

JACKSON: Well, I guess it means violence against people, unprovoked violence—lower-class behavior. Sex without love, making unwanted babies—lower-class behavior. Taking what belongs to other people—lower-class behavior. Filling your nose full of cocaine, driving drunk—lower-class behavior. That's not lower-class behavior, Dr. Murray, that's immoral.

It seems to me that whether it is stealing in the suites or stealing in the streets, whether it is happening in ghetto, barrio, reservation, or suburb, we should condemn lower-class behavior. Cain killing Abel, brother killing brother, is lower-class behavior because it's low morals, it's unethical, it's not right. Whether they're welfarized or subsidized, people should not engage in lower-class behavior. Is it more moral for a business executive to sniff cocaine than a welfare recipient?

MURRAY: If you are saying that rich white people can be lousy, I agree. But my point is that if we continue to pretend that all poor people are victims, if we do not once again recognize in social policy the distinctions that have been recognized all along on the street, we will continue to victimize those poor people who most deserve our respect and our help.

Parents, black or white, who are working at lousy jobs but who are *working*, paying the rent, teaching their kids how to behave—yes, those people are behaving differently, and certainly in a more praiseworthy way, than parents who fail to do those things. Poor people fall into very different classes, distinguished by differences in work behavior, such as chronic unemployment whether there are jobs or not. And there are differences in child rearing. Working-class people pay a lot of attention to how their children are doing; they talk to them, ask how they're doing in school. But there are children who come to school at the age of five and do not know, for example, the words for the colors; nobody's talked to them, they've been utterly neglected. Finally, when there is divorce among the working class the man takes continued responsibility for supporting the children. Lower-class behavior, on the other hand, is characterized by serial monogamy or promiscuity and a failure of the man to take responsibility for his children.

JACKSON: Dr. Murray, the lady who lived across the street from us while I was growing up ran what they called a "bootleg house." She was a woman of high character: she was a seamstress, and all her children graduated from college. But on the weekend people came over to her house to drink and gamble, and so Mrs. X was considered an outcast. Now, another lady named Mrs. Y, who lived about three blocks from us, owned a liquor store; because she was white she could get a liquor license. Mrs. Y was an entrepreneur, Mrs. X was a moral outcast. But something told me early in the game that the only difference between Mrs. X and Mrs. Y was a license.

Men and women would come over to Mrs. X's house sometimes and have sex down in the basement: promiscuity, also a sign of lower-class behavior, and another reason why people looked down on her. Well, I began working at the hotel in town; I was paid to carry in the booze for the men who would meet women there, often other people's wives, sometimes even their friends' wives. They'd each leave at a different time and by a different door to maintain their respectability, but I knew where they lived because I used to cut their grass and rake their leaves. This is distinctly lower-class behavior—sleeping with other people's wives.

MURRAY: No, engaging in sexual behavior, even promiscuity, does not make you lower class. What makes you lower class is having kids you can't or don't take care of.

JACKSON: Now, Dr. Murray, are you saying that a lawyer who has sex with his partner's wife and uses a prophylactic is engaging in behavior that's higher class than that of someone who does the same thing but does not have the sense or ability to use a prophylactic?

185

MURRAY: Look, I'm not against sex. I'm not even necessarily against sex outside of marriage.

JACKSON: Now, don't get too swift on me here. The act of going to bed with another man's wife is adultery.

MURRAY: Fine.

JACKSON: It ain't fine. It's *immoral.* It's lower-class behavior, and whether it takes place in the White House, statehouse, courthouse, outhouse, your house, my house, that behavior is unethical.

MURRAY: But that has nothing to do with what I'm saying.

JACKSON: It shows a certain attitude: if you do something and it's subsidized, it's all right; if others do it and it's welfarized, it's not so good.

I was in inner-city Washington several months ago, talking to a gym full of high school kids. I challenged those who had taken drugs to come down front. About 300 came down. Next day the *Washington Post* published three pictures and the headline "Jackson does phenomenal thing—kids admit drug usage." Editorial: "It's a great thing that Jackson did, but you know he has a special way with black kids." Next day I went to a school in Maryland—in one of the richest counties in America, about 97 percent white, single-family dwellings, upper middle class, and all that. The principal said to me, "Well, you can make your pitch, but of course it won't work here." So I made my pitch. I said, "Taking drugs is morally wrong, except in controlled medical situations; it's morally wrong and ungodly." Six hundred students were present. I said, "Those who have tried drugs, come forward." About 200 came forward. This was a junior high school; these kids were thirteen, fourteen years old. The principal was in a daze. Now *that's* lower-class behavior and upper-class economic status. Rich folks embezzle and poor folks steal; rich folks prevaricate and poor folks lie. But I think a lie is a lie is a lie.

MURRAY: If we agree that lying is lying and stealing is stealing, that doesn't help the little old lady who is trying to get from her apartment to the grocery store without getting her Social Security check ripped off. If we take the attitude that white-collar crime is just as bad as street crime, so let's not go after the street criminals when we let the embezzlers get away, the problem is that we ignore that little old lady, who is not in much immediate danger from embezzlers. Poor people, first of all, need safety. We'll take care of the white-collar criminals as well as we can, but first I want to make it safe in the neighborhoods. And if that requires putting a whole lot of people behind bars, let's do it.

JACKSON: We should remember that four years at a state university in New York costs less that $25,000; four years at Attica costs $104,000. I am more inclined to take these young kids and lock them up in dormitories, give them years of mind expansion and trade development. It costs too much to leave them around for years without education, hope, or training.

The present welfare system should be replaced with a human development system. As presently constructed, the welfare system has built-in snares: there's no earn-incentive, no learn-incentive to get out. Assume you are locked into this box: a girl with a tenth-grade education and a baby. If she's making, say, $200 a month on welfare, why not provide some positive incentives? If she went back to school and got her junior college degree, she should get $240, $250. Why? Because that's making her employable, moving her closer to the market, where she can earn her own money. She can go back to junior college and study computer science, or learn cosmetology or business. The way it is now in most states, if she went out and found a job and made $200, they would take away $200 from welfare. So why earn the $200? Maybe if she earns $200 she should keep at least $100.

The point is that incentives to earn and learn must be built into the system. As it is now, if the young man who fathered the child doesn't have a job but comes back to live with the mother, she loses her check. So there's an incentive to keep the father away. And one of the few ways she can get any extra money is by engaging in an activity that may get her an extra child.

Now, this young girl—white, black, Hispanic, Asian, Indian—is the victim of a system that is not oriented toward human development. We must take away the punishment and threats and disincentives and move toward a sense of optimism and increasing options.

MURRAY: One part of me endorses what you're saying in principle. But when I think of all the practical difficulties, I get depressed. Most of all, it is extremely difficult to make much progress with youngsters who already have certain behavior patterns. If we go to a poor part of New York City, white or black, and pick a hundred kids who really have problems—drugs, illegitimate kids, the rest of it—and I say, "Here's a blank check; hire the best people, use the latest technologies, do whatever you can," at the end of three or four or even five years, if you start with seventeen- or eighteen-year-olds, *maybe* you will be able to point to ten or fifteen out of the hundred who show any major signs of getting somewhere.

Human beings aren't plastic. We don't know how to deal with certain kinds of problems after a certain age. The only route we have is prevention. So if you're hearing me say we're going to have to write off a generation, you can certainly back me into that corner.

JACKSON: Dr. Murray, I have seen these same kids, who you say can't do anything, volunteer for the Army, and in six to eight months they are building bridges, assuming responsibility. Why? Because it's an effective program that teaches, inspires, and sets clear goals.

So many young people step into sex and have babies because of ignorance, lack of discipline, and the like. If there was sex education before the fact, as well as the teaching of moral values, then there'd be less debate about abortion after the fact. Today, there is this whole group of people who *love* the fetus; they march across America to save a fetus and march right back to cut off aid for a baby.

Aid to women for prenatal care has a lot of value. The Head Start program saved and salvaged a whole generation. The drive to wipe out malnutrition by Senators McGovern and Hollings in the food stamp program actually worked; it brought about balanced diets where there had been none. We should drop programs that aren't working, not those that are.

MURRAY: It is beginning to percolate into the consciousness of policy-makers that we just don't know how to affect large numbers of people who are leading blighted lives. The only way we can deal with this is by prevention.

JACKSON: I agree that there are ways to change this situation without just paying another top-heavy layer of overseers and administrators who'd be sending paperwork back to Albany. I would take 500 young people and say, "How many of you would like this neighborhood to be cleaner?" Most hands would go up. "How many of you would like to have windows in your buildings in the wintertime?" Hands would go up. "How many of you would like to make $12 to $20 an hour?" Many hands. "Then here's what you must do if you want to make $12 to $20 an hour. We'll teach you how to be a mason. You can lay bricks and not throw them. You can learn how to be a glazier, how to be a plasterer. And at the end of this time we'll get you certified in a trade union. You will then have the skill to build where you live; if the floor's buckling in your gymnasium, you can fix it."

And so these young men and women would be empowered and enfranchised: they would much rather make $20 an hour than be on welfare. Just to do things *for* them while keeping them economically disenfranchised is no systemic change at all. And, Dr. Murray, people who can lay bricks and carpet and cut glass have no intention of going back on welfare.

MURRAY: I should point out that in my ideal world, by God, any black youngster who wants to can become a glazier, any poor youngster can learn a trade. And, Reverend Jackson, in my ideal world I would also clone *you*, because I've heard you speak to these kids.

JACKSON: But why do you think black kids everywhere are playing basketball so well? I submit to you that they're playing basketball and football and baseball so well and in such great numbers because there is a clear and obvious reward; there's a carrot. Do this and you'll be in the paper, on the radio, on television. And you'll get a college scholarship. And if you're real good, you'll get a professional contract. So these same kids that you say are unreachable and unteachable will gravitate to a carrot if they can see it. There must be a way out. And right now we must come up with ways out.

MURRAY: Yes, education and training opportunity—the carrots—are absolutely central. But once you have those, you have to have a support system, and this is where we've got a real problem. For example, let's say a youngster graduates from high school without many skills. He gets into a good job-training program, one that will really teach him a skill if he buckles down. But the youngster has never learned good work habits, so he flunks out of the training program. For that youngster to come out of high school ready to take advantage of a training program, there must be changes in the school he came from.

Now, what about the youngster who is offered an opportunity but who is below average in intelligence? I mean, half the country is below average in intelligence, and in industriousness.

JACKSON: Does that apply all the way through the government?

MURRAY: Let's just say this youngster is no great shakes, not much of anything. How is this youngster going to have a life that lets him look back when he's sixty and say, "Well, I did O.K., given what I had. At least I always supported myself and raised my kids and so on." The only way that eighteen-year-old kid is ever going to get to that position is by taking jobs that aren't much fun and don't pay much money. In order to reach the point where he feels good about supporting himself and his family, he's got to survive those years of eighteen, nineteen, twenty, when kids want to do things which make a whole lot of sense when you're that age but turn out to have been real stupid by the time you're thirty. Here is where, after you've provided the opportunities, which I am for in abundance, you've still got to worry.

JACKSON: But Dr. Murray, democracy must first guarantee opportunity. It doesn't guarantee success. Now, why do you think these ghetto and barrio youngsters are doing so well in athletics?

MURRAY: Because they see people just like them, who came out of those same streets, making a whole lot of money doing it.

JACKSON: So successful role models are a great motivator.

MURRAY: They make a huge difference. Now, how do we get the Jesse Jacksons of the world to be more visible role models?

JACKSON: Well, I've been working on that for a few years. But the point is that where the rules are clear, even though the work is hard, the locked-out tend to achieve. Ain't no low-class and high-class touchdowns. But there are no black baseball managers and no black professional football coaches. Why? Because in those areas where the decisions are made behind closed doors and where the rules are not so clear, those who are locked out don't do well.

That is basically true in the private economy: the more subjective the rules, the less the penetration. When people go behind closed doors to, say, determine who the dean of the medical school will be, eight people who are doctors, all of them graduated from the same school, tend to come up with someone from the same lineage. Why are there so many blacks in government? Because if you do well on the test, you can get in, and the rules of seniority are established.

MURRAY: In 1983, the New York City Police Department gave a sergeant's exam, and 10.6 percent of the white candidates passed but only 1.6 percent of the blacks. So it was decided that even though the rules were clear, some blacks who had failed the test would be promoted in order to fill a quota. Now, either you assume that the test measured nothing relevant to being a sergeant and that skill is randomly distributed, so it didn't make any difference that a whole bunch of blacks were arbitrarily promoted despite the fact that they didn't pass the test, or you assume that the test did in fact measure abilities that are important to advancement. If that's true, a few years down the road very few of the black sergeants will become lieutenants. This ensures, in an almost diabolically clever way, that no matter how able blacks become, they will continue to be segmented, and whites will always be looking at black co-workers who aren't quite as good at their jobs as the whites are. You build in an appearance of inferiority where none need exist.

Now, your son went to St. Albans and my daughters go to National Cathedral. These are among the finest schools in Washington. Your son, when he applies for a job, doesn't need or want any special consideration. The fact that he's black is irrelevant.

JACKSON: You're making dangerous comparisons here, Doctor, which tend to inflame weak minds. My son is not a good example because, like his father, his achievements are above average. The fact is that all of America, in some sense, must be educated about its past and must face the corrective surgery that is needed.

When there's moral leadership from the White House and from the academy, people tend to adjust. When Lyndon Johnson said—with the moral authority of a converted Texan—that to make a great society we must make adjustments, people took the Voting Rights Act and affirmative action and said, "Let's go."

There are a lot of positive examples around the country where integrated schools have worked, where busing has worked, where affirmative action has worked, when that spirit of moral leadership was present. The same school where the National Guard had to take two blacks to school in 1961—the University of Georgia—is where Herschel Walker won the Heisman Trophy. Later he was able to marry a white woman without protest in rural Georgia. Why? Because people had been taught that it was all right.

MURRAY: You've got the cart before the horse. By the mid-1960s, white folks finally, after far too long, had had their consciousnesses raised. They said to themselves, "We've done wrong. We have violated a principle that's one of the taproots of America; we haven't given people a fair shot just because their skin's a different color." A chord was struck that triggered a strong desire not only to stop doing the bad things but also to help people make up for lost ground.

That additional response was, from the very beginning, sort of pushing it. The principle that had actually been violated was that of the fair shot; but the black civil rights movement isn't feeding off that important nutrient anymore. It's gone beyond that.

192

Today, when white folks aren't making public pronouncements, I hear far too many of them saying things which are pretty damned racist. I see a convergence of the old racism, which is still out there, with a new racism, from people who are saying, "Well, gee, it's been twenty years now. You'd think they'd be catching up by now."

JACKSON: They're getting strong signals from the highest pulpit in the nation. When the White House and the Justice Department close their doors to the Afro-American leadership; when the Congressional Black Caucus cannot meet with the President of the United States; when the government closes its doors to the NAACP, the SCLC, the Urban League, Operation PUSH; when the White House will not meet with the Conference of Black Mayors; when those who work in the vineyards daily will not even engage in the dialogue you and I have engaged in today—that's reprehensible behavior. It sends out signals that hurt people. When leadership is present, people behave differently.

MURRAY: In addition to spending a lot of time talking to white people in general, I also spend a lot of time talking to conservatives. And I happen to know that their passion for a color-blind society is not just rhetoric.

JACKSON: Are you a consultant for an optometrist? Because the only people who would benefit from people going color-blind would be optometrists.

Nobody wants to be that way, man. We don't *need* to be color-blind; we need to affirm the beauty of colors and the diversity of people. I do not have to see you as some color other than what you are to affirm your person.

MURRAY: I mean that the ideal of giving everybody a fair shot—of not saying to anyone, "Because you're black I'm going to refuse to give you a chance"—is something which a lot of conservatives feel more passionately about than a lot of your putative friends do.

JACKSON: But if two people are in a one-mile race and one starts off with a half-mile head start and one starts off at point zero—okay, now let's take the chains off, every man for himself—well, such a race is not just. We are starting out behind. I mean, of the top 600 television executives, fewer than 15 are black.

MURRAY: I had a talk with somebody from one of the networks a few weeks ago, as a matter of fact. He said to me: "Well, we figured we ought to have a black producer, so we went out and hired the best one we could find. But he really isn't very good, so we do most of his work for him." Now, insofar as people aren't allowed to be TV producers because they're black, that's bad. But insofar as white people go around saying, "We had to get our black TV producer, so we brought in someone who can't make it on his own," they are not doing blacks a service.

JACKSON: Man, for most of my life I have seen black people train white people to be their boss. Incompetent whites have stood on the shoulders of blacks for a long time. Do you know how impressed I am when a white rock singer who is selling millions of records explains how he got his inspiration from a black artist, who can't even afford to come to the white man's concert? A few months ago *Time* said in an article that Gary Hart was the only Democrat who has run a coast-to-coast campaign. I was on the cover of *Time* twice during the 1984 campaign. But Hart's the only one. Isn't that a strange phenomenon? It's like Ralph Ellison's invisible man: they look at you but they don't see you.

By and large, the black people the White House sees are those one or two exceptions who did something great. They take a Hispanic kid or a black person and try to impose that model on the nation. I could take the position, "Well, if I can make it from a poor community in South Carolina, explain to me how a white person can be in poverty," and it would be absurd. But I could argue it and get lots of applause.

MURRAY: I'm willing to grant that we shouldn't make so much of the exception if you grant me that just because folks may be against certain kinds of programs, it doesn't mean that they're mean-spirited, or don't care about problems.

JACKSON: If we can avoid the demagogy and turn debate into dialogue and stereotypes into creative thinking, we can begin to develop ideas. I mean, I agree that this welfare system hurts people fundamentally. Many of the things that come from this Administration, like the enterprise zone idea, have a lot of validity. If an enterprise zone creates a green line instead of a red line, where if you live in that area you get certain incentives—that idea has merit. It may mean that a young man or a young woman teaching school will want to move to a district because of a tax incentive, or perhaps a doctor or a lawyer will want to move his office there. You establish an incentive for people to locate there, through the tax system or otherwise; you begin to shift capital, and the people who live there have first option on the new jobs. But the Administration has never really discussed this idea with those who would have to communicate with the masses about it.

So that idea has merit. Together we could make sense of such an idea. I'm anxious to open up the door of social policy, and I'm impressed with this opportunity today.

AN INNER-CITY COUNTER-REALITY

(AUGUST 1991)

James Traub

HERE IS HOW a story travels on *The Gary Byrd Show:* one morning
last January, about a week before the beginning of the Persian Gulf
war, Byrd, the host of the most popular black radio talk show in New
York City, asked his live audience at the Apollo Theatre in Harlem,
"Did anybody hear about that young black brother that got shot in
the head?" The incident involved a Marine stationed in Saudi Arabia
who had been killed by a bullet fired by a fellow soldier. The dead
man, Lance Corporal Anthony Stewart, had complained of racism in
letters home; the shooter was apparently "a European or a Latino,"
said Byrd. The following day Byrd added that the Marine Corps had
changed the cause of death from suicide to an accident; the family was
challenging the account. Byrd wasn't saying murder, but he made that
conclusion sound inescapable. A caller had already said that the killing
proved that blacks could depend on no one save one another—not
even Latinos.

Two weeks later a spokesman for the Stewart family, Stonewall
Odom, appeared on the show. The family, said Odom, had learned
that the soldier who shot their son was an unstable character given to

waving his gun at fellow Marines. Stewart, apparently, was the victim not of racism but of criminal recklessness. But the germ had already escaped into the atmosphere. The week after Odom's appearance, I was talking to a guy sitting in the row in front of me at the Apollo about a black scholar who had had the temerity to suggest that the military had begun to purge itself of racism. "He's full of shit," said my interlocutor. "He's reading from a script. You know about that lance corporal got shot in the back of the head by a white guy? So he's full of shit."

You probably have never even heard of Lance Corporal Stewart. In New York the story was carried in only one of the mainstream newspapers, *Newsday*, which is the only one that shows consistent interest in black affairs. It's not clear exactly what the significance of the soldier's story is, but on *The Gary Byrd Show* the lance corporal has joined the pantheon of martyrs to racism. The facts will soon be forgotten.

Talk radio, as Gary Byrd put it to me with typical delicacy, "has been very much a forum for the venting of emotions and perspectives and so forth." Only in the last two decades, however, have blacks had the financial power to own their own radio stations, and thereby vent their own emotions and perspectives over the airwaves. According to Janice Graham, founder of the National Council of Black Talk Radio and host of the talk show *Our Common Ground* on WPBR in West Palm Beach, Florida, about half a dozen other programs can claim an impact similar to Byrd's. She mentions *The Ty Wansley Show* on WVON in Chicago, as well as shows in St. Louis and Houston.

The Gary Byrd Show goes out over WLIB-AM, which is owned by New York's largest black media company, Inner City Broadcasting. Inner City was established by Percy Sutton, a former borough president of Manhattan. That the station—and Byrd's show—reaches an audience that matters in New York was underscored this past spring when Mayor David Dinkins, having concluded that his core support in the black community was dissolving, decided to pay a visit to the Apollo, where he endured shouted criticisms and insults from the audience with his usual combination of dignity, restraint, and vagueness. The show plays too significant a role in the formation of black opinion to be dismissed. During the prolonged agony of the Tawana Brawley case, Brawley's advisers and attorneys, Al Sharpton, Alton Maddox, and C. Vernon Mason, spoke to Byrd almost weekly. When the three appeared at the Apollo to criticize Governor Mario Cuomo's selection of a special prosecutor in this case, Cuomo himself called in to defend the choice, an act of calculated bravado.

You can drop by the Apollo and take in the show from ten in the morning until two every day from Monday to Thursday. The trip itself is instructive, since middle-class Manhattanites rarely find a reason to visit 125th Street. The elegant stone facades along the south side of the street recall the era when Harlem was a bourgeois, largely German-Jewish neighborhood, and the succeeding era when white shopkeepers catered to an increasingly black clientele. Now the street is lined with the sort of tacky discount stores that cater to poor people. The only big buildings are the ones that house federal and state government offices. Lassitude has won out over entrepreneurial vigor as the dominant mood of the street. On a windy day, trash and even shards of glass tumble out of the vacant lots and pinwheel down the sidewalks.

Each day about a hundred people—and pretty much the *same* hundred—can be found in the Apollo, an elegant throwback to the era of the Harlem Renaissance. The balconies are still plush, and gilded urns and laurel leaves form a noble border to the high proscenium arch. It's an oddly mellow atmosphere, considering the violence of the polemics issuing from the stage. On my first few visits, I made a point of smiling graciously at everyone and always kept my *New York Times* carefully hidden beneath a copy of the *Amsterdam News,* the largest of the city's black newspapers. But after a while I realized that, while I was considered an oddity and even an object of suspicion, nobody was going to hassle me—that wasn't the mood of the show. Had I been a black reporter sitting in the audience of, say, Radio Bensonhurst, I might have felt a good deal less comfortable.

On my first visit to the Apollo, the subject of the day was the

Tawana Brawley case. It was the Brawley case that had first brought home to many New Yorkers the feeling that whites and blacks had come to live in parallel psychic universes. The facts that finally emerged led to the conclusion that Tawana Brawley had invented her story of abduction and rape by a group of whites in Wappingers Falls, New York, in November 1987. But since her story, like Lance Corporal Stewart's, had proved something many blacks already believed to be true, and since the idea that she had lied seemed like a rebuke, a second set of facts had emerged, facts that seemed to vindicate her story. There was a white reality and a black reality, a white meaning and a black meaning. A few days before I visited *The Gary Byrd Show* I had had a bizarre conversation with a group of people, all black, waiting to get into the Central Park jogger trial. I had thought that I was fairly deeply versed in the Brawley case, but everyone on line knew of details I had never heard that definitively proved the theory of rape and cover-up. I had been reading the white media, they had been reading the black media—and listening to Gary Byrd.

It was, I was told, "press day" on the show, and I envisioned a group of reporters, white and black, kicking around the racial resonances of the Brawley case, à la *Washington Week in Review*. I had the wrong show. Sitting up on the Apollo stage with Byrd were the publishers of three Harlem newspapers, including Wilbert Tatum, owner of the *Amsterdam News*. Byrd began by checking whether all agreed that the grand jury report and the press accounts of the Brawley affair had been transparent, racist falsehoods. All did. Then Tatum took the stage to praise Tawana Brawley as a latter-day African princess and to accuse the white press of deliberately lying in order to substitute a black villain for a white one. The crowd in the Apollo hooted with derision.

The real target of the day was the *New York Times*. Six reporters at the *Times* had written a book called *Outrage*, which painstakingly laid out their hunt for the facts in the Brawley case. In their book the reporters had illustrated the racial gulf by using as a choral voice a group of black men who regularly met at a Brooklyn coffee shop. They had been described with careful deference. Three of the men had agreed to appear on the show, and they vied with one another to attack the book. One of them, a seventy-year-old college professor named William Mackey, Jr., told the audience that the one black *Times* reporter, E. R. Shipp, was a lesbian—otherwise, how account for her hatred of Tawana, a fellow black woman?

Here was a counter-reality, a counter-mythos, with alternative facts and alternative motives. And yet it was something much more complex than the inchoate ranting that Eric Bogosian captured in *Talk Radio*. As I began returning to the show, I discovered that part of its special fascination was that I could watch the counter-reality take shape. One day, after the lance corporal cycle had been completed, I heard Byrd interview Sonny Carson, a notorious "community activist" in Brooklyn who had helped organize an interminable boycott of a Korean grocer who had allegedly assaulted a Haitian woman. Carson appeared on the show the day after a jury had acquitted the Korean man on all charges. Apparently it was Tawana Brawley all over again. The moral that Byrd drew from the trial was that the word of a black woman "ultimately meant nothing." The boycott, Carson said, would go on, would widen.

Carson analyzed the situation historically. "The Jews," he explained, "when they left, they made sure that they turned those stores over to people who would continue the trickery." Oppression took new forms but was ever the same. Byrd, who sometimes plays a very deft devil's advocate, said that some people wondered why blacks didn't shop in their own stores. Maybe the Koreans just sell better produce? That was another one of the lies, said Carson; "the fish that's fried in Korean stores is fish that's ready to go bad."

Carson, thinking on his feet, seemed to have plucked those fish out of a side pocket. But it had the same effect as Mackey's slur on E. R. Shipp: it nullified the threat of objective reality, in this case the reality that the Koreans simply play by the rules of the marketplace. It vindicated the counter-reality of "the Jews" and the eternal recurrence of trickery. A few minutes later a young woman from Newark called to say that a raid on a local Korean grocer had found a freezer "full of skinned rats and cats, with onions on the other side," all to be mixed together into the soy sauce. The audience groaned as one. First the bad fish, then the skinned rats and cats. The little stories sustain the big truth. The woman said that she and others were organizing a protest.

The little stories and the big truths need each other; on *The Gary Byrd Show* they mingle and take on added force. I grew accustomed to hearing these skinned-cats-and-rats stories, usually volunteered by members of the audience whom Byrd invites up to one of two microphones stationed in front of the stage. Black Cabbage Patch dolls cost ten dollars more than white ones. The Central Park jogger couldn't have been raped because no signs of trauma were found. The Constitution still says that a black man is only three fifths of a person. Africans were the first people to worship one God. Africans were already here when Columbus "discovered" America.

The stories were true because they were True—because they corroborated a big truth. Conspiracy theories require the soil of such an overwhelming truth in order to take root. I was sometimes reminded of my friend Vince, an insanely rabid Pittsburgh Pirates fan who is convinced that the Pirates and then the Oakland A's were bribed by the mob to roll over in front of the Cincinnati Reds last year. Otherwise, how could you explain the lowly Reds beating the great Pirates in the pennant and the A's in the World Series? The same mental process was no doubt at work when President Reagan described the Contras as the moral equivalent of the Founding Fathers, or when the Palestinians persuaded themselves that Saddam Hussein was trouncing the coalition forces. The underlying emotion dictates the facts; no fact can be too strange if it vindicates the emotion.

But, of course, the Palestinians *have* been deprived of a homeland, and blacks have been enslaved and oppressed and isolated—thus the rhetorical force of the conspiracy theories. One morning I heard a sobbing mother tell the story of her daughter Shereema, a tiny woman of ninety-two pounds. When a crack dealer stole Shereema's radio, the girl's fiancé flagged down a police car. The officers, irritated at being stopped for so trivial an offense, beat up the fiancé and broke Shereema's arm. The distraught mother begged the Reverend Al

Sharpton, sitting on the stage with Byrd, to use his powers to intervene. Sharpton delivered on cue, bellowing, "They declared war on us! Where is the manhood in our community that should stand up for a young woman like this?" Sharpton vowed to fight, even unto death if need be.

It all seemed like theater to me, and I turned around to ask two girls sitting behind me what they thought about the story. One girl said that her boyfriend had gotten kicked around by the cops. The other said that, only the week before, the police had stopped her as she went through the non-paying gate in the subway, even though she had flashed her student card. The Shereema story sounded true to them; it confirmed a truth they had already felt. Indeed, a few days before, I had heard a man named Frank Budd vividly describe an attack made on him by a gang of Hasidic Jews who mistakenly thought that he had hit a child with his station wagon; later, in the hospital, the police treated him as if he had been at fault. It sounded like the nightmare of every black person in New York. The story sounded true to me, and perhaps the Shereema story would have sounded true as well had I not assumed that the police do not break the arms of black women out of pique. What is the psychic gulf between blacks and whites, after all, but a vivid reflection of the experiential gulf that lies between them? Whites are isolated from black reality as blacks are isolated from white reality.

During a break in the show one day I was being harangued by Melvin Green, a member of the Trotskyist New Alliance Party, and a younger, bigger, angrier man, who said that I could call him "X." They lectured me on the need for massive reparations for black people, on the jogger case, the S&Ls, and the Gulf war. I mentioned that I was against the war myself. They both looked stunned.

"Do you assume that all white people think the same way?" I asked Melvin.

"Yes."

"Really?" Melvin looked at me like I was trying to pull his leg. *Of course* all white people think the same way. It occurred to me that Melvin had probably not had many more political conversations with whites recently than most whites are likely to have with blacks.

The conversation ended in an unexpected way. As we were walking out the door, X, who seemed almost unhinged, was storming about the white media and integration and "that Jewboy Robert Abrams." (Abrams, New York's attorney general, was the special prosecutor appointed by Cuomo in the Brawley case.) He sheared off, still shouting, but Melvin suddenly rejoined me as I was heading down into the subway. He wanted to know what I had thought about the show.

It was an honest question, so I told him that I was disturbed by the way in which dubious rumors instantly took on the solidity of facts. To my surprise he murmured, "We reach out too soon." And then, either thinking of what I had said or of X, he suddenly added, "You probably noticed a lot of anger." He realized, he said, that the anger could help discredit some serious black activism.

The Gary Byrd Show offers consolation and reassurance to a bitter and frustrated audience, but Byrd himself is neither bitter nor frustrated. The Imhotep, as he calls himself—Imhotep was an Egyptian sage and scholar—has been a successful radio personality since he was seventeen and, he told me, a well-paid one too. He is a friendly interviewer and an active listener. While I spoke with him he was fiddling with his ever-present laptop computer; I noticed that the embroidery of his African cap matched the embroidery running down his jersey shirt. He is self-evidently a man to whom professional values matter. The more I asked him about the Reverend Sharpton and global white supremacy and so on the more gently agitated he became. He wanted to remind me that the show is carefully laid out—on his laptop—to flow from racial billingsgate to segments on education and culture, personal health and numerology, and the occasional dramatic performance. Byrd said that he kept a professional eye on radio shows like *A Prairie Home Companion*. "I don't do the show to get off on a vicarious dynamic of controversy," he said. "That's not really what I am."

That, in fact, is exactly what makes the show so powerful in its way. Byrd has the gift of evoking anger without himself ever becoming angry or even altering the modulation of his voice. His professionalism and his silken manner have the effect of legitimizing the outrageous things said on the show and making them sound practically normal. He can prompt a guest into saying that public school authorities are waging a conscious campaign to destroy black youth and make it sound like a colloquy on farm prices. And Byrd knows where to draw the line. When one of the house lunatics gets up to start ranting about Mayor Dinkins's secret membership in the Trilateral Commission, Byrd will say, "Now, hold on, brother," and then conclude, "but the brother has touched on a very important issue."

The show has a distinctly intellectual tone, which is more than can be said for most of the Imhotep's competition. Indeed, *The Gary Byrd Show* is one of the few radio programs with an ideology of its own, an ideology whose fundamental premise is that life is a Darwinian struggle for racial advantage. Dr. Leonard Jeffries, a professor of African studies at City College who has enjoyed some notoriety for his theory that blacks are a benign "people of the sun" while whites are malevolent "ice people," came on the show to explain that Christopher Columbus had exported to the New World the European system of "institutionalized genocide and enslavement." Over the centuries the system ramified into chattel slavery, and then into wage slavery, and then into debt slavery. Now, said Jeffries, we are witnessing "the death throes of the European system." The next era will be the era of Africa—so long as black people come together to devise "an African world agenda."

Here was the principle of eternal recurrence in meta-historical form. Sonny Carson had suggested that the Koreans were the Jews in a new form; the Reverend Al had said that Yusuf Hawkins, the black teenager killed in a racial attack in Bensonhurst in the summer of 1989, was the new Emmett Till. Nothing changed; domination simply assumed a new shape. I discovered this principle reductio ad absurdum one morning when I turned on the show to hear Dr. Frances Cress Welsing, a psychiatrist, expound her theory that racism is a consequence of white fear of genetic annihilation through race-mixing—a fear, in other words, of pigment vulnerability. The "Cress Theory," as it's called, has the immense virtue of bringing racism down to a biological level, a level at which everything is inevitable and hopes for amelioration are ludicrous. "Their own behavioral data suggests that they cannot stop what they are doing," Dr. Welsing explained to the audience.

I asked Byrd if he believed in the Cress Theory himself. After first asking me to explain the theory in order to make sure I had grasped its nuances, Byrd said, "I think it's possible." No one, he said, had convincingly refuted the theory. But he didn't agree with Cress that persuasion could do nothing to improve race relations. "Communications science," Byrd said, using "behavior modification," could bring people around. I think this was Byrd's convoluted way of saying that shows like his could advance the debate. This struck me as unlikely.

The simple fact is that no middle ground is permitted on the show. Since the ideology presumes that white reality is unitary, black reality must likewise be unitary. It's as if one took President Reagan's mind for a model. Almost from the time I first started listening to the show, I noticed that Byrd was on a kick about Martin Luther King. King was an "elder," in Byrd's Afrocentric phraseology, a figure of uncontested greatness. But there was one problem: many white people felt that way as well. This convergence clearly pointed to the possibility of an unacceptable middle ground—the middle ground of integration, of the liberal hopes that now look so naive—and so Byrd labored to eliminate it. "Dr. King," as the Imhotep said one day, "is one of the most misquoted, perspective-wise, people." Byrd talked about King's opposition to the Vietnam War, his growing stridency toward the end of his life. One day C. Vernon Mason explained that King was moving toward Pan-Africanism at the time of his death. "He was killed because he was evolving in a direction of being a person who would change the world."

On the day Dr. King's birthday was celebrated last January, the Apollo was more crowded than I'd ever seen it. Many people wanted to come to the mike to talk about Dr. King's influence on them; their words were filled not only with bitterness and dark conspiracies but with a terrible sense of vanished possibility. Who could fill that luminous space now? For a moment I deluded myself that I was hearing a yearning for the lost middle ground. An elderly man got up to tell a heartrending story of segregation in Mississippi and his own dawning consciousness. Then he said, "They never would have killed Martin if Malcolm was alive. Malcolm would have torn this country apart. And it's the same with the Reverend Farrakhan now . . ."

Martin was Malcolm: that was the real point. Another speaker, Dr. Sharshi McIntyre, said that "Martin was a warrior invoked with the spirit of his Africanness." "Malcolm was educated, but Martin was miseducated." Her manner was quicksilver, incantatory, almost breathtaking. The audience was deeply moved. Byrd summed up: "Far less separates a Martin Luther King and a Malcolm X than we have been led to believe." A hero had been wrested from false consciousness, from white reality, from the unbroachable suggestion of a shared destiny.

During the time that I was regularly listening to the show, the Gulf war came to crowd out almost all other obsessions. On what he called his "Power Play in the Gulf" series, Byrd brought on an array of journalists, scholars, and activists to explain that President Bush's "New World Order" was code language for global white supremacy. (Conspiracy theorists have a way of flattering the powerful by taking them more seriously than anyone else does.) There were precedents galore, and Byrd got quite hung up on a conference held by the European powers in 1884 in order to carve up Africa. It was carving time again, only now the Middle East was on the platter.

Israel was probably at the bottom of a lot of it. One day I fell into conversation with a scholarly-looking character named Richard Caillout, who said that he had written an unpublished book about Christopher Columbus, the bringer of slavery and imperialism, and an unpublished play about Nelson Mandela.

"There's only one state in that area that's expanded its borders, and that's Israel," he said. Israel was a "colonial settler state," just like South Africa. Oh, come on, I said; Israel is morally no different from South Africa? "No." At least Caillout didn't take the semi-official view that the Iraqis, as dark-skinned people, should be considered cousins rather than Visigoths. He just thought Iraq was no worse than Israel.

Meanwhile, up onstage, Betty Dopson of the Committee to Eliminate Media Offensive to African People was saying that according to a CEMOTAP poll, based on interviews with one hundred respondents in local community meetings, churches, and supermarkets, more than 80 percent of blacks opposed the war, and 87 percent didn't believe other polls saying that blacks were evenly divided on the subject. Here was a black poll designed to counter the white poll. Byrd then made a telephone call to a Dr. Milton Morris, the vice president of research for the Joint Center for Political and Economic Studies, in Washington, to talk about the situation of blacks in the military. I had the feeling that something was amiss when Byrd asked Dr. Morris, with exaggerated politesse, if he would prefer using the word "black" to "African-American." Morris said that, yes, that would be more natural to him.

What about blacks in the military? Byrd asked. Morris said his research showed that "the military is the most hospitable environment in this country for people of color." Inside the Apollo there was a stunned silence such as I had never heard before. Someone in the back hooted. Morris continued, citing figures that showed blacks were twice as heavily represented in the officer corps of the various services as they had been a decade earlier.

Apparently the good doctor had wandered in off another planet. To anyone else his findings might have seemed awfully modest, but on *The Gary Byrd Show* they seemed to threaten the whole mythic construct. Byrd didn't quite know what to do. "Of course," he said, "those numbers would have to be factored in with the issue of racism." Dr. Morris agreed as to how that might be true. Then Byrd asked his other guests if they wished to comment. Don Rojas, executive editor of the *Amsterdam News,* said, icily polite, "What do you mean by 'the military is the most hospitable . . . '?" The audience, finding an outlet for their feelings, clapped and jeered. Dr. Morris repeated his findings; I thought I heard him use the words "African-American."

The mask of courtesy on the Apollo stage began to fall away. Betty Dopson asked if Dr. Morris had surveyed the population of minorities in military prisons. Morris seemed baffled by the question, so Dopson said that she had heard that the ratio in military prison was the same as in civilian life: 80 to 85 percent black and Latino. Dr. Morris said that he had made no such study. The audience groaned in disgust. Byrd, ever smooth, launched into a general discussion of the misuse of statistics and then said: "That particular statistic would put an almost completely different slant on the information you have offered."

"There is no credible challenge to this data," said Morris stiffly.

And so it went, a dialogue of the deaf. Dr. James McIntosh, another official from CEMOTAP, asked Morris what definition of racism he was using. Morris said that he wasn't using any definition of racism; he tried to explain the principle of scholarly objectivity. The idea was obviously alien. Rojas asked Morris what the "objective" of the study had been. Dopson asked who had been behind his funding. Byrd asked where the information had come from. I had never before heard a sharp exchange on the show; I had never seen a black man ill-treated. In every question there was the unspoken belief that Morris had committed an act of betrayal. Morris himself, perhaps as a point of intellectual pride, kept up to the very end the pretense that he was engaged in a scholarly discussion.

Byrd finally threw the microphones open. The first woman to speak was choked with rage. "I advise young people not to go into the military," she said, "because there's nothing for you there, and there's nothing for you when you come home." To my horror I saw X advancing to the other mike. "For this Dr. Tom from D.C. I got a couple of questions," he shouted. Byrd told him to cool it, but he took off on a polemical rampage anyway. A silver-haired man next to me, a photographer for the *Muslim Journal*, recoiled from the vitriol. "He's been honest," he murmured. "He's just speaking the facts." It was the guy in front of me who had said that the story of Lance Corporal Stewart proved that Morris was a stooge.

Byrd was now torn between two tenets of his show's ideology: the universality of white racism and the principle of brotherhood with all people of color. Finally he attempted a typically polished flanking maneuver. "Where are you from, sir?"

"I would like to know if it is relevant."

"Are you from the Caribbean?"

"I was *born* in the Caribbean, yes." That, presumably, explained his immigrant identification with American benevolence. But Byrd wanted to lead him to another issue: if the U.S. Army and its high-ranking black officers attacked your Caribbean island, that might change your view, mightn't it? "That might be what you would call the bending of a statistic?"

"That wasn't my point at all."

"What was your point?"

"Achievement has to be taken into account when we go out and talk about how much racism there is."

My story, oddly enough, has a sort of happy ending. After I had just about had it with the nth iteration of global white supremacy and skinned cats and rats, I went back to the show one last time with two friends. As we were leaving, Melvin Green caught up with us and joined us for coffee in the Mart 125 across the street. Ever since his comment about black anger, Melvin had toed the line ideologically in our conversations. Now, over coffee, he explained to my slightly incredulous friends how the power structure had brought Arabs over to serve as shopkeepers in black neighborhoods, the better to destroy black-Arab relations; how the FBI had harassed him; how Christopher Columbus hadn't discovered America; and so on.

There was something shifting uneasily beneath the flow of Melvin's thoughts, though none of us noticed it. He turned to me and said, "I'm going to say something that's really going to shock you." I thought he meant that he was going to go off the deep end. But he said, "I've been trying to make myself hate for two years." That, he felt, was what his politics required; that was what *The Gary Byrd Show* seemed to ask of him. But it wasn't quite working. It was hard for him to take things like the Cress Theory seriously. He was looking for another way. And then Melvin began talking about, of all things, *agape,* the pure love that asks nothing in return, and about the kinship he had once felt in the military with a white soldier.

It would have been embarrassing had it not been so sincere. I thought I had known Melvin, but evidently I hadn't. He was one of those two-dimensional objects that suddenly turn to one side to reveal a third dimension. Probably he couldn't have said himself exactly what he thought. He believed the whole litany; but he didn't want to believe it. Perhaps he was in transit from it to something else. *Agape* must have sounded to Melvin like a suitably high-minded and selfless destination; but even if he was headed to someplace more secular— especially if he was—he was leaving behind the temple of received wisdom. He was looking for the middle ground. It may be that no such piece of territory exists anymore, but at least Melvin was looking.

I'M BLACK, YOU'RE WHITE, WHO'S INNOCENT?

(JUNE 1988)

Shelby Steele

IT IS A warm, windless California evening, and the dying light that covers the redbrick patio is tinted pale orange by the day's smog. Eight of us, not close friends, sit in lawn chairs sipping chardonnay. A black engineer and I (we had never met before) integrate the group. A psychologist is also among us, and her presence encourages a surprising openness. But not until well after the lovely twilight dinner has been served, when the sky has turned to deep black and the drinks have long since changed to scotch, does the subject of race spring awkwardly upon us. Out of nowhere the engineer announces, with a coloring of accusation in his voice, that it bothers him to send his daughter to a school where she is one of only three black children. "I didn't realize my ambition to get ahead would pull me into a world where my daughter would lose touch with her blackness," he says.

Over the course of the evening we have talked about money, infidelity, past and present addictions, child abuse, even politics. Intimacies have been revealed, fears named. But this subject, race, sinks us into one of those shaming silences where eye contact terrorizes. Our host looks for something in the bottom of his glass. Two women stare into the black sky as if to locate the Big Dipper and point it out to us. Finally, the psychologist seems to gather herself for a challenge, but it is too late. "Oh, I'm sure she'll be just fine," says our hostess, rising from her chair. When she excuses herself to get the coffee, the two sky gazers offer to help.

With three of us now gone, I am surprised to see the engineer still silently holding his ground. There is a willfulness in his eyes, an inner pride. He knows he has said something awkward, but he is determined not to give a damn. His unwavering eyes intimidate me. At last the host's head snaps erect. He has an idea. "The hell with coffee," he says. "How about some of the smoothest brandy you ever tasted?" An idea made exciting by the escape it offers. Gratefully we follow him back into the house, quickly drink his brandy, and say our good-byes.

An autopsy of this party might read: death induced by an abrupt and lethal injection of the American race issue. An accurate if superficial assessment. Since it has been my fate to live a rather integrated life, I have often witnessed sudden deaths like this. The threat of them, if not the reality, is a part of the texture of integration. In the late 1960s, when I was just out of college, I took a delinquent's delight in playing the engineer's role, and actually developed a small reputation for playing it well. Those were the days of flagellatory white guilt; it was such great fun to pinion some professor or housewife or, best of all, a large group of remorseful whites, with the knowledge of both their racism and their denial of it. The adolescent impulse to sneer at convention, to startle the middle-aged with doubt, could be indulged under the guise of racial indignation. And how could I lose? My victims—earnest liberals for the most part—could no more crawl out from under my accusations than Joseph K. in Kafka's *Trial* could escape the amorphous charges brought against him. At this odd moment in history the world was aligned to facilitate my immaturity.

About a year of this was enough: the guilt that follows most cheap thrills caught up to me, and I put myself in check. But the impulse to do it faded more slowly. It was one of those petty talents that is tied to vanity, and when there were ebbs in my self-esteem the impulse to use it would come alive again. In integrated situations I can still feel the faint itch. But then there are many youthful impulses that still itch, and now, just inside the door of mid-life, this one is least precious to me.

In the literature classes I teach, I often see how the presence of whites all but seduces some black students into provocation. When we come to a novel by a black writer, say Toni Morrison, the white students can easily discuss the human motivations of the black characters. But, inevitably, a black student, as if by reflex, will begin to set in relief the various racial problems that are the background of these characters' lives. This student's tone will carry a reprimand: the class is afraid to confront the reality of racism. Classes cannot be allowed to die like dinner parties, however. My latest strategy is to thank that student for his or her moral vigilance, and then appoint the young man or woman as the class's official racism monitor. But even if I get a laugh—I usually do, but sometimes the student is particularly indignant, and it gets uncomfortable—the strategy never quite works. Our racial division is suddenly drawn in neon. Overcaution spreads like spilled paint. And, in fact, the black student who started it all does become a kind of monitor. The very presence of this student imposes a new accountability on the class.

I think those who provoke this sort of awkwardness are operating out of a black identity that obliges them to badger white people about race almost on principle. Content hardly matters. (For example, it made no sense for the engineer to expect white people to sympathize with his anguish over sending his daughter to school with *white* children.) Race indeed remains a source of white shame; the goal of these provocations is to put whites, no matter how indirectly, in touch with this collective guilt. In other words, these provocations I speak of are *power* moves, little shows of power that try to freeze the "enemy" in self-consciousness. They gratify and inflate the provocateur. They are the underdog's bite. And whites, far more secure in their power, respond with a self-contained and tolerant silence that is, itself, a show of power. What greater power than that of non-response, the power to let a small enemy sizzle in his own juices, to even feel a little sad at his frustration just as one is also complimented by it. Black anger always, in a way, flatters white power. In America, to know that one is not black is to feel an extra grace, a little boost of impunity.

I think the real trouble between the races in America is that the races are not just races but competing power groups—a fact that is easily minimized perhaps because it is so obvious. What is not so obvious is that this is true quite apart from the issue of class. Even the well-situated middle-class (or wealthy) black is never completely immune to that peculiar contest of power that his skin color subjects him to. Race is a separate reality in American society, an entity that carries its own potential for power, a mark of fate that class can soften considerably but not eradicate.

The distinction of race has always been used in American life to sanction each race's pursuit of power in relation to the other. The allure of race as a human delineation is the very shallowness of the delineation it makes. Onto this shallowness—mere skin and hair—men can project a false depth, a system of dismal attributions, a series of malevolent or ignoble stereotypes that skin and hair lack the substance to contradict. These dark projections then rationalize the pursuit of power. Your difference from me makes you bad, and your badness justifies, even demands, my pursuit of power over you—the oldest formula for aggression known to man. Whenever much importance is given to race, power is the primary motive.

But the human animal almost never pursues power without first convincing himself that he is *entitled* to it. And this feeling of entitlement has its own precondition: to be entitled one must first believe in one's innocence, at least in the area where one wishes to be entitled. By innocence I mean a feeling of essential goodness in relation to others and, therefore, superiority to others. Our innocence always inflates us and deflates those we seek power over. Once inflated we are entitled; we are in fact licensed to go after the power our innocence tells us we deserve. In this sense, *innocence is power*. Of course, innocence need not be genuine or real in any objective sense, as the Nazis demonstrated not long ago. Its only test is whether or not we can convince ourselves of it.

I think the racial struggle in America has always been primarily a struggle for innocence. White racism from the beginning has been a claim of white innocence and, therefore, of white entitlement to subjugate blacks. And in the 1960s, as went innocence so went power. Blacks used the innocence that grew out of their long subjugation to seize more power, while whites lost some of their innocence and so lost a degree of power over blacks. Both races instinctively understand that to lose innocence is to lose power (in relation to each other). Now to be innocent someone else must be guilty, a natural law that leads the races to forge their innocence on each other's backs. The inferiority of the black always makes the white man superior; the evil might of whites makes blacks good. This pattern means that both races have a hidden investment in racism and racial disharmony, despite their good intentions to the contrary. Power defines their relations, and power requires innocence, which, in turn, requires racism and racial division.

I believe it was this hidden investment that the engineer was protecting when he made his remark—the white "evil" he saw in a white school "depriving" his daughter of her black heritage confirmed his innocence. Only the logic of power explained this—he bent reality to show that he was once again a victim of the white world and, as a victim, innocent. His determined eyes insisted on this. And the whites, in their silence, no doubt protected their innocence by seeing him as an ungracious troublemaker—his bad behavior underscoring their goodness. I can only guess how he was talked about after the party. But it isn't hard to imagine that his blunder gave everyone a lift. What none of us saw was the underlying game of power and innocence we were trapped in, or how much we needed a racial impasse to play that game.

When I was a boy of about twelve, a white friend of mine told me one day that his uncle, who would be arriving the next day for a visit, was a racist. Excited by the prospect of seeing such a man, I spent the following afternoon hanging around the alley behind my friend's house, watching from a distance as this uncle worked on the engine of his Buick. Yes, here was evil and I was compelled to look upon it. And

I saw evil in the sharp angle of his elbow as he pumped his wrench to tighten nuts, I saw it in the blade-sharp crease of his chinos, in the pack of Lucky Strikes that threatened to slip from his shirt pocket as he bent, and in the way his concentration seemed to shut out the human world. He worked neatly and efficiently, wiping his hands constantly, and I decided that evil worked like this.

I felt a compulsion to have this man look upon me so that I could see evil—so that I could see the face of it. But when he noticed me standing beside his toolbox, he said only, "If you're looking for Bobby, I think he went up to the school to play baseball." He smiled nicely and went back to work. I was stunned for a moment, but then I realized that evil could be sly as well, could smile when it wanted to trick you.

Need, especially hidden need, puts a strong pressure on perception, and my need to have this man embody white evil was stronger than any contravening evidence. As a black person you always hear about racists but never meet any. And I needed to incarnate this odious category of humanity, those people who hated Martin Luther King, Jr., and thought blacks should "go slow" or not at all. So, in my mental dictionary, behind the term "white racist," I inserted this man's likeness. I would think of him and say to myself, "There is no reason for him to hate black people. Only evil explains unmotivated hatred." And this thought soothed me; I felt innocent. If I hated white people, which I did not, at least I had a reason. His evil commanded me to assert in the world the goodness he made me confident of in myself.

In looking at this man I was *seeing for innocence*—a form of seeing that has more to do with one's hidden need for innocence (and power) than with the person or group one is looking at. It is quite possible, for example, that the man I saw that day was not a racist. He did absolutely nothing in my presence to indicate that he was. I invested an entire afternoon in seeing not the man but my innocence through the man. *Seeing for innocence* is, in this way, the essence of racism—the use of others as a means to our own goodness and superiority.

The loss of innocence has always to do with guilt, Kierkegaard tells us, and it has never been easy for whites to avoid guilt where blacks are concerned. For whites, *seeing for innocence* means seeing themselves and blacks in ways that minimize white guilt. Often this amounts to a kind of white revisionism, as when President Reagan declares himself "color-blind" in matters of race. The President, like many of us, may aspire to racial color blindness, but few would grant that he has yet reached this sublimely guiltless state. The statement clearly revises reality, moves it forward into some heretofore unknown America where all racial determinism will have vanished. I do not think that Ronald Reagan is a racist, as that term is commonly used, but neither do I think that he is capable of seeing color without making attributions, some of which may be negative—nor am I, or anyone else I've ever met.

So why make such a statement? I think Reagan's claim of color blindness with regard to race is really a claim of racial innocence and guiltlessness—the preconditions for entitlement and power. This was the claim that grounded Reagan's campaign against special entitlement programs—affirmative action, racial quotas, and so on—that black power had won in the Sixties. Color blindness was a strategic assumption of innocence that licensed Reagan's use of government power against black power.

I do not object to Reagan's goals in this so much as the presumption of innocence by which he rationalized them. I, too, am strained to defend racial quotas and any affirmative action that supersedes merit. And I believe there is much that Reagan has to offer blacks. His emphasis on traditional American values—individual initiative, self-sufficiency, strong families—offers what I think is the most enduring solution to the demoralization and poverty that continue to widen the gap between blacks and whites in America. Even his de-emphasis of race is reasonable in a society where race only divides. But Reagan's posture of innocence undermines any beneficial interaction he might have with blacks. For blacks instinctively sense that a claim of racial innocence always precedes a power move against them. Reagan's pretense of innocence makes him an adversary, and makes his quite reasonable message seem vindictive. You cannot be innocent of a man's problem and expect him to listen.

I'm convinced that the secret of Reagan's "teflon" coating, his personal popularity apart from his policies and actions, has been his ability to offer mainstream America a vision of itself as innocent and entitled (unlike Jimmy Carter, who seemed to offer only guilt and obligation). Probably his most far-reaching accomplishment has been to reverse somewhat the pattern by which innocence came to be distributed in the Sixties, when outsiders were innocent and insiders were guilty. Corporations, the middle class, entrepreneurs, the military—all villains in the Sixties—either took on a new innocence in Reagan's vision or were designated as protectors of innocence. But again, for one man to be innocent another man must be bad or guilty. Innocence imposes, *demands*, division and conflict, a right/wrong view of the world. And this, I feel, has led to the underside of Reagan's achievement. His posture of innocence draws him into a partisanship that undermines the universality of his values. He can't sell these values to blacks and others because he has made blacks into the bad guys and outsiders who justify his power. It is humiliating for a black person to like Reagan because Reagan's power is so clearly derived from a distribution of innocence that leaves a black with less of it, and the white man with more.

Black Americans have always had to find a way to handle white society's presumption of racial innocence whenever they have sought to enter the American mainstream. Louis Armstrong's exaggerated smile honored the presumed innocence of white society—I will not bring you your racial guilt if you will let me play my music. Ralph Ellison calls this "masking"; I call it bargaining. But whatever it's called, it points to the power of white society to enforce its innocence. I believe this power is greatly diminished today. Society has reformed and transformed—Miles Davis never smiles. Nevertheless, this power has not faded altogether; blacks must still contend with it.

Historically, blacks have handled white society's presumption of innocence in two ways: they have bargained with it, granting white society its innocence in exchange for entry into the mainstream; or they have challenged it, holding that innocence hostage until their demand for entry (or other concessions) was met. A bargainer says, *I already believe you are innocent (good, fair-minded) and have faith that you will prove it.* A challenger says, *If you are innocent, then prove it.* Bargainers *give* in hope of receiving; challengers *withhold* until they receive. Of course, there is risk in both approaches, but in each case the black is negotiating his own self-interest against the presumed racial innocence of the larger society.

Clearly the most visible black bargainer on the American scene today is Bill Cosby. His television show is a perfect formula for black bargaining in the Eighties. The remarkable Huxtable family—with its doctor/lawyer parent combination, its drug-free, college-bound children, and its wise yet youthful grandparents—is a blackface version of the American dream. Cosby is a subscriber to the American identity, and his subscription confirms his belief in its fair-mindedness. His vast audience knows this, knows that Cosby will never assault their innocence with racial guilt. Racial controversy is all but banished from the show. The Huxtable family never discusses affirmative action.

The bargain Cosby offers his white viewers—I will confirm your racial innocence if you accept me—is a good deal for all concerned. Not only does it allow whites to enjoy Cosby's humor with no loss of innocence, but it actually enhances their innocence by implying that race is not the serious problem for blacks that it once was. If anything, the success of this handsome, affluent black family points to the fair-mindedness of whites who, out of their essential goodness, changed society so that black families like the Huxtables could succeed. Whites can watch *The Cosby Show* and feel complimented on a job well done.

The power that black bargainers wield is the power of absolution. On Thursday nights, Cosby, like a priest, absolves his white viewers, forgives and forgets the sins of the past. (Interestingly, Cosby was one of the first blacks last winter to publicly absolve Jimmy the Greek for his well-publicized faux pas about black athletes.) And for this he is rewarded with an almost sacrosanct status. Cosby benefits from what might be called a gratitude factor. His continued number-one rating may have something to do with the (white) public's gratitude at being offered a commodity so rare in our time; he tells his white viewers each week that they are okay, and that this black man is not going to challenge them.

When a black bargains, he may invoke the gratitude factor and find himself cherished beyond the measure of his achievement; when he challenges, he may draw the dark projections of whites and become a source of irritation to them. If he moves back and forth between these two options, as I think many blacks do today, he will likely baffle whites. It is difficult for whites to either accept or reject such blacks. It seems to me that Jesse Jackson is such a figure—many whites see Jackson as a challenger by instinct and a bargainer by political ambition. They are uneasy with him, more than a little suspicious. His powerful speech at the 1984 Democratic convention was a masterpiece of bargaining. In it he offered a Kinglike vision of what America could be, a vision that presupposed Americans had the fair-mindedness to achieve full equality—an offer in hope of a return. A few days after this speech, looking for rest and privacy at a lodge in Big Sur, he and his wife were greeted with standing ovations three times a day when they entered the dining room for meals. So much about Jackson is deeply American—his underdog striving, his irrepressible faith in himself, the daring of his ambition, and even his stubbornness. These qualities point to his underlying faith that Americans can respond to him despite his race, and this faith is a compliment to Americans, an offer of innocence.

But Jackson does not always stick to the terms of his bargain—he is not like Cosby on TV. When he hugs Arafat, smokes cigars with Castro, refuses to repudiate Farrakhan, threatens a boycott of major league baseball, or, more recently, talks of "corporate barracudas," "pension-fund socialism," and "economic violence," he looks like a challenger in bargainer's clothing, and his positions on the issues look like familiar protests dressed in white-paper formality. At these times he appears to be revoking the innocence so much else about him seems to offer. The old activist seems to come out of hiding once again to take white innocence hostage until whites prove they deserve to have it. In his candidacy there is a suggestion of protest, a fierce insistence on his *right* to run, that sends whites a message that he may secretly see them as a good bit less than innocent. His dilemma is to appear the bargainer while his campaign itself seems to be a challenge.

There are, of course, other problems that hamper Jackson's bid for the Democratic presidential nomination. He has held no elective office, he is thought too flamboyant and opportunistic by many, there are rather loud whispers of "character" problems. As an individual he may not be the best test of a black man's chances for winning so high an office. Still, I believe it is the aura of challenge surrounding him that hurts him most. Whether it is right or wrong, fair or unfair, I think no black candidate will have a serious chance at his party's nomination, much less the presidency, until he can convince white Americans that he can be trusted to preserve *their* sense of racial innocence. Such a candidate will have to use his power of absolution; he will have to flatly forgive and forget. He will have to bargain with white innocence out of a genuine belief that it really exists. There can be no faking it. He will have to offer a vision that is passionately raceless, a vision that strongly condemns any form of racial politics. This will require the most courageous kind of leadership, leadership that asks all the people to meet a new standard.

Now the other side of America's racial impasse: How do blacks lay claim to their racial innocence?

The most obvious and unarguable source of black innocence is the victimization that blacks endured for centuries at the hands of a race that insisted on black inferiority as a means to its own innocence and power. Like all victims, what blacks lost in power they gained in innocence—innocence that, in turn, entitled them to pursue power. This was the innocence that fueled the civil rights movement of the Sixties, and that gave blacks their first real power in American life—victimization metamorphosed into power via innocence. But this formula carries a drawback that I believe is virtually as devastating to blacks today as victimization once was. It is a formula that binds the victim to his victimization by linking his power to his status as a victim. And this, I'm convinced, is the tragedy of black power in America today. It is primarily a victim's power, grounded too deeply in the entitlement derived from past injustice and in the innocence that

Western/Christian tradition has always associated with poverty.

Whatever gains this power brings in the short run through political action, it undermines in the long run. Social victims may be collectively entitled, but they are all too often individually demoralized. Since the social victim has been oppressed by society, he comes to feel that his individual life will he improved more by changes *in* society than by his own initiative. Without realizing it, he makes society rather than himself the agent of change. The power he finds in his victimization may lead him to collective action against society, but it also encourages passivity within the sphere of his personal life.

This past summer I saw a television documentary that examined life in Detroit's inner city on the twentieth anniversary of the riots there in which forty-three people were killed. A comparison of the inner city then and now showed a decline in the quality of life. Residents feel less safe than they did twenty years ago, drug trafficking is far worse, crimes by blacks against blacks are more frequent, housing remains substandard, and the teenage pregnancy rate has skyrocketed. Twenty years of decline and demoralization, even as opportunities for blacks to better themselves have increased. This paradox is not peculiar to Detroit. By many measures, the majority of blacks—those not yet in the middle class—are further behind whites today than before the victories of the civil rights movement. But there is a reluctance among blacks to examine this paradox, I think, because it suggests that racial victimization is not our real problem. If conditions have worsened for most of us as racism has receded, then much of the problem must be of our own making. But to fully admit this would cause us to lose the innocence we derive from our victimization. And we would jeopardize the entitlement we've always had to challenge society. We are in the odd and self-defeating position where taking responsibility for bettering ourselves feels like a surrender to white power.

So we have a hidden investment in victimization and poverty. These distressing conditions have been the source of our only real power, and there is an unconscious sort of gravitation toward them, a complaining celebration of them. One sees evidence of this in the near happiness with which certain black leaders recount the horror of Howard

Beach and other recent (and I think over-celebrated) instances of racial tension. As one is saddened by these tragic events, one is also repelled at the way some black leaders—agitated to near hysteria by the scent of victim-power inherent in them—leap forward to exploit them as evidence of black innocence and white guilt. It is as though they sense the decline of black victimization as a loss of standing and dive into the middle of these incidents as if they were reservoirs of pure black innocence swollen with potential power.

Seeing for innocence pressures blacks to focus on racism and to neglect the individual initiative that would deliver them from poverty—the only thing that finally delivers anyone from poverty. With our eyes on innocence we see racism everywhere and miss opportunity even as we stumble over it. About 70 percent of black students at my university drop out before graduating—a flight from opportunity that racism cannot explain. It is an injustice that whites can *see for innocence* with more impunity than blacks can. The price whites pay is a certain blindness to themselves. Moreover, for whites *seeing for innocence* continues to engender the bad faith of a long-disgruntled minority. But the price blacks pay is an ever-escalating poverty that threatens to make the worst off of them a permanent underclass. Not fair, but real.

Challenging works best for the collective, while bargaining is more the individual's suit. From this point on, the race's advancement will come from the efforts of its individuals. True, some challenging will be necessary for a long time to come. But bargaining is now—today— a way for the black individual to *join* the larger society, to make a place for himself or herself.

"Innocence is ignorance," Kierkegaard says, and if this is so, the claim of innocence amounts to an insistence on ignorance, a refusal to know. In their assertions of innocence both races carve out very functional areas of ignorance for themselves—territories of blindness that license a misguided pursuit of power. Whites gain superiority by *not* knowing blacks; blacks gain entitlement by *not* seeing their own responsibility for bettering themselves. The power each race seeks in relation to the other is grounded in a double-edged ignorance, ignorance of the self as well as the other.

The original sin that brought us to an impasse at the dinner party I mentioned at the outset occurred centuries ago, when it was first decided to exploit racial difference as a means to power. It was the determinism that flowed karmically from this sin that dropped over us like a net that night. What bothered me most was our helplessness. Even the engineer did not know how to go forward. His challenge hadn't worked, and he'd lost the option to bargain. The marriage of race and power depersonalized us, changed us from eight people to six whites and two blacks. The easiest thing was to let silence blanket our situation, our impasse.

I think the civil rights movement in its early and middle years offered the best way out of America's racial impasse: in this society, race must not be a source of advantage or disadvantage for anyone. This is fundamentally a *moral* position, one that seeks to breach the corrupt union of race and power with principles of fairness and human equality: if all men are created equal, then racial difference cannot sanction power. The civil rights movement was conceived for no other reason than to redress that corrupt union, and its guiding insight was that only a moral power based on enduring principles of justice, equality, and freedom could offset the lower impulse in man to exploit race as a means to power. Three hundred years of suffering had driven the point home, and in Montgomery, Little Rock, and Selma, racial power was the enemy and moral power the weapon.

An important difference between genuine and presumed innocence, I believe, is that the former must be earned through sacrifice, while the latter is unearned and only veils the quest for privilege. And there was much sacrifice in the early civil rights movement. The Gandhian principle of non-violent resistance that gave the movement a spiritual center as well as a method of protest demanded sacrifice, a passive offering of the self in the name of justice. A price was paid in terror and lost life, and from this sacrifice came a hard-earned innocence and a credible moral power.

Non-violent passive resistance is a bargainer's strategy. It assumes the power that is the object of the protest has the genuine innocence

to morally respond, and puts the protesters at the mercy of that innocence. I think this movement won so many concessions precisely
because of its belief in the capacity of whites to be moral. It did not so
much demand that whites change as offer them relentlessly the opportunity to live by their own morality—to attain a true innocence based
on the sacrifice of their racial privilege, rather than a false innocence
based on presumed racial superiority. Blacks always bargain with or
challenge the larger society; but I believe that in the early civil rights
years, these forms of negotiation achieved a degree of integrity and
genuineness never seen before or since.

In the mid-Sixties all this changed. Suddenly a sharp *racial* consciousness emerged to compete with the moral consciousness that had
defined the movement to that point. Whites were no longer welcome
in the movement, and a vocal "black power" minority gained dramatic
visibility. Increasingly, the movement began to seek racial as well as
moral power, and thus it fell into a fundamental contradiction that
plagues it to this day. Moral power precludes racial power by
denouncing race as a means to power. Now suddenly the movement
itself was using race as a means to power, and thereby affirming the
very union of race and power it was born to redress. In the end, black
power can claim no higher moral standing than white power.

It makes no sense to say this shouldn't have happened. The sacrifices
that moral power demands are difficult to sustain, and it was
inevitable that blacks would tire of these sacrifices and seek a more
earthly power. Nevertheless, a loss of genuine innocence and moral
power followed. The movement, splintered by a burst of racial militancy in the late Sixties, lost its hold on the American conscience and
descended more and more to the level of secular, interest-group politics. Bargaining and challenging once again became racial rather than
moral negotiations.

You hear it asked, why are there no Martin Luther Kings around
today? I think one reason is that there are no black leaders willing to
resist the seductions of racial power, or to make the sacrifices moral
power requires. King understood that racial power subverts moral
power, and he pushed the principles of fairness and equality rather

than black power because he believed those principles would bring blacks their most complete liberation. He sacrificed race for morality, and his innocence was made genuine by that sacrifice. What made King the most powerful and extraordinary black leader of this century was not his race but his morality.

Black power is a challenge. It grants whites no innocence; it denies their moral capacity and then demands that they be moral. No power can long insist on itself without evoking an opposing power. Doesn't an insistence on black power call up white power? (And could this have something to do with what many are now calling a resurgence of white racism?) I believe that what divided the races at the dinner party I attended, and what divides them in the nation, can only be bridged by an adherence to those moral principles that disallow race as a source of power, privilege, status, or entitlement of any kind. In our age, principles like fairness and equality are ill-defined and all but drowned in relativity. But this is the fault of people, not principles. We keep them muddied because they are the greatest threat to our presumed innocence and our selective ignorance. Moral principles, even when somewhat ambiguous, have the power to assign responsibility and therefore to provide us with knowledge. At the dinner party we were afraid of so severe an accountability.

What both black and white Americans fear are the sacrifices and risks that true racial harmony demands. This fear is the measure of our racial chasm. And though fear always seeks a thousand justifications, none is ever good enough, and the problems we run from only remain to haunt us. It would be right to suggest courage as an antidote to fear, but the glory of the word might only intimidate us into more fear. I prefer the word *effort*—relentless effort, moral effort. What I like most about this word are its connotations of everydayness, earnestness, and practical sacrifice. No matter how badly it might have gone for us that warm summer night, we should have talked. We should have made the effort.

BLACK LIKE . . . SHIRLEY TEMPLE

(FEBRUARY 1992)

Gerald Early

IT WAS TWO years ago, the summer that my daughters gave up their Afros and had their hair straightened, that I decided to watch every Shirley Temple film available on video with them. This included nineteen Twentieth Century Fox films that were made during her heyday—1934 to 1938—and several short Baby Burlesks.

I am not quite sure why I did this. I do not like Shirley Temple movies. I did not like them much as a child. But my daughters—Linnet, then age ten, and Rosalind, then age seven—after having seen a colorized version of *Our Little Girl,* a perfectly wretched Temple vehicle (even Temple herself admits this in her autobiography), on the Disney channel one evening, very much wanted to do this summer project. We watched each of the films at least three times. The project appealed to me because I felt I could share something with my children while exercising parental control. I would seem to be a kid while retaining my status and authority as father.

Perhaps I associate my children's change in hairstyle with our Shirley Temple phase because so much was made of Temple's hair, her curls, during her years of stardom. My daughters liked Temple's hair very much.

During the summer that we watched these films together, my relationship with my daughters changed. At first I saw the films merely as vehicles for parental instruction—black parental instruction, I should say, for I had prepared to give a history of black actors in Hollywood in the 1930s and provide information on the lives of the black dancer Bill "Bojangles" Robinson, the actress Hattie McDaniel, and some of the other blacks who appeared in Temple films. I was never given much of an opportunity.

"I don't want to hear your old lectures, Daddy," Linnet said. "We want to watch the movies. This isn't school. You make being black seem like a lesson."

When they laughed uproariously at some graceless thing that Stepin Fetchit or Willie Best did, Rosalind turned to me, knowing that I was aghast, and said:

"Don't worry, we know they aren't real black people."

"But do you know what you're laughing at?" I asked, chagrined.

"Yeah," Rosalind said, "clowns, not black people."

Eventually, I was told that if all I wanted to do was talk about the movies or analyze them, then I would not be permitted to watch. Besides, they were more than capable of judging the films themselves. So I grew quiet as the summer went on. I did not want to be banished.

It was during this summer that they abandoned their Afro hairstyles for good. They had had a hard time of it in school the previous year; their hair had been the subject of jokes and taunts from both black and white children. Moreover, I suppose they wanted straightened hair like their mother.

When they both burst through the door that evening with their hair newly straightened, beaming, looking for all the world like young ladies, I was so taken aback in a kind of horror that I could only mutter in astonishment when they asked, "How do you like it?" It was as if my children were no longer mine, as if a culture that had convinced them they were ugly had taken them from me. I momentarily looked at my wife as if to say, "This is your doing. If only you would wear your hair as you did when we first met, this would not have happened."

My wife's response was, "They wanted their hair straightened and they thought they were old enough for it. Besides, there is no virtue in wearing an Afro. I don't believe in politically correct hair. Who was the last white woman you saw who didn't have something done to her hair? Most white women don't wear their hair the way God put it on their heads. It's been dyed, moussed, permed, teased, spiked, shagged, curled, and coiffed. What do you think, Shirley Temple was born with those curls? I've got news for you. Her mom had to work like heck to get those curls set just right. I want the same privilege to do to my hair what white women can do to theirs. It's my right to self-expression."

Right after this happened, late in the summer, I began to find excuses not to watch the Shirley Temple movies. After about two or three weeks, Linnet, who was particularly upset by my lack of approval, asked me why I would not watch the movies with them any-more. I said that I thought the films were for children, not adults; that I was, in effect, intruding. Besides, I had work to do. Eventually, we got around to her new hairstyle.

"I like my hair like this," she said. "This is the way I want to wear it."

"Do you care if I like it?" I asked.

She paused for a moment. "No," she said, bravely. "I want to wear my hair the way I like."

"To get the approval of other people?" I asked unkindly.

"Well," she said, "a little. I don't like to be called dumb. I don't like to be called ugly. I want to be like everybody else. I wear my hair some for me and some for other people. I don't think I'm Shirley Temple or a white girl, but I want to look like a girl, not like a boy. When you write, Daddy, don't you want approval from other people, too?"

Before the discussion ended, she said, "I wish you would watch the movies with us. It's more fun when you watch, too."

About two weeks later, the weekend before the start of school, I received in the mail a Shirley Temple video we hadn't seen, some early shorts that mimicked adult-genre movies, in which she and the other children went around dressed in diapers. I thought this might make a good truce, and so I brought it to my daughters' room and offered to watch it with them. Just before the video started I made a gesture that surprised even me: I stood above Linnet, bent over, and smelled her hair. It had just been washed and freshly straightened ("touched up," my wife said), and it smelled a bit like shampoo, a bit like pressing oil, and very slightly burned, much like, during my childhood, my mother's, my sisters', my aunts' hair smelled. It was a smell that I had, in some odd way, become fond of because, I suppose, it was so familiar, so distressingly familiar, like home.

THE COLORINGS OF CHILDHOOD

(JANUARY 1992)

David Updike

FIVE OR SIX years ago, when my older sister revealed to the rest of our family her intention of marrying her boyfriend, from Ghana, I remember that my reaction, as a nervous and somewhat protective younger brother, was something like "Well, that's fine for them—I just wonder about the children." I'm not sure what I was wondering, exactly, but it no doubt had to do with the thorny questions of race and identity, of having parents of different complexions, and a child, presumably, of some intermediate shade, and what that would mean for a child growing up here, in the United States of America.

I had no idea, at the time, that I, too, would one day marry an African, or that soon thereafter we would have a child, or that I would hear my own apprehensions of several years before echoed in the words of one of my wife's friends. She was a white American of a classic liberal mold—wearer of Guatemalan shawls, befriender of Africans, espouser of worthy causes—but she was made uneasy by the thought of Njoki, her friend from Kenya, marrying me, a white person. She first asked Njoki what my "politics" were and, having been assured that they were okay, went on to say, "Well, I'm sure he's a very nice person, but before you get married I just hope you'll think about the children."

I recognized in her remarks the shadow of my own, but when it is one's own marriage that is being worried about, one's children, not yet conceived, one tends to ponder such comments more closely. By this time, too, I was the uncle of two handsome, happy boys, Ghanian-American, who, as far as I could tell, were suffering no side effects for having parents of different colors. Njoki, too, was displeased.

"What is she trying to say, exactly—that *my* child will be disadvantaged because he looks like me?" my wife asked. "So what does she think about me? Does she think *I'm* disadvantaged because I'm African?"

I responded that our liberal friend was trying to get at the complicated question of identity, knowing, as she did, that the child, in a country that simplifies complicated, racial equations to either "black" or "white," wouldn't know to which group he "belonged."

"To both of them," Njoki answered, "or to neither. He will be Kenyan-American. The ridiculous part is that if I was marrying an African she wouldn't mind at all—she wouldn't say, 'Think of the children,' because the child would just be black, like me, and it wouldn't be her problem. She wouldn't have to worry about it. Honestly," she finally said, her head bowed into her hand in resignation, "this country is so complicated."

But her friend's reaction is not, I suspect, an uncommon one, even among those who think of themselves as progressive and ideologically unfettered: they don't mind, in principle, the idea of interracial unions, but the prospect of children clouds the issue, so to speak, and raises the identity issue—if not for the child, the *beheld*, then for us, the beholders. For as I slowly pondered the woman's remarks, it occurred to me that she was not saying "He won't know who he is," but something closer to "*I* won't know who he is—I won't know to which group this child belongs, the black people or the white." Added to this is the suppressed, looming understanding that, however the child sees himself, however we see the child, the country at large will perceive the child as "black," and, consequently, this son or daughter of a friend, this child to whom we might actually be an aunt or uncle, parent or grandparent, cousin or friend, this person whom we love and wish the best for in life, will grow up on the opposite side of the color line from us and, as such, will be privy to a whole new realm of the American Experience, which we, by virtue of our skin color, have previously avoided; and this—for the vast majority of white Americans—is a new and not altogether comforting experience.

Harlem, Anacostia, Roxbury, Watts: in every major city in America, and most minor ones, there is a neighborhood that most whites have never been to, will never go to, and regard, from a distance, with an almost primordial fear, akin to the child's apprehension of the bogey-man. They have read about this place in the paper and heard on the nightly news of the crime and violence there, but the thought of actually going there for a visit is almost unthinkable; if they ever found themselves there—got off at the wrong subway stop or took an ill-fated wrong turn—they imagine they would be set upon by hordes of angry, dark people with nothing better to do than sit around waiting for hapless white people to amble into their lair. Most white Americans, I suspect, would be more comfortable walking through the streets of Lagos, or Nairobi, or Kingston, than they would be walking through any predominantly black neighborhood in America.

For a couple of years Njoki lived in Harlem, on Riverside Drive and 145th Street, and was visited there one evening by a couple of our friends and their one-year-old child. When it came time to leave, after dark, the woman asked Njoki if she would walk them to the corner, to hail a cab—as if the presence of a black person would grant them free passage and protect them from the perils of the neighborhood. Njoki explained that it was okay, that the neighborhood was quite safe and they wouldn't be singled out for special attention because they were white.

"It's okay for us," the friend explained. "I just wouldn't want anything to happen to the baby."

Njoki relented and walked them over to Broadway, but as they went she wondered what made her friends think the residents of Harlem wanted to attack a couple with a baby, or why she, an African and a stranger to this country, was called upon to somehow protect her American friends from their own countrymen. At the corner they hailed a cab, and they were whisked off to some safer corner of the city, leaving Njoki to walk back alone to her apartment, at far greater risk, as a single woman, than any group of people, white or black, would ever be.

Which is not to say that I myself felt at perfect ease walking through the streets of Harlem, but simply that the more time I spent there the more I realized that no one was particularly interested, or concerned, that a pale man in collegiate tweeds was walking through the neighborhood. During the two years that my wife lived there, I walked often from her apartment down to City College, where I taught, and from there to Columbia University, and I was never bothered or heckled by anyone. As a friend of mine, a resident of Harlem, said to me once, "Black people are around white people all the time."

But as a child growing up in a small New England town, I was almost never around black people. My impressions of the world beyond, or of African-Americans, were mostly gleaned from television and magazines and movies, from which, it seems to me, it is nearly impossible not to acquire certain racist assumptions about people, however slight and subtle; and even when one has become aware of them they are nearly impossible to shed entirely. Like astronomers who can hear the "background radiation" that marks the beginning of the universe, so can one hear, in the background of one's own thoughts, the persistent, static hiss of American history.

By the time my second nephew was born I had written two children's books, both about a boy and his dog and their various adventures in the small New England town where they lived. As I began to think about a third book in this series, it occurred to me that the boy could now have a friend, and if he was to have a friend it might be nice if his complexion was somewhat closer to that of my two nephews, so that when they read the book they would find a character who, in this regard, looked somewhat like themselves. I wrote such a book and sent in the manuscript with a letter explaining that, although there was no reference to race in the book, I would like the second boy to appear darker than his friend in the illustrations.

A few weeks later I received the editor's response: he liked the plot and story line, he said, but was confused by this new character, which seemed underdeveloped and vague. The editor didn't understand what this character was doing in a small New England town. I ran the risk, too, of being accused of "tokenism" by some of the members of the library associations—black women especially, he pointed out—who were on the lookout for such things.

I wrote back and, among other things, suggested that children are less encumbered by problems of race and ethnicity than their parents or teachers, and I thought it unlikely they would worry what he was doing in a small New England town. I was willing to run the risk of being accused of tokenism either by reviewers or watchdogs of the children's-book world. In the end, we agreed on a few small editorial changes, and when the book came out the character in question was indeed of brown skin, and I never heard another word about it either from teachers or reviewers or disgruntled children. But this editorial skirmish gave me a taste of the children's-book world I had not quite imagined, and I've since had dealings with several other publishers, most of whom, it seemed to me, exhibited a kind of heightened vigilance when it came to books about "children of color," so wrought were editors with anxieties about tokenism and marketing and whatever other obstacles lie between them and a slightly broader vision of what constitutes suitable subject matter for children.

Njoki is often asked what my family thinks of my being married to an African woman, a black woman, but she is almost never asked what her family thinks of her being married to a "mzungu"—a white person. Her interviewers are surprised to learn that my parents don't mind and that hers don't either, and that her parents regret much more that neither she nor I is a practicing Catholic. They are also surprised to learn that there would be much more apprehension and mutual suspicion had she married a Kenyan of another ethnic group, or an African of another country. And I am married to an African, not an African-American, and in my case, too, the suspicions and animosities of history are diffused by the absence of a common and adversarial past. And, similarly, for Njoki, the thought of her being married to a white Kenyan—the descendants of Karen Blixen (more commonly known as Isak Dinesen) and her ilk—is almost laughable.

Several summers ago we spent six weeks in Kenya and passed much of our time there in a middle-class suburb of Nairobi called Karen, named after this same Karen Blixen, who once lived here in the shadow of the Ngong Hills. One night we were invited to dinner at the house of a neighbor—a couple in the tourist industry who had invited a group of traveling Americans over to their house for dinner. Their home was in the typically grand style of the Kenyan middle class, the "grounds" surrounded by a tall barbed-wire and electrified fence, and further protected by an all-night watchman and several roaming dogs. But inside the floors were polished wood parquet, the furniture was tasteful, and, aside from a few African prints, we could have been in an upper-middle-class dwelling in Los Angeles, or Buenos Aires, or Rome. The other guests had already arrived, and sat on couches eating and drinking and talking with their hosts. As it turned out, all of the guests were African-American, mostly from New Jersey and New York; we were introduced, and joined them, but it became clear that some were not very happy to find me, a white American, here in the home of an African, 8,000 miles from the country they and I so uneasily shared. When I tried to speak to one of the African-American women, she would answer in clipped monosyllables and stare into distant corners of the room; another woman had brought a tape recorder, with which to record some of the conversations, but whenever I spoke, it was observed, she would turn off the machine and wait for my polluting commentary to pass. I did find one woman who was not, outwardly, troubled by my presence, and spent much of the evening talking with her, but my otherwise chilly reception had not been lost on Njoki's sister and brother-in-law and niece, who were both mystified and amused. On the car ride home we tried to explain—about the history of the United States, and slavery, and about African-Americans' identification with Africa as the place from which their ancestors were taken, stolen, for hundreds of years. Njoki tried to explain how their visit here was a kind of homecoming, a return to the continent they probably would have never left, were it not for the unpleasant fact of slavery.

"Yes, but that was West Africa—it has nothing to do with here. And besides, they're Americans now—and you're American, too."

"Yes, but . . ."

"And you're a guest. You have as much right to be here as they do."

"Yes, but . . ."

It is difficult to accurately convey the complexities of race in America to someone who has never been here, and they remained unconvinced. Our American dinner companions, I suspect, would have been saddened, if not maddened, by our sour postmortem of the evening, and I was sorry to have been, as far as they were concerned, in the wrong place at the wrong time, was sorry to have diminished their enjoyment of their visit. But I still felt that I had more in common with my fellow African-American guests than either of us did with our Kenyan hosts—an idea to which they might have heartily objected. They shared with our hosts a genetic and, to some extent, cultural "Africanness," and the experience of being mistreated by peoples of European ancestry; I shared with my hosts the experience of growing up in a place where people of one's own ethnicity, or color, were in the majority; but with my fellow guests I shared the more immediate experience of having grown up in America, where our experiences have been rather different, where we also live, as uneasy acquaintances, on opposing sides of the same, American coin.

I am asked, sometimes, either directly or by implication, how it is that both my sister and I—New Englanders of northern European extraction—came to marry Africans, people of another culture and color and continent. I have never had much of an answer for these people, except to say that both my sister and I are compatible with our respective spouses in ways neither of us had been with previous companions, all of whom were far closer to our own complexions. When I was five or so, and my sister seven, my family lived for two months on a small island in the Caribbean, and it is my mother's rather whimsical theory that it was from impressions gleaned during this trip—for my sister from the somewhat older boys she played with in an old, rusty model T that sat beside our house, and for me from the long-limbed, beautiful baby-sitters who used to take care of us—that led us both, thirty years later, to marry Africans. Nor do I think that it was any strain of "jungle fever" that caused us to marry who we did. More likely, my sister and I both married Africans because, as children, we were not conditioned not to, were not told that this was not one of life's options, and so, when the opportunity arose, there were no barriers—neither our own nor our parents'. And in the "white liberal" world in which I grew up, it would have been uncouth to make any outward show of disapproval—though I suspect some amused speculation went on behind closed doors about my sister's and my choice of mates, and I believe some of my parents' friends expressed quiet concern, but I have never personally received any negative commentary, neither from friends nor passersby. It had been more of an issue for Njoki, who has some friends who believe marrying a white man is a "sellout" of some kind, a "betrayal" of the race, and that with it comes the loss of some strain of political correctness. But such friends either tend to adjust or to fade away into a world more cleanly divided between black and white, where they will be irritated and confused no more.

By some unexpected confluence of genes our son Wesley's hair is, to our surprise, relatively straight—long, looping curls that tighten slightly when it rains—and this, too, will mean something in America, means something already to the elderly neighborhood women who tell us, with a smile, that he has "good" hair, and to other people, friends and strangers both, who tell us he looks like he is from Central America, or India, or the Middle East, implicitly meaning *rather than black*. Children, however, are less circumspect in their observations, and I have no doubt my son will be called a few names while growing up, both by white children and by brown; he may be told that he is really "black," and he may be told that he thinks he's "white"; in

Kenya, I have been assured, he will be considered "half-caste"—an unpleasant linguistic relic from colonial days. He may also be treated badly by teachers prone to impatience, or a lack of empathy, with students of lighter, or darker, complexions than their own. He may be embarrassed by the sound of his mother's language; he may be embarrassed by my whiteness. He may go through a time when he is, indeed, confused about his "identity," but in this respect I don't think he will be much different from other children, or teenagers, or adults. There is no way of my knowing, really, what his experience as a multiracial child will be, or, for that matter, how helpful I or his mother will be to him along the way. We can only tell him what we think and know, and hope, as all parents do, that our words will be of some use.

We are not bothered by mothers in the park who seem to get a little nervous, overly vigilant, when their children begin to commiserate with other, darker children, as if their children are in some sort of subtle, ineffable danger—too close for comfort. Their fears seem laughable, absurd, and one comes to almost pity the children who will grow up in the shadow of such fearful, narrow people, from whom they will inherit the same nervous bundle of apprehensions and pathologies. Many of them will be sent to private schools, not because the public schools in our city are not very good but because of the subconscious assumption that schools with so many children of other races *can't* be that good: such schools and students will hold their own children back somehow. But in the end, these people tend to recede, not disappear, exactly, but shrink before the simple, overwhelming presence of your child, who shrieks with joy at something as simple as the sound of your key turning in the door.

Wesley will visit Africa and live there for a time, and will know the Kenyan half of his family there and the American half here, and into the bargain will know his Ghanian uncle and his Ghanian-American cousins and a whole West African branch of his extended family. And it may just be that, contrary to the assumptions of concerned friends, this child of a "mixed" marriage will suffer no great disadvantages at all, but rather will enjoy advantages denied the rest of us; for as the child of two cultures he will "belong" to neither of them exclusively but both of them collectively, will be a part of my Americanness and Njoki's Africanness, and will be something neither she nor I ever will be—African-American—and as such will be a part of a rich and varied culture that will always hold me at arm's length. And in these layers of identity lies an opportunity for a kind of expansion of the world, a dissolution of the boundaries and obstacles that hold us all in a kind of skittish, social obeisance, and he thus may be spared the suspicions and apprehensions that plague those of us who have grown up with an exclusive, clearly defined sense of belonging. In the end, my son will be, simply, an American child, an American adult. His will be a wider, more complicated world than mine was, and to him will fall the privilege and burden, as it falls to us all, of making of it what he will.

ABOUT THE AUTHORS

Maya Angelou (1928–) is a novelist and poet. Her works include *Just Give Me a Cool Drink of Water 'Fore I Diiie*, *Gather Together in My Name*, and *I Know Why the Caged Bird Sings*.

James Baldwin (1924–1987) is the author of *Go Tell It on the Mountain*, *Giovanni's Room*, and *Harlem Quartet*, among other works. He was working on a study of the life of Martin Luther King, Jr., at the time of his death.

Arna Bontemps (1902–1973) was among the novelists and poets who formed the Harlem Renaissance of the 1920s and 1930s. Later, he taught in the Afro-American Studies Department at Yale and was librarian at Fisk University. His works include *Black Thunder*, *God Sends Sunday*, and *Free at Last: The Life of Frederick Douglass*.

Priscilla Butler (1909–) worked for many years as a domestic in Alabama. She was interviewed in *Telling Memories Among Southern Women: Domestic Workers and Their Employers in the Segregated South*, by Susan Tucker. Tucker is the librarian for the Newcomb College Center for Research on Women.

Robert Coles (1929–) is a professor of psychiatry and medical humanities at Harvard University. He is the author of numerous books on the inner life of children and won the 1973 Pulitzer Prize for Volumes II and III of *Children of Crisis*.

Orde Coombs (1939–1984) is the author of *Do You See My Love for You Growing?* and, with Chester Higgins, Jr., *Some Time Ago; A Historical Portrait of Black Americans From 1850–1950*.

Gerald Early (1952–) is a professor in the English Department at Washington University, in St. Louis. He is the author of *Tuxedo Junction: Essays on American Culture.*

Ralph Ellison (1914–) won the 1953 National Book Award for his novel *Invisible Man.* He is the Albert Schweitzer Professor in the Humanities Emeritus at New York University.

William Faulkner (1897–1962) won the Nobel Prize in Literature in 1949. His novels include *The Sound and the Fury, As I Lay Dying,* and *Light in August.*

Henry Louis Gates, Jr., (1950–) is the W.E.B. Du Bois Professor of the Humanities at Harvard, where he is also the chairman of the Afro-American Studies Department. He is the author of *Figures in Black: Words, Signs, and the "Racial" Self, The Signifying Monkey: Towards a Theory of Afro-American Literary Criticism,* and, most recently, *Loose Canons: Notes on the Culture Wars.*

Jesse Jackson (1941–) is the chairman of the National Rainbow Coalition, the former director of the Southern Christian Leadership Conference's Operation Breadbasket, and the founder of Operation PUSH. He sought the Democratic presidential nomination in 1984 and in 1988.

Charles Murray (1943–) is a Bradley Fellow at the American Enterprise Institute. He is the author of *Losing Ground: American Social Policy 1950–1980* and *In Pursuit: Of Happiness and Good Government.*

Itabari Njeri is a contributing editor to *The Los Angeles Times Magazine* and the author of *Every Goodbye Ain't Gone,* which won the 1990 American Book Award. She is currently at work on a book about ethnic identity and conflict in America.

Mary Richie is the author of two novels, *A Romantic Education* and *Loving Upward.* She has just completed a new novel.

Shelby Steele (1946–) is professor of English at San Jose State University, in California. His book of essays, *The Content of Our Character,* won the National Book Critics Circle Award for general non-fiction.

William Styron (1925–) won the 1968 Pulitzer Prize for his novel *The Confessions of Nat Turner.* His other books include *Lie Down in Darkness, Sophie's Choice,* and, most recently, *Darkness Visible.*

James Traub (1954–) is the author of *Too Good to be True: The Outlandish Story of Wedtech.* He is currently working on a book about the City College of New York.

Mark Twain (1825–1910), one of America's greatest writers, is the author of numerous books. Among the most widely read are *The Adventures of Tom Sawyer, The Adventures of Huckleberry Finn,* and *Life on the Mississippi.*

David Updike (1957–) has published a collection of short stories entitled *Out on the Marsh,* along with several children's books.

Roger Wilkins (1932–) is the Robinson Professor of History and American Culture at George Mason University and the author of *A Man's Life: An Autobiography.*

ACKNOWLEDGMENTS

"Slavery in Hannibal," by Mark Twain, was written in 1910.

"This Quiet Dust." From *This Quiet Dust and Other Writings,* by William Styron. Copyright © 1953, 1961, 1962, 1963, 1964, 1965, 1968, 1972, 1974, 1975, 1976, 1977, 1980, 1981, 1982 by William Styron. Reprinted by permission of Random House, Inc.

"My White Father." From *Telling Memories Among Southern Women: Domestic Workers and Their Employers in the Segregated South,* by Susan Tucker. (Schocken, 1990) Reprinted by permission of the author and editor.

"Why I Returned," by Arna Bontemps. Copyright © 1965 by Arna Bontemps. Reprinted by permission of the Estate of Arna Bontemps.

"Harlem Is Nowhere." From *Shadow and Act,* by Ralph Ellison. Copyright © 1964 by Ralph Ellison. Reprinted by permission of Random House, Inc.

"I Know Why the Caged Bird Sings." From *I Know Why the Caged Bird Sings,* by Maya Angelou. Copyright © 1969 by Maya Angelou. Reprinted by permission of Random House, Inc.

"Race and Fear," by William Faulkner. Copyright © 1956 by William Faulkner. Reprinted from *Gentlemen, Scholars and Scoundrels,* Harper & Brothers (1959).

"When Morpheus Held Him." From *Every Good-bye Ain't Gone,* by Itabari Njeri. (Times Books, 1990). Copyright © 1990 by Itabari Njeri. Reprinted by permission of Russell & Volkening, Inc., agent for the author.

"In Search of Martin Luther King, Jr.," by James Baldwin. Copyright © 1961 by James Baldwin. Used by arrangement with the James Baldwin Estate.

"Voices From the South," by Robert Coles. Copyright © 1965 by Robert Coles. Reprinted by permission of the author.

"Confessions of a Blue-Chip Black," by Roger Wilkins. Copyright © 1962 by Roger Wilkins. Reprinted by permission of the author.

"A Paleness of Heart," by Mary Richie. Copyright © 1973 by Mary Richie. Reprinted by permission of the author.

"Soul in Suburbia," by Orde Coombs. Copyright © 1972 by Orde Coombs.

"Portraits in Black," by Henry Louis Gates, Jr. Copyright © 1976 by Henry Louis Gates, Jr. Reprinted by permission of the author.

"An Inner-City Counter-Reality," by James Traub. Copyright © 1991 by James Traub. Reprinted by permission of the author.

"I'm Black, You're White, Who's Innocent?", by Shelby Steele. Copyright © 1988 by Shelby Steele. Reprinted by permission of the author.

"Black Like . . . Shirley Temple," by Gerald Early. Copyright © 1992 by Gerald Early. Reprinted by permission of the author.

"The Colorings of Childhood," by David Updike. Copyright © 1992 by David Updike. Reprinted by permission of the author.